A
DEVOUT
&
HOLY
LIFE

A
DEVOUT
&
HOLY
LIFE

William Law

Whitaker House

All Scripture quotations are from the *King James Version* (KJV) of the Bible.

A DEVOUT AND HOLY LIFE

ISBN: 0-88368-463-2
Printed in the United States of America
Copyright © 1996 by Whitaker House

Whitaker House
580 Pittsburgh Street
Springdale, PA 15144

1 2 3 4 5 6 7 8 9 10 11 12 / 06 05 04 03 02 01 00 99 98 97 96

CONTENTS

THE NATURE OF CHRISTIAN DEVOTION

D evotion is not prayer, but prayer is part of devotion. Devotion signifies a life given, or devoted, to God. The devout man, therefore, is one who lives no longer to his own will or to the way and spirit of the world, but solely to the will of God. He considers God in everything, and he serves God in everything; he makes every aspect of his common life into an aspect of piety, by doing everything in the name of God and to His glory.

Prayer, whether public or private, is simply an instance of devotion. We readily acknowledge that God alone is to be the rule and measure of our prayers, that in them we are to look wholly unto Him and act wholly for Him. We know that we are to pray only in such a manner, for such things, and to such ends, as are suitable to His glory.

Now, if a man were simply to find out the reason why he is to be so strictly pious in his prayers, he will also find out why he must be as strictly pious in all the other areas of his life. For the very reasons why we should make God the rule and measure of our prayers, why we should look wholly unto Him and pray according to His will, are the same reasons why we should also make Him the rule and measure of all the other actions of our lives. Any way of life, any employment of our talents—whether of our time or our money—that is not strictly according to the will of God, that is not carried out for His glory, is as great an absurdity as prayers that are not according to the will of God.

There is no other reason why our prayers should be according to the will of God, why they should have nothing in them but what is wise and holy and heavenly; there is no other reason for this, but that our lives may be of the same nature, full of the same wisdom, holiness, and heavenly qualities—that we may live unto God in the same spirit that we pray unto Him. If it were not our strict duty to live by reason, to devote all the actions of our lives to God; if it were not absolutely necessary to walk before Him in wisdom and holiness and all heavenly conversation, doing everything in His name and for His glory; there would be no excellency or wisdom in the most heavenly prayers. No, such prayers would be absurdities; they would be like prayers for wings, when it was never our privilege to fly.

Therefore, as surely as there is wisdom in praying for the Spirit of God, so are we to make that Spirit the rule of all our actions; as surely as our duty is to look wholly unto God in our prayers, so is it our duty to live wholly unto God. Just as we cannot be said to pray unto God unless our prayers look wholly to Him, so we cannot be said to live unto God unless we live unto Him in all the ordinary actions of our lives, and unless He is the rule and measure of all our ways. Unreasonable and absurd ways of life, whether in labor or recreation, whether they consume our time or our money, are like unreasonable and absurd prayers, and they are as truly an offense to God.

It is because we fail to even consider this, that e see such a mixture of ridicule in the lives of many people. They are very strict about having certain times and places of devotion, but when the service of the church is over, they are like those who seldom or never come there. In their way of life, in their manner of spending their time and money, in their cares and fears, in their pleasures and indulgences, in their work and recreation, they are like the rest of the world.

This causes the wanton and reckless part of the world to make a general mockery of those who are devout, because they see their devotion goes no farther than their prayers. When their prayers are over, they live no more unto God, but they live by the same whims and fancies, and in as full an enjoyment of all the follies of life, as other people, until the time of prayer returns again. They are the jest and scorn of careless and worldly people, not because they are really devoted to God, but because they appear to have no other devotion but that of occasional prayers.

Julius[1] is a man very fearful of missing prayers; the entire congregation supposes him to be ill if he is not at church. However, he spends the remainder of his time following his every whim. He is a companion of people who engage in silly pleasures; he gives himself up to idle, gossiping conversation; he allows himself foolish hatred and resentment against certain people without considering that he is to love everybody as himself (see Leviticus 19:18); and he never puts his conversation, his time, and his money under the rules of

---

[1] Julius: the suggestion is that Caesar is the worldly power, as opposed to God. The notes in this edition simply aim at explaining the names of the allegorical characters and at giving the sense of words whose connotations have altered in the course of time.

religion. The whole body of Scripture stands directly against such a life: one who lives such a course of idleness and folly does not live according to the religion of Jesus Christ. If Julius were to read the New Testament from the beginning to the end, he would find his course of life condemned in every page of it.

Indeed, I cannot imagine anything more absurd than to add wise, sublime, and heavenly prayers to a life of vanity and folly, where neither labor nor entertainment, neither time nor money, are under the wise and heavenly direction of our prayers. Suppose we were to see a man pretending to act wholly with regard to God in everything that he did—a man who would neither spend time nor money, nor engage in any work or leisure, unless he could act according to strict principles of reason and piety. Suppose that the same man neglected all prayer, whether public or private. Would we not be amazed at such a man, and wonder how he could have so much folly along with so much religion?

This man's actions are as unreasonable as pretending to be strict in devotion, being careful to observe certain times and places of prayer, and yet letting the rest of your life—your time and labor, your talents, and your money—be disposed of without any regard to piety and devotion. You cannot have holy prayers and divine petitions without a holiness of life suitable to them; and you cannot have a holy and divine life without prayers. For to be weak and foolish in spending our time and money, is no greater a mistake than to be weak and foolish in relation to our prayers. And to allow ourselves to live in such ways that neither are, nor can be, offered to God, is the same irreligion as to neglect our prayers or use them in a manner unworthy of God.

The point of the matter is this: either reason and religion prescribe rules for all the ordinary actions of our life, or they do not. If they do, then it is as necessary to govern all our actions by those rules, as it is to worship God. For if religion teaches us anything concerning eating and drinking (1 Cor. 10:31), or spending our time (Eph. 5:16) and money (1 Tim. 6:8–10); if it teaches us how we are to use and despise the world (1 John 2:15); if it tells us what attitude we are to have in common life, or how we are to be disposed toward all people (Eph. 4:31–32); if it tells us how we are to behave toward the sick, the poor, the old, the destitute; if it tells us whom we are to treat with a particular love and whom we are to regard with a particular esteem; if it tells us how we are to treat our enemies (Matt. 5:44) and how we are to mortify (Col. 3:5) and deny ourselves (Matt. 16:24)—a person must be very weak to think these aspects of religion are not to be observed with as much exactness as any doctrines that relate to prayer.

There is not one command in the whole Gospel for public worship, and perhaps it is a duty that is insisted on in Scripture less than any other. The entire New Testament never so much as mentions that we should make it a matter of daily heedfulness, whereas the religion or devotion that is to govern the ordinary actions of our lives is found in almost every verse of Scripture.

Those Scriptures that deal with Christ or His apostles, are filled with doctrines that relate to daily living. They call us to renounce the world; to differ in every attitude and way of life from the spirit and the way of the world; to renounce all its goods, fear none of its evils, reject its joys, and have no value for its happiness; to be as newborn babes (1 Pet. 2:2), born into a new state of things; to live as pilgrims (1 Pet. 2:11) in spiritual watching, in holy fear, and in heavenly aspirations for another life; to take up our daily cross and deny ourselves (Matt. 16:24); to profess the blessedness of mourning (Matt. 5:4) and to seek the blessedness of poverty of spirit (Matt. 5:3); to forsake the pride and vanity of riches (1 Tim. 6:17); to take no thought for the morrow (Matt. 6:34); to live in the profoundest state of humility (James 4:10); to rejoice in worldly sufferings (1 Pet. 4:12–13); to reject the lust of the flesh, the lust of the eyes, and the pride of life (1 John 2:16); to bear injuries (Matt. 5:44); to forgive and bless our enemies (Matt. 5:43–44); to love mankind as God loves them (Eph. 5:2); to give up our hearts and affections entirely to God (James 4:7); and to strive to enter through the strait[2] gate (Matt. 7:13) into a life of eternal glory.

This is the common devotion that our blessed Savior taught, in order to make it the common life of all Christians. Is it not therefore very strange that people give so much weight to public worship, concerning which there is not one precept of our Lord's to be found, and yet they neglect these common duties of ordinary life, which are commanded in every page of the Gospel? I call these duties the devotion of everyday life, because if they are to be practiced, they must be made part of our lives every day; they can have no place anywhere else.

---

[2]The spelling here is actually correct, meaning *narrow* or *closely fitting*.

If heavenly affection and contempt of the world are necessary to the character of Christians, it is necessary that this mind-set appear in the whole course of their lives and in their manner of using the world, because it can have no place anywhere else. If self-denial is a condition of salvation, everyone who would be saved must make it a part of his daily life. If humility is a Christian duty, then the everyday life of a Christian is to be a constant course of humility in all its kinds. If poverty of spirit is necessary, it must be the spirit and attitude of every day of our lives.

If we are to relieve the naked, the sick, and the prisoner, it must be the common charity of our lives, as far as we can render ourselves able to perform it. If we are to love our enemies, we must make our lives a visible exercise and demonstration of that love every day. If contentment and thankfulness and the patient bearing of evil are duties to God, then they are the duties of every day and in every circumstance of our lives. If we are to be wise and holy as the newborn sons of God, we cannot be so unless we renounce everything that is foolish and vain in every part of our lives. If we are to be new creatures in Christ (2 Cor. 5:17), we must show that we are so, by having new ways of living in the world. (See Romans 12:2.) If we are to follow Christ, it must be in our way of spending every day.

It is the same for all the virtues and holy qualities of Christianity; they are not ours unless they are the virtues and qualities of our daily lives. Christianity does not leave us to live in the common ways of life, conforming to the folly of customs and gratifying the passions and desires in which the spirit of the world delights. Christianity does not indulge us in any of these things. All its virtues, which it makes necessary to salvation, are only so many ways of living above and contrary to the world in all the actions of our lives. If our lives are not every day a course of humility, self-denial, renunciation of the world, poverty of spirit, and heavenly affection, then we do not live the lives of Christians.

However, although a uniform, open, and visible practice of all these virtues is clearly what Christianity is, yet there is little or nothing of this to be found even among the better sort of people. You often see them at church, pleased with the fine preachers; but look into their lives, and you will see that they are the same sort of people as those who make no pretenses to devotion. The difference that you find between them is only the difference of their natural temperaments.

They have the same taste of the world, the same worldly cares, fears, and joys as the rest of the world; they have the same frame of mind, equally vain in their desires. They have the same fondness for luxurious living and material goods, the same pride and vanity of dress, the same self-love and indulgence, the same foolish friendships and groundless hatreds, the same levity of mind and trifling of spirit, the same fondness for entertainment, the same idle dispositions and vain ways of spending their time in visiting and conversation, as those who never intended to be devout.

This comparison is not between people who seem to be good and those who are known to be indulgent; but it is among people of moderate lives. Let us take an instance in two modest women. Suppose that one of them is careful about her times of devotion, and observes them through a sense of duty. And suppose that the other has no concern about it, but attends church seldom or often, just as it happens.

Now, it is easy to see the difference between these two women, but apart from this, can you find any further difference between them? Are not the customs, manners, and attitudes of the one, the same as the customs, manners, and attitudes of the other? Do they live as if they belonged to different worlds, had different ideas in their heads, and had different rules by which they governed all their actions? Do they not have the same goods and evils? Are they not pleased and displeased in the same manner, about the same things? Do they not live in the same course of life? Does one seem to be of this world, looking at the things that are temporal, and the other to be of another world, looking wholly at the things that are eternal (2 Cor. 4:18)?

If you examine their predominant attitudes in the greatest areas of life or in the greatest doctrines of Christianity, you will not find the least difference imaginable. In that case, you must look into their everyday lives and consider them with regard to the use of the world, because that is what everybody can see.

Now, you know that having the right ideas about God is necessary to religion, yet it is also necessary to have right ideas about this world. It is entirely possible for a man to have his affections set upon this world, and yet be considered a good Christian. And yet, if Christianity has not changed a man's mind and spirit with relation to these things, what can we say that it has done for him? For if the doctrines of Christianity were practiced, they would make a man as different from other people—as to all worldly temperaments, sensual pleasures, and the pride of life—as a wise man is different from an idiot. It would be as easy a thing to know a Christian by his outward way of life, as it is now difficult to find anybody who lives the Christian life.

Indeed, it is well known that Christians are now not only like other men in their frailties and infirmities (this might be in some degree excusable), but they are also like the world in all the most important aspects of their lives. They live every day in the same attitudes, the same designs, and the same indulgences as those who neither know God nor the happiness to be found in another life.

Everyone who is capable of any reflection must have observed that this is generally the state of devout people, whether men or women. You may see them as different from other people, inasmuch as they have specific times and places of prayer, but they are generally like the rest of the world in all the other parts of their lives: that is, they add Christian devotion to a heathen life.

I have the authority of our blessed Savior to say, "Take no thought, saying, What shall we eat? or, What shall we drink? or, Wherewithal shall we be clothed? (For after all these things do the Gentiles seek)" (Matt. 6:31–32). If being this concerned even with the necessities of this life shows that we are not yet of a Christian spirit, but are like the heathen, then surely to enjoy the vanity and folly of the world as they do—to be like them in the chief qualities and attitudes of our lives, in self-centeredness and indulgence; in sensual pleasures and diversions; in the vanity of dress and the love of show and greatness—is a much greater sign of a heathen spirit. Consequently, one who adds devotion to such a life, may be said to pray as a Christian, but he lives as a heathen.

16

Chapter Two

WHY WE FALL SHORT

I t may now be reasonably inquired, "How is it that even the lives of the better sort of people are thus strangely opposed to the principles of Christianity?" Before I give a direct answer to this, I think we should explore why swearing is so common a vice among Christians. If we can find the reason why the majority of men live in this notorious vice, we will have found the reason why even the majority of the better sort of people live so contrary to Christianity.

Indeed, swearing is more common among men than it is among women. However, this sin is so common among men that there are perhaps more than two in three that are guilty of it through the whole course of their lives, swearing just as it happens, some constantly, others only now and then.

Now, why is it that two out of three men are guilty of so gross and profane a sin as this? There is neither ignorance nor human infirmity to blame for it; it is against an express commandment and one of the most distinct doctrines of the Scriptures (Exod. 20:7). Rather, the reason is because men do not have so much as the intention to please God in all their actions. For, if one of those men had just enough piety as to intend to please God in all his actions, considering it the happiest and best thing in the world, he would never swear again. It would

17

be as impossible for him to swear, while he feels this intention within himself, as it is impossible for a man who intends to please his king to go up and abuse him to his face.

It seems like such a small part of devotion to have such a sincere intention, but it is absolutely necessary. A Christian who has not reached this degree of piety has no reason to consider himself a disciple of Christ. And yet, it is purely because so many men lack this degree of piety, that you see such a mixture of sin and folly even in the lives of the better sort of people. It is because they lack this intention that you see men profess religion yet live in swearing and sensuality; that you see clergymen given to pride, covetousness, and worldly enjoyments.

It is because they lack this intention that you see women profess devotion yet live in all the folly and vanity of dress, wasting their time in idleness and pleasures, and in every instance of luxury that their money can buy. For if a woman were simply to feel her heart full of this intention, she would find it impossible to primp and preen; she would no more desire to shine at balls or assemblies, or to be recognized among those who are most finely dressed, than she would desire to dance on a rope to please spectators. Instead, she would know that the one is as far from the wisdom and excellency of the Christian spirit as the other.

It was this general intention that made the first Christians such eminent instances of piety. Stop here and ask yourself, "Why am I not as pious as the first Christians were?" Your own heart will tell you that it is neither through ignorance nor inability, but purely because you never thoroughly intended it. You observe the same Sunday worship that they did, and you are strict in it because it is your full intention to be so. Nevertheless, when you fully intend to be as they were in their ordinary lives, when you intend to please God in all your actions, you will find it as possible as being strictly exact about attending church.

Now, can someone who lacks this general, sincere intention still be considered a Christian? Well, if the sincere intention to serve God were among Christians, it would change the whole face of the world: true piety and exemplary holiness would be as common and visible as buying and selling.

If a gentleman of birth and fortune would simply have this intention to please God, he would be carried from every appearance of evil to every instance of piety and goodness. He would not live in idleness and indulgence, in pleasures and intemperance, in vain expenses and high living, because these things cannot be turned into means of piety and holiness, or made into parts of a wise and religious life. The more he would remove himself "from all appearance of evil" (1 Thess. 5:22), the more he would hasten and aspire after every instance of goodness.

He would not ask what is allowable and pardonable, but he would ask what is commendable and praiseworthy. He would not ask whether God will forgive the folly of his life, the madness of his pleasures, the vanity of his expenses, the richness of his possessions, and the careless consumption of his time; but he would ask whether God is pleased with these things or whether these are the appointed ways of gaining His favor.

He would not inquire whether it is pardonable to hoard up money, adorn himself with gold, and gild his chariots, while the widow and the orphan, the sick and the prisoner, desperately need relief; but he would ask whether God has required us to give Him these things, whether we will be called to account for them at the Last Day (Matt. 25:31–46). It would not be his intention to live in ways that God may perhaps pardon, but he would intend to be diligent in ways that God will infallibly reward.

He would not look at the lives of Christians to learn how he ought to spend his money and time, but he would look into the Scriptures and make every doctrine, parable, precept, or instruction that relates to rich men, a law to himself. He would have nothing to do with costly apparel, because the rich man in the gospel of Luke was clothed with purple and fine linen (Luke 16:19–31). He would deny himself the pleasures and indulgences that his resources could procure for him, because our blessed Savior says, "Woe unto you that are rich! for ye have received your consolation" (Luke 6:24). He would spend all that he could for charity, because "the Judge of quick and dead" (Acts 10:42) has said that all that is so given, is given to Him (Matt. 25:40).

He would have no hospitable table for the rich and wealthy to come and feast with him in good eating and drinking, because our Lord says,

> When thou makest a dinner or a supper, call not thy friends, nor thy brethren, neither thy kinsmen, nor thy rich neighbours; lest they also bid thee again, and a recompense be made thee. But when thou makest a feast, call the poor, the maimed, the lame, the blind: and thou shalt be blessed; for they cannot recompense thee: for thou shalt be recompensed at the resurrection of the just.
>
> (Luke 14:12–14)

He would not be carried from pleasure to pleasure in expensive materialism, because

> *All that is in the world, the lust of the flesh,*
> *and the lust of the eyes, and the pride of life,*
> *is not of the Father, but is of the world.*
> *(1 John 2:16)*

Do not look upon this as an imaginary description of charity, that looks fine in the mind but cannot be put into practice. This is so far from being an imaginary, impracticable form of life, that it has been practiced in former ages by great numbers of Christians, who were glad to turn their whole lives into a constant course of charity. And it is so far from being impossible now, that if we can find any Christians who sincerely intend to please God in all their actions—whether they are young or old, single or married, men or women—if they have this intention, it will be impossible for them to do otherwise. This one principle will infallibly carry them to this height of charity, and they will find themselves unable to stop short of it.

For how is it possible for a man to bury his money in needless finery, in covering himself or his horses with gold, when he intends to please God in the use of his money, and intends it because he judges it to be his greatest happiness? How is it possible for anyone intent on pleasing God to waste his money, while there are works of piety and charity to be done with it, or ways of spending it well? This is as impossible as it would be for a man who intends to please God in his words, to go into company on purpose to swear and lie. For just as all waste and unreasonable expense is done intentionally and with deliberation, so no one whose constant intention is to please

21

God in the use of his money, can be guilty of waste.

I have chosen to explain this matter by appealing to this intention, because it makes the case so plain, and because we may see it in the clearest light and feel it in the strongest manner simply by looking into our own hearts. Everyone can as easily tell how he spends his money and whether he considers how to please God in it, as he can tell where his resources are and whether they are in money or land. There is no plea left for ignorance or frailty as to this matter; everyone is in the light, and no one can fail except the person who does not intend to please God in all that he has.

Think of two persons: one is regular in public and private prayer; the other is not. Now, the reason for this difference is not that one has strength and power to observe prayer, and the other does not; rather, one intends to please God in the duties of devotion, and the other has no intention of that kind.

The case is the same in the right or wrong use of our time and money. You might see one person throwing away his time in sleep and idleness, in visiting and diversions, and his money in the most vain and unreasonable expenses. You see another being careful about every day, dividing his hours by rules of reason and religion, and spending all his money in works of charity. The difference is not that one has strength and power to do things this way, and the other has not; but it is that one intends to please God in the right use of all his time and money, and the other does not.

Here, therefore, let us judge ourselves sincerely. We should not so easily accept the common disorders of our lives, the vanity of our expenses, the folly of our diversions, the pride of our habits, the idleness of our lives, and the wasting of our time, thinking that these are the imperfections we must fall into through the unavoidable weakness and frailty of our natures. Rather, let us be assured that these disorders of our everyday lives are due to the fact that we do not intend to please God in all the actions of our lives. We must not look upon ourselves as in a state of common and pardonable imperfection, but in a state that needs the first and most fundamental principle of Christianity, that is, an intention to please God in everything.

The problem is not that we desire to be good and perfect but fall short of it through the weakness of our nature. Rather, the problem is that we do not have enough piety to intend to be as good as we can, or to please God in all the actions of our lives. We see this plainly in the case of one who spends his time in sports when he should be at church; it is not that he needs more power, but that he lacks the intention or desire to be there.

The case is obviously the same in every other folly of human life. A woman who spends her time and money in the unreasonable ways and fashions of the world, does not do so because she needs power to be wise and religious in the management of her time and money, but because she has no intention or desire of being so. When she feels this intention, however, she will find it quite possible to manage her time and money wisely, because it will be her concern and desire to do so.

This doctrine does not suppose that we have no need of divine grace, or that it is in our own power to make ourselves perfect. It only supposes that, through the lack of a sincere intention to please God in all our actions, we fall into irregularities of life that we would have power to avoid by the ordinary means of grace. It only teaches us that we do not have the perfection that our present state of grace makes us capable of, because we do not so much as intend to have it.

The reason why we see no real self-sacrifice or self-denial, no eminent charity, no profound humility, no heavenly affection, no true contempt of the world, no Christian meekness, no sincere zeal, no eminent piety in the lives of Christians, is because Christians do not so much as intend to be exact and exemplary in these virtues. As we will see in the next chapter, this is not only foolish, but it is also dangerous to the Christian walk.

Chapter Three

THE PRACTICE OF CHRISTIAN VIRTUES

The goodness of God and His rich mercies in Christ Jesus are a sufficient assurance to us that He will be merciful to our unavoidable weaknesses, that is, to the failings that are the effects of our ignorance. However, we have no reason to expect the same mercy toward us for those sins that we have lived in and have had no intention to avoid. For instance, a common swearer seems to have no claim to the divine mercy, because he can no more plead weakness as his excuse than the man that hid his talent in the earth (Matt. 25:24–29) could plead that he lacked the strength to keep it out of the earth.

Now, if this is right reasoning in the case of a common swearer—that his sin is not to be considered a pardonable frailty because he has no weakness to plead in its excuse—why then do we not carry this way of reasoning to its true extent? Why do we not condemn every other error of life in the same way? For if swearing is bad because we might avoid it if we sincerely intended to, must not all other erroneous ways of life also cause us guilt if we live in them, not through weakness and inability, but because we never sincerely intended to avoid them?

Perhaps you have made no progress in the most important Christian virtues: you have scarcely gone halfway in humility and charity.

Now, if your failure in these duties is due to your lack of intention to perform them in any true degree, do you not have then as little to say for yourself as the common swearer? Are you not as much without excuse? Why, then, do you not examine your conscience with regard to these things? Do you not think it as dangerous to live in defects that are in your power to amend, as it is for a common swearer to live in the breach of that duty that is in his power to observe? Are not negligence and the lack of a sincere intention as blameworthy in one case as in another?

You will perhaps say that everyone falls short of the perfection of the Gospel (Rom. 3:23), and that you are therefore content with your failings. However, that is a pointless statement. The question is not whether gospel perfection can be fully attained, but whether you come as near it as a sincere intention and careful diligence can carry you. Are you not now in a much lower state than you might be if you sincerely intended and carefully labored to advance yourself in all Christian virtues?

If you are moving as forward in the Christian life as your best endeavors can move you, then you may legitimately hope that your imperfections will not be laid to your charge; but if your defects in piety, humility, and charity are due to your negligence and lack of sincere intention to be as eminent as you can in these virtues, then you leave yourself as much without excuse as one who lives in the sin of swearing because he has no sincere intention to depart from it.

The salvation of our souls is set forth in Scripture as a thing of difficulty, a thing that requires all our diligence and is to be worked out with fear and trembling (Phil. 2:12). We are told that "strait is the gate, and narrow is the way, which leadeth unto life, and few there be that find it" (Matt. 7:14). We are also told that "many are called, but few are chosen" (Matt. 22:14), and that many will miss their salvation, although they seem to have taken some pains to obtain it, as in these words: "Strive to enter in at the strait gate: for many, I say unto you, will seek to enter in, and shall not be able" (Luke 13:24).

Our Lord commands us to strive to enter in, because many who only seek to enter will fail. By this, we are clearly taught that religion is a state of labor and striving, and that many will fail to obtain salvation—not because they took no pains to care about it, but because they did not take pains to care enough; they only sought, but did not strive, to enter in. Every Christian, therefore, should examine his life by these doctrines as well as he examines it by the commandments.

If my religion is only a formal compliance with the modes of worship that are in fashion where I live; if it costs me no pains or trouble; if it puts me under no rules and restraints; if I have no careful thoughts and sober reflections about it; is it not great weakness to think that I am striving to enter in at the strait gate? If I am seeking everything that can delight my senses and feed my appetites; if I am spending my time and fortune in leisure, entertainment, and worldly enjoyments; if I am a stranger to fasting and prayer and self-denial; how can it be said that I am working out my salvation with fear and trembling (Phil. 2:12)? If there is nothing in my life that shows me to be different from nonbelievers; if I use the world and worldly enjoyments as the majority of people now do, and in all ages have done; why should I think that I am

27

among those few who are walking in the narrow way to heaven?

And yet, if the way is narrow, if none can walk in it except those that strive, should I not ask myself whether I am taking a path that is narrow enough, or whether the pains I take are sufficient? Should this not be at least as important as my observing the second and third commandments?

The sum of this matter is this: Our salvation depends on the sincerity and perfection of our endeavors to obtain it. Weak and imperfect men will, notwithstanding their frailties and defects, be received as having pleased God, if they have done their utmost to please Him. The rewards of charity, piety, and humility will be given to those whose lives have been a careful labor to exercise these virtues in as high a degree as they could.

We cannot offer God the service of angels; we cannot obey Him as man in a state of perfection could. But, fallen men can do their best, and this is the perfection that is required of us; it is only the perfection of our best endeavors, a careful labor to be as perfect as we can. However, if we stop short of this, for all we know, we stop short of the mercy of God and leave ourselves nothing to plead from the terms of the Gospel. In the Scriptures, God has made no promises of mercy to the slothful and negligent. His mercy is only offered to our frail and imperfect but nonetheless best endeavors to practice all manner of righteousness. The law to angels is angelic righteousness; the law to perfect beings is strict perfection; therefore, the law to our imperfect natures is the best obedience that our frail nature is able to perform.

It seems right that the measure of our love to God is the measure of our love of every virtue. We are to love and practice Christian virtues with all our heart, with all our soul, with all our mind, and with all our strength. (See Mark 12:30.) When we cease to live with this regard to virtue, we live below our nature, and, instead of being able to plead our infirmities, we stand guilty of negligence.

It is for this reason that we are exhorted to work out our salvation with fear and trembling (Phil. 2:12). For unless our hearts are eagerly bent on the work of our salvation, unless holy fears animate our endeavors and keep us constantly examining how we live and how ready we are to die, we will in all probability fall into a state of negligence and become far too comfortable with a life that will never carry us to the rewards of heaven.

If you will consider that a just God can only make allowances that are suitable to His justice, and that your works are all to be examined by fire (1 Cor. 3:13), you will find that fear and trembling are proper attitudes for drawing near so great a trial. Indeed, there is no probability that you will be able to do all that is expected of you, or that you will make the progress in piety that the holiness and justice of God require of you, unless you are constantly afraid of falling short of it.

Now, this is not intended to make believers anxious or discontent in the service of God. Rather, it is meant to fill them with a just fear of living in sloth and idleness, and in the neglect of virtues that they will want at the Day of Judgment. It is meant to excite them to an earnest examination of their lives, to such zeal and care and concern after Christian perfection as that which would be used in any matter that has gained their hearts and affections. It is only asking them to be very apprehensive of their state, very humble in their opinion of themselves, very earnest after higher degrees of piety, and very fearful of falling short of happiness, as the apostle Paul was when he wrote to the Philippians,

> *Not as though I had already attained, either were already perfect...but this one thing I do, forgetting those things which are behind, and reaching forth unto those things which are before, I press toward the mark for the prize of the high calling of God in Christ Jesus.* (Phil. 3:12–14)

And then he added in verse 15, "Let us therefore, as many as be perfect, be thus minded."

If the apostle thought it necessary for those who were in his state of perfection to be "thus minded"—that is, laboring, pressing, and aspiring after some degree of holiness to which they were not then arrived—surely it is much more necessary for us, who are born in these last days and laboring under great imperfections, to be "thus minded." That is, we must be earnest and strive after such degrees of a holy and divine life as we have not yet attained. The best way for anyone to know how much he ought to aspire after holiness, is to consider, not what will make his present life easy, but what will make things easier for him at the hour of death. For at that hour, every person will wish that he had been as perfect as human nature can be.

Is this not enough to excite both our wishes for that perfection and our laboring after it, so that we will not have regrets on our deathbed? Is it not excessively foolish for us to be content with a course of piety that we already know cannot content us on our day of death? How can we carry a more severe condemnation against ourselves than to believe that, at the hour of death, we will wish that we had been among the first servants of God, and yet to adopt no methods of practicing Christian virtues while we are alive?

This may be an absurdity that we can easily pass over at present, while the health of our bodies, the passions of our minds, the noise, the hurry, the pleasures, and the business of the world lead us on with eyes that see not and ears that hear not (Jer. 5:21); yet, at death, it will set itself before us in a dreadful magnitude, it will haunt us like a dismal ghost, and our consciences will never let us take our eyes off it.

We often see a man of the world who is hardly able to forgive himself when he has been brought into any calamity or disgrace purely by his own folly. Self-condemnation quickly becomes a torment to him. The affliction is made doubly tormenting because he must place all the blame on himself, for he has acted against the nature and reason of things, and contrary to the advice of all his friends. From this we may in some degree guess how terrible the pain of that self-condemnation will be, when a man finds himself in the miseries of death. His self-condemning conscience must charge all his distress upon his own folly and madness, for he has acted against the sense and reason of his own mind, against all the doctrines and precepts of religion, and contrary to all the instructions, calls, and warnings of both God and man.

Imagine standing at the bedside when some particular acquaintance or relation of yours lies in distress and agony, lamenting the folly of his past life. He very much regrets how he has neglected and

31

disregarded the piety of the Gospel and the terms of salvation. Not only does he have his frailties and imperfections to lament at this time, but he must acknowledge that he has thoroughly neglected all religious improvement and all consideration of what God has required of him. What pain do you think a man must feel when his conscience lays all this folly before him, when it shows him how regular, exact, and wise he has been in small matters that are passed away like a dream, and how stupidly and senselessly he has lived, without any reflection, without any rules, in eternal things?

We often think of death as a miserable separation from the enjoyments of this life. Yet, what is miserable or dreadful about death except the consequences of it? When a man is dead, what does anything mean to him except the state he is in then? Feasts and pleasures and enjoyments seem great things to us while we are thinking of nothing higher; but as soon as we add death to them, they all sink into an equal littleness.

Again, if you were to stand by the bedside when your poor friend lay in agony, it would in all likelihood teach you wisdom that never before entered your heart. You might consider how often you yourself could have been surprised in a state of negligence, and your heart would be softened, and you would turn the remainder of your own life into a regular course of piety. The whole of your Christian life, if you will seriously consider it, is to be a course of striving after piety and perfection.

Chapter Four

DEVOTING YOUR WORK TO GOD

I n the first chapter I wrote about the general nature of devotion, and we saw that it does not imply any form of prayer, but it is a certain form of life that is offered to God. We also saw that devotion is not meant for particular times or places, but for every place and in everything. I will now draw your attention to some particulars, to show how we are to devote our labor and employment, our time, and our money to God.

A Christian should consider every place as holy, because God is there. Likewise, he should look upon every part of his life as a matter of holiness, because everything is to be offered to God. We understand that the profession of a clergyman is a holy profession because it is a ministration in holy things, an attendance at the altar. However, worldly business is also to be made holy unto the Lord, by being done as a service to Him and in conformity to His divine will. Every person, place, or thing in the world that is devoted to divine service belongs to God; all things are to be used and all persons are to act for the glory of God.

Men of worldly business, therefore, must not look upon themselves as free to live to themselves, their own whims, and their own states of mind simply because their employment is of a worldly nature. Rather, they must consider that the world and all worldly professions belong to God as truly as persons and things that are devoted to the altar. It is as much the duty of men in worldly business to live wholly unto God, as it is the duty of those who are devoted to divine service.

All men are obliged to act for God with all their powers and faculties because every person receives his powers and faculties from Him. Men will, obviously, hold various jobs and employments, yet they must all work for the same end: to be dutiful servants of God in the right and pious performance of their various callings. Clergymen must live wholly unto God in the exercise of holy offices, in the ministration of prayers and sacraments, and in a zealous distribution of spiritual goods. Men of other employments are, in their particular ways, as much obliged to act as servants of God and to live wholly unto Him in their various callings.

It is true that clergymen, who have devoted themselves to God a second time (besides their baptismal vows) to be His servants, are to keep themselves as separate and different from the common life of other men as an altar is kept separate from tables of common use. Yet, as all Christians are by their baptism devoted to God, so they all, in their various occupations, are to live as holy and heavenly persons, doing everything as a service to God. For things spiritual and temporal, sacred and common, must, like men and angels, like heaven and earth, all join together to glorify God.

As there is but one God and Father of us all (Eph. 4:6), whose glory gives light and life to everything that lives, whose presence fills all places, whose power supports all beings, whose providence rules all events (Ps. 103:19); so all that live, whether in heaven or earth—whether thrones or principalities, men or angels—must, with one spirit, live wholly to the praise and glory of this one God and Father of them all (see Psalm 150:6): angels as angels, in their heavenly ministrations; men as men, women as women, bishops as bishops, priests as priests, and deacons as deacons; some with spiritual things and some with temporal things, offering to God the daily sacrifice of a reasonable life, wise actions, purity of heart, and heavenly affections.

This is something that everyone needs to do while in this world. It is not necessary for women to trifle away their time in the follies and impertinences of a fashionable life, nor is it necessary for men to resign themselves to worldly cares and concerns. The rich need not gratify their passions in the indulgences and pride of life, and the poor need not vex and torment their hearts with their impoverished condition.

Instead, men and women, rich and poor, must, with bishops and priests, walk before God in the same wise and holy spirit, in the same denial of all vain states of mind, and in the same discipline and care of their souls—not only because they all have the same rational nature and are servants of the same God, but because they all need the same holiness to make them fit for the happiness to which they are all called. It is therefore absolutely necessary for all Christians, whether men or women, to consider themselves devoted to holiness. From there, they must order their everyday ways of life by such rules of reason and piety that may turn them into continual services unto God Almighty.

Now, to do this, we must have the same spirit that is required in any work of piety. For, if "whether...[we] eat, or drink, or whatsoever [we] do," we are to "do all to the glory of God" (1 Cor. 10:31); if we are to "use this world, as not abusing it" (1 Cor. 7:31); if we are to "present [our] bodies a living sacrifice, holy, acceptable unto God" (Rom. 12:1); if we are to live "by faith, not by sight" (2 Cor. 5:7); if we are to have "our conversation...in heaven" (Phil. 3:20)—then it is necessary that our lives, in every position, be made to glorify God by the same dispositions that make our prayers and adorations acceptable to Him. For if we are worldly or earthly-minded in our employments, if they are carried on with vain desires and covetous spirits, only to satisfy ourselves, we can no more be said to live to the glory of God than gluttons and drunkards can be said to eat and drink to the glory of God.

Whatever we do to the glory of God must be done with a spirit suitable to that glory. The same state of mind that makes our alms and devotions acceptable, must also make our labor a proper offering to God. If a man works to be rich, and pursues his business that he may raise himself to a position of fame and fortune in the world, he is no longer serving God in his employment. Rather, he is acting under other masters, and he no more deserves a reward from God than one who gives alms that he may be seen, or prays that he may be heard of men (Matt. 6:3–5).

Vain and earthly desires are no more allowable in our employments than in our alms and devotions. Temperaments of worldly pride and vainglory are not only evil when they mix with our good works, but they have the same evil nature and make us odious to God when they enter into our business employment. If it were allowable to indulge covetous or vain passions in our worldly employments, it would then be allowable to be vainglorious in our devotions. However, as our alms and devotions are not an acceptable service unless they proceed from a heart truly devoted to God, so our work cannot be considered a service to Him unless it is performed with the same piety of heart.

Most of the employments of life are lawful in themselves. They may be made a substantial part of our duty to God, as long as we remember to engage in them only insofar as is suitable to beings that are to live above the world. This is the only spiritual application to worldly business: it must have no more of our hands, our hearts, or our time than is consistent with a hearty, daily, careful preparation of ourselves for another life.

Christians must renounce this world to prepare themselves, by daily devotion and universal holiness, for an eternal state of quite another nature. They must look upon worldly employments as they look upon worldly desires and bodily infirmities—as things not to be desired, but only to be endured and suffered until death and the resurrection have carried us to an eternal state of real happiness.

Whoever does not look at the things of this life in this degree of littleness, cannot be said either to feel or believe the greatest truths of Christianity. For if he thinks there is anything great or important in human business, how can he feel or believe the Scriptures, which represent this life and the greatest things of life as vapors, dreams, and shadows? (See James 4:14 and 1 Chronicles 29:15.) If he thinks appearance and show and worldly glory are the proper happiness of a Christian, how can he be said to feel or believe the doctrine, "Blessed are ye, when men shall hate you, and when they shall separate you from their company, and shall reproach you, and cast out your name as evil, for the Son of man's sake" (Luke 6:22)?

Surely, if there were any real happiness in appearances, show, and worldly glory—if these things deserved our thoughts and care—it could not be a matter of the highest joy when we are torn from them by persecutions and sufferings. If, therefore, a man will live as to show that he feels and believes the most fundamental doctrines of Christianity, he must live above the world. He must do the business of life and yet live wholly unto God, going through his worldly employment with a heavenly mind.

The farmer who tills the ground is employed in an honest business—one that is necessary in life and very capable of being made an acceptable service unto God. However, if he labors and toils, not to serve any reasonable ends of life, but in order to have his plow made of silver and to have his horses harnessed in gold, the honesty of his employment is lost to him, and his labor becomes his folly.

One who works that he may be rich and live in pleasure and indulgence, lives no more to the glory of God than one who gambles for the same ends. For though there is a great difference between working and gambling, most of that difference is lost when men do their work for the same ends that others gamble. Charity and fine dressing are very different things, but if men give to the poor for the same reasons that others dress finely—only to be seen and admired—then charity is like the vanity of fine clothes. If the same motives that make some people hardworking and industrious in their trades also cause others to be constantly gambling, the two activities become one and the same.

The majority of working people, especially in the cities, are buried in business all week long, unable to think of anything else. Then they spend their Sundays in idleness and refreshment, in visits and jovial meetings that often make it the worst day of the week. Of course, they do not live this way because they cannot live apart from their work, but they live this way because they want to grow rich and maintain their families in a degree of finery for which a reasonable Christian life has no need.

If we could remove this frame of mind, people in all kinds of work would find themselves at leisure to live every day like Christians, to be careful of every duty of the Gospel, to live in a visible course of religion, and to be strict observers both of public and private prayer. The only way to do this is to have people consider their employment as something that they are obliged to devote to the glory of God, something that they are to do only as a duty to Him. Nothing can be right in business that is not under these rules.

The apostle Paul commanded servants to be obedient to their masters

> in singleness of...heart, as unto Christ; not
> with eyeservice, as menpleasers; but as the
> servants of Christ, doing the will of God
> from the heart; with good will doing service,
> as to the Lord, and not to men. (Eph. 6:5-7)

This passage sufficiently shows that all Christians are to live wholly unto God in every state and condition, doing the work of their calling as part of their devotion or service to God. For, certainly, if slaves are to look to God in all their actions, and serve in singleness of heart as unto the Lord, surely men of other employments and conditions are as much obliged to go through their businesses with the same singleness of heart—not pleasing the vanity of their own minds, not gratifying their own selfish and worldly desires, but living as the servants of God in all that they have to do.

No one would say that a slave is to devote his life to God and make the will of God the sole rule and end of his service, without saying that a businessman must act with the same spirit of devotion in his business. It is therefore absolutely certain that no Christian is to enter any further into business, nor for any other ends, unless he can in singleness of heart offer it to God as a reasonable service. (See Romans 12:1.) For the Son of God has redeemed us that we should, by a life of reason and piety, live to the glory of God (Luke 1:68–75). This is the only rule and measure for every order and state of life. Without this rule, the most lawful employment becomes a sinful state of life.

Take this away from the life of a clergyman, and his holy profession serves only to expose him to a greater damnation. Take this away from businessmen, and businesses become merely houses of greediness and filthy profits. Take this away from gentlemen, and the course of their lives becomes a course of sensuality, pride, and corruption. Take this rule from our tables, and all falls into gluttony and drunkenness. Take this measure from our manner of dress, and all is turned into such paint and glitter and ridiculous ornaments, so as to shame the wearer. Take this away from the use of our money, and you will find people spending liberally in everything except charity. Take this away from our leisure time, and you will find no sports too silly and no entertainments too vain and corrupt to be the pleasure of Christians.

If, therefore, we desire to live unto God, it is necessary to bring our lives completely under this law, to make His glory the sole rule and measure of every employment of life. There is no other true devotion except that of living in devotion to God in the everyday business of our lives.

Men must not content themselves with the lawfulness of their employments, but they must consider whether they use them as they are to use everything—as strangers and pilgrims (1 Pet. 2:11) who are baptized into the resurrection of Jesus Christ (Col. 2:12), who are to follow Him in a wise and heavenly course of life (1 Pet. 1:15–16), in the conscious denial of all worldly desires and in purifying and preparing their souls (Eph. 5:26–27) for the blessed enjoyment of God. Vanity, pride, covetousness, or ambition in the common course of business is as contrary to these holy qualities of Christianity as cheating and dishonesty. A Christian is not only required to be honest, but he must be of a Christian spirit and make his life an exercise of humility, repentance, and heavenly affection.

Proud views and vain desires in our worldly employments are as truly vices and corruptions as hypocrisy in prayer, or vanity in almsgiving (Matt. 6:3–5). These things make us repulsive to God, just as any other kind of pride would do. One who labors and toils in a calling so that he may gain fame and popularity, is as far from the pious humility of a Christian as one who gives to charity for show. Pride and vanity in our prayers and offerings make them unacceptable services to God, not because there is anything particular in prayers and alms that cannot allow for pride, but because pride is in no respect made for man. Pride destroys the piety of our prayers and alms because it destroys the piety of everything that it touches and renders every action that it governs incapable of being offered to God.

God requires us to show humility in all our actions and designs, just as we would show truth and honesty. A man is not honest and true because he is so to a great many people, or upon several occasions. Rather, a man is honest and true because truth and honesty are the measure of all his dealings. Likewise, humility must be the general ruling habit of our minds, extending to all our actions.

We sometimes talk as if a man might be humble in some things and proud in others—humble in his dress, but proud of his learning; humble in his person, but proud in his views and designs. Nevertheless, though this may pass in common discourse, where few things are said according to strict truth, it cannot be allowed once we look into the nature of our actions.

It is very possible for a man who lives by cheating, to be very punctual in paying for what he buys. At the same time, everyone is assured that he does not do so out of any principle of true honesty. It is also very possible for a man who is proud of his estate, ambitious in his views, or conceited about his learning, to dress humbly, as a truly humble man would do. However, to suppose that he does so out of a principle of religious humility, is as absurd as supposing that a thief pays for what he buys out of a principle of religious honesty. Just as dishonesty destroys our claim to an honest principle of mind, so does pride destroy our claim to a humble spirit.

There is no doubt that prayers and alms that proceed from pride and ostentation are abominable to God. Yet, that pride is as pardonable there as anywhere else. Suppose God rejects pride in our prayers and alms, but bears with pride in our dress, our persons, or our estates. It would be the same as supposing that God condemns falsehood in some actions, but allows it in others. Pride in one thing differs from pride in another thing as much as the robbing of one man differs from the robbing of another. In other words, there is no real difference.

Again, if pride and ostentation are so abhorrent that they destroy the merit and worth of the most reasonable actions, surely pride must be equally repugnant in those actions that are founded only in the weakness and feebleness of our natures. For instance, alms are commanded by God as excellent in themselves, as true instances of a divine temperament, but clothes are only allowed to cover our shame (Gen. 3:7). Surely, therefore, it must be at least as hateful to be vain in our clothes as to be vain in our alms.

A regular and uniform piety, one that extends itself to all the actions of our lives, is absolutely necessary. We must eat and drink and dress and discourse according to the sobriety of the Christian spirit. We should engage in no employments except those we can truly devote to God, nor pursue them any farther than contributes to the reasonable ends of a holy, devout life. We must be honest, not only on particular occasions or when it is favored by the world, easy to be performed, and free from danger or loss, but out of a living principle of justice that makes us love truth and integrity in all its instances, and that makes us follow it through all dangers and against all opposition.

For we know that the more we pay for any truth, the better is our bargain, and our integrity becomes a pearl when we have parted with all to keep it. We must be humble, not only in such instances as are expected in the world, or suitable to our temperaments, or confined to particular occasions, but in a humility of spirit that renders us meek and lowly in the whole course of our lives. Humility must show itself in our dress, our person, our conversation, our enjoyment of the world, the tranquillity of our minds, our patience under injuries, our submission to superiors, our condescensions to those that are below us, and in all the outward actions of our lives.

We must not only devote times and places to prayer, but be everywhere in the spirit of devotion. With hearts always set toward heaven, we must look up to God in all our actions and do everything as His servants. We must live in the world as in a holy temple of God, always worshipping Him, though not with our lips, yet with the thankfulness of our hearts, the holiness of our actions, and the pious and charitable use of all His gifts. We must not only send up petitions and thoughts to heaven, but we must go through all our worldly business with a heavenly spirit, as members of Christ's mystical body—so that, with new hearts and new minds, we may turn an earthly life into a preparation for a life of greatness and glory in the kingdom of heaven.

Now, the only way to arrive at this piety of spirit is to bring all your actions under the same rule as your devotions and alms. You know very well what it is that makes the piety of your alms or devotions; now the same rules, the same regard to God, must render everything else that you do, a fit and acceptable service unto God. I hope I have written enough to show you the necessity of introducing religion into all the actions of your everyday life, and of living and acting with the same regard to God, in all that you do, as in your prayers and alms.

If, at every meal, the head of each family were to make a solemn adoration of God, in a manner suitable to a devout mind, he would turn this ordinary action of animal life into a piety to God by making every meal to begin and end with devotion. We yet see some remains of this custom in Christian families, but, indeed, it is now generally performed more like a mockery upon devotion than any solemn application of the mind unto God. So, if in these days of general corruption this part of devotion falls into a mock ceremony, it is because sensuality and intemperance have too great a power over us for us to add any devotion to our meals. Nevertheless, when we are as pious as Jews and heathens of all ages have been, we will think it proper to pray at the beginning and end of our meals.

I have appealed to this pious custom of all ages of the world, as a proof that religion is to be the rule and measure of all the actions of ordinary life. For surely, if we are to eat only under such rules of devotion, then whatever else we do, must, in its proper way, be done with the same regard to the glory of God and according to the principles of a devout and pious mind.

Chapter Five

DEVOTING EVERYTHING TO GOD

As we saw in the previous chapter, no one is to live in his employment according to his own pleasure, but he is to do all his business as a service unto God. However, many people are free from the necessities of labor and employments, and they have their time and money at their own disposal. Are they, likewise, expected to glorify God through their business, when they have no employment?

Those who have no particular employment, who seem left at greater liberty to live to themselves, to pursue their own desires, and to spend their time and fortunes as they please—they are actually under greater obligations of living wholly unto God in all their actions. The freedom of their condition puts them under a greater necessity of always choosing and always doing the best things. They are those of whom much will be required, because much is given to them (Luke 12:48).

A slave can only live unto God in one particular way, that is, by religious patience and submission in his state of slavery. Even so, all ways of holy living, all instances and all kinds of virtue, lie open to those who are masters of themselves, their time, and their money. It is therefore the duty of such persons to make a wise use of their liberty, to devote themselves to all kinds of virtue, to aspire after everything that is holy and pious, to endeavor to be eminent in all good works, and to please God in the highest and most perfect manner.

If you are neither laborer nor businessman, neither merchant nor soldier, consider yourself, therefore, as placed in a state similar to that of the angels, who are sent into the world as ministering spirits for the general good of mankind, to assist, protect, and minister to them who will be heirs of salvation (Heb. 1:13–14). For the more you are free from the common necessities of men, the more you are to imitate the higher perfections of angels.

Those who must work for a living have a duty to serve and glorify God by humility, obedience, and faithfulness in their various employments. When the time comes for men to be rewarded for their labors by the great "Judge of quick and dead" (Acts 10:42), the Lord will receive these humble and obedient ones, saying,

> *Well done, thou good and faithful servant: thou hast been faithful over a few things, I will make thee ruler over many things: enter thou into the joy of thy lord.   (Matt. 25:21)*

However, if you have been placed above the necessities of life, with nothing to do but to make the best use of a variety of blessings to the honor of God—then it is your duty to imitate the greatest servants of God, to inquire how the most eminent saints have lived, to study all the arts and methods of perfection, and to set no bounds on your love and gratitude to the bountiful Author of so many blessings. It is your duty to turn your five talents into five more (Matt. 25:16) and to consider how your time, leisure, health, and money may be made into the means of purifying your own soul and carrying you at last to the greatest heights of eternal glory.

Your soul is to be the object of daily care and attendance. Be sorry for its impurities, its spots, and its imperfections, and study all the holy arts of restoring it to its natural and primitive purity. Delight in its service, and beg of God to adorn it with every grace and perfection. Nourish it with good works; give it peace in solitude; get it strength in prayer; make it wise with reading; enlighten it by meditation; make it tender with love; sweeten it with humility; humble it with repentance; enliven it with psalms and hymns; and comfort it with frequent reflections upon future glory. Keep it in the presence of God, and teach it to imitate those guardian angels who, though they attend on human affairs and the lowest of mankind, yet "always behold the face of [our] Father which is in heaven" (Matt. 18:10).

God has but one command to all mankind, whether they are bound or free, rich or poor: that they live up to the excellency of that nature that He has given them; that they live by reason; that they walk in the light of religion, use everything as wisdom directs, glorify God in all His gifts, and dedicate every condition of life to His service. If you work for a living, you are to be reasonable and pious and holy in all your labors. However, if you have both time and money in your own power, you are obliged to have the same reason, holiness, and piety in the use of all your time and all your fortune. The right religious use of every thing and every talent, is the indispensable duty of every being that is capable of knowing right and wrong.

Because we are all of the same nature, we must always act according to the reason of our nature. Because every one of us is a servant of the same God, we must do everything as the servants of that God. Because every place is full of His presence, we must live in every place as in His presence. And because everything is equally His gift, we must use everything as we would use those things belonging to God. Either we must have this piety, wisdom, and devotion in every area of life, extending to the use of everything, or we must have it in no part of life. If we forget God in one thing, or if we disregard our reason and live by our fancies at a particular time or place, it would be as lawful to forget God in everything and to disregard our reason all the time and in every place.

Some people are grave and solemn at church, but silly and frantic at home. Some live by principles on Sunday, but they spend the rest of the week by chance. Some have fixed times of prayer, but they waste the rest of their time as they please. Some people give money to charity, but they squander away the rest however they wish. Such people have not considered enough the nature of religion or the true reasons for piety. For he that, using principles of reason, can tell why it is good to be wise and heavenly-minded at church, can tell that it is always desirable to have the same attitude in all other places. He that truly knows why he should spend any time well, knows that it is never allowable to throw any time away. He that rightly understands the reasonableness and excellency of charity, will know that it can never be excusable to waste any of our money in pride and folly, or in any needless expenses.

Every argument that shows the wisdom and excellency of charity, proves the wisdom of spending all our money well. Every argument that proves the wisdom and reasonableness of having times of prayer, shows the wisdom and reasonableness of losing none of our time. If we did not always need to act as if we were in the divine presence, if we did not need to consider and use everything as the gift of God, if we did not always need to live by reason and make religion the rule of all our actions—then we would never need to act as if we were in the presence of God, and we would never need to make religion and reason the measure of any of our actions.

If, therefore, we are to live unto God at any time or in any place, we are to live unto Him at all times and in all places. If we are to use anything as the gift of God, we are to use everything as His gift. If we are to do anything by strict rules of reason and piety, we are to do everything by those rules. Reason, wisdom, and piety are as much the best things at all times and in all places, as they are the best things at any time or in any place.

If it is our glory and happiness to have a rational nature that is endued with wisdom and reason and that is capable of imitating the divine nature, then it must be our glory and happiness to improve our reason and wisdom, to live up to the excellency of our rational nature, and to imitate God in all our actions, to the utmost of our power. Those who confine religion to times and places and little rules, who think that it is being too strict and rigid to introduce religion into everyday life because it will put limits on all their actions and ways of living—those people mistake the whole nature of religion. For surely they cannot think any part of their lives is made easier for being free from religion. That is like misinterpreting the whole nature of wisdom by not thinking it desirable to be always wise. Anyone who thinks it too much to be pious in all his actions has not learned the nature of piety. Likewise, anyone who does not earnestly desire to live in everything according to reason does not sufficiently understand what reason is.

If we had a religion comprised of absurd superstitions that had no regard to the perfection of our nature, people might be glad to have some part of their lives excused from it. However, the religion of the Gospel is only the refinement and exaltation of our best faculties. It requires a life of the highest reason. It teaches us to use this world as in reason it ought to be used (see 1 Corinthians 7:31), to live in the attitudes that are the glory of intelligent beings, to walk in such wisdom as exalts our nature, and to practice such piety as will raise us to God. With that, who can think it grievous to live always in the spirit of such a religion, to have every part of his life full of it, except someone who would think it grievous to be as the angels of God in heaven?

Furthermore, as God is one and the same Being, always acting according to His own nature, so it is the duty of every being that He has created, to live according to the nature that He has given it and always to act as it was created to act. It is therefore an immutable law of God that all rational beings should act reasonably in all their actions, not at this time, or in that place, or upon this occasion, or in the use of some particular thing, but at all times, in all places, on all occasions, and in the use of all things. This is a law that is as unchangeable as God, and can no more cease to be than God can cease to be a God of wisdom and order. When, therefore, any being endued with reason does any unreasonable thing, it sins against the great law of its nature, abuses itself, and sins against God, the Author of that nature.

As a result, anyone who pleads for indulgences and vanities, for any foolish fashions, customs, or pleasures of the world, for the misuse of either time or money, pleads for a rebellion against his own nature, and for a rebellion against God, who has given us reason for no other purpose than to make it the rule and measure of all our ways. Consequently, when you are guilty of any folly or extravagance or indulgence, do not consider it a small matter. It may seem so if compared to some other sins, but when you consider it as contrary to your nature, you will see that nothing that is unreasonable can be considered small. All unreasonable ways are contrary to the nature of all rational beings, whether men or angels. When rational beings act according to the reason and excellence of their nature, then they are acceptable to God.

We are unlike the angels; the weaknesses of human life make food and clothing necessary for us. Yet, it is no more allowable for us to turn these necessities into follies, and indulge ourselves in the luxury of food or the vanities of dress, than it is allowable for angels to act below the dignity of their proper state. A reasonable life, in which wisdom is applied to the human condition, is as much the duty of all men as it is the duty of all angels and intelligent beings. As rational beings, all men are obliged to live by reason and glorify God by a continual right use of their various talents and faculties.

Although we are not angels, we may know, by considering the state and perfection of angels, for what ends and by what rules we are to live and act. Our blessed Savior has clearly turned our thoughts this way by making this petition a constant part of all our prayers: "Thy will be done in earth, as it is in heaven" (Matt. 6:10). This is certain evidence that the obedience of men is to imitate the obedience of angels, and that rational beings on earth are to live to God as rational beings in heaven live to Him.

Therefore, when you begin to think about how Christians ought to live, and in what degrees of wisdom and holiness they ought to use the things of this life, you must not look at the world. Instead, you must look up to God and the society of angels, and think what wisdom and holiness is fit to prepare you for such a state of glory, whether you are employed or not. You must look to all the highest precepts of the Gospel, examine yourself by the spirit of Christ, think how the wisest men in the world have lived, and think how departed souls would live if they were again to act the short part of human life. Even more importantly, you must think what degrees of wisdom and holiness you will wish for when you are leaving the world.

Now, I am not proposing any needless perfection. In fact, I am simply complying with the apostle's advice, where he said,

> *Finally, brethren, whatsoever things are true, whatsoever things are honest, whatsoever things are just, whatsoever things are pure, whatsoever things are lovely, whatsoever things are of good report; if there be any virtue, and if there be any praise, think on these things.* (Phil. 4:8)

No one can come near the doctrine of this passage, except one who intends to do everything in this life as the servant of God; to live by reason in everything that he does; and to make the wisdom and holiness of the Gospel the rule and measure of his desires and his use of every gift of God, including his time and his money.

Chapter Six

THE WISE AND CORRUPT USES OF MONEY

The holiness of Christianity requires us to aspire after a universal obedience, doing and using everything as the servants of God. We are especially obliged to observe this religious exactness in the use of our money and possessions, and in all states and employments of our lives. The reason for this would be very clear to us if we were only to consider that our possessions are as much the gifts of God as our eyes or our hands. Our belongings are no more to be buried or wasted upon pleasure, than our eyes are to be put out or our limbs are to be cut off as we please.

But, besides this consideration, there are several other important reasons why we should be religiously exact in the use of our resources. First, the manner of spending one's money or using one's estate enters so far into the business of every day, and makes up so much of one's everyday life, that daily life takes on the same nature as one's usual way of spending his money. If reason and religion govern us in this, then reason and religion will have control of our lives. On the other hand, if humor, pride, and fancy are the measures of how we spend our money, then humor, pride, and fancy will have control of the greater part of our lives.

Another reason for devoting our money to right uses, is because it has the potential of being used to the most excellent purposes and as a great means of doing good. If we waste it, we do not waste a trifle that signifies little, but we waste that which might be made as eyes to the blind, as a husband to the widow, as a father to the orphan; we waste that which not only enables us to minister worldly comforts to those who are in distress, but also that which might purchase for ourselves everlasting treasures in heaven. (See Matthew 6:19–20.) If we part with our money in foolish ways, we part with a great power of comforting our fellow creatures, and of making ourselves forever blessed.

If nothing is so glorious as doing good, if nothing makes us so like to God, then nothing can be so glorious in the use of our money as to use it all in works of love and goodness. To make ourselves as friends, fathers, and benefactors to all our fellow creatures, is to imitate divine love and to turn all our power into acts of generosity, care, and kindness to those who are in need of it.

Suppose a man had extra eyes and hands and feet that he could give to those who needed them. If he should either lock them up in a chest or please himself with some needless or ridiculous use of them, instead of giving them to his brothers who were blind and lame, would we not justly consider him an inhuman wretch? If he chose to amuse himself with furnishing his house with those things, rather than to entitle himself to an eternal reward by giving them to those who needed eyes and hands, might we not justly consider him mad?

Money has very much the nature of eyes and feet: if we lock it up in chests or waste it in needless and ridiculous expenses, while the poor and distressed are in need of it; if we consume it in the ridiculous ornaments of apparel, while others are starving in nakedness; then we are not far from the cruelty of one who chooses to adorn his house with hands and eyes instead of giving them to those who need them. If we choose to indulge ourselves in expensive enjoyments that have no real use in themselves or that satisfy no real need, rather than to entitle ourselves to an eternal reward by disposing of our money well, then we are guilty of the same madness. For after we have satisfied our own reasonable needs, all the rest of our money is but spare eyes or hands; it is something that we cannot keep to ourselves without being foolish in the use of it, something that can only be used well by giving it to those who need it.

Thirdly, if we waste our money, we are not only guilty of wasting a talent that God has given us; we are not only guilty of making useless a powerful means of doing good; but we do ourselves further harm by turning this useful talent into a powerful means of corrupting ourselves. This is because money that is spent in wrong ways is spent in support of some wrong spirit, in gratifying some vain and unreasonable desires, in conforming to the pride and fashions of the world that Christians, as reasonable men, are obliged to renounce.

A man with a fine wit ought to be strictly devoted to piety, lest he be led into greater follies by trifling it away. Likewise, money, if it is not used strictly according to reason and religion, can not only be trifled away, but it will betray people into greater follies and make them live a more extravagant and silly life than they would have without it. If, therefore, you do not spend your money in doing good to others, then you spend it to your own injury. You become like a man who refuses to give medicine to a sick friend. This is the case of having more than enough money: if you give it to those who need it, it is like a medicine; if you spend it on yourself in something that you do not need, it only disorders your mind and makes you worse than you would have been without it.

Consider again the aforementioned comparison. If the man who would not make a right use of spare eyes and hands happens to spoil his own eyes and hands by continually trying to use the spare ones himself, we might justly accuse him of still greater madness. Now, this is truly the case of riches spent on ourselves in vain and needless expenses: in trying to use them where they have no real use, nor any real need, we only use them to our great injury—creating unreasonable desires, nourishing ill tempers, indulging our passions, and supporting a worldly, vain turn of mind.

Eating and drinking, fine clothes, fine houses, high social positions, fine appearance, entertainment, and pleasures naturally hurt and disorder our hearts. They are the food and nourishment of all the folly and weakness of our nature, and are certain to make us vain and worldly. They all support something that should not be supported; they are contrary to that sobriety and piety of heart that relishes divine things. They are like weights upon our minds, making us less able and less inclined to raise up our thoughts and affections to the things that are above.

Money thus spent is not merely wasted or lost, but it is spent to bad purposes and miserable effects, to the corruption and disorder of our hearts, and to making us less able to live up to the sublime doctrines of the Gospel. It is like keeping money from the poor to buy poison for yourself. Whatever is spent in the vanity of dress may be considered spent to set vanity in your mind. Whatever is laid out for idleness and indulgence may be considered given to make your heart dull and irreligious. Whatever is spent to increase your fame or finery of appearance may be considered spent to dazzle your own eyes and render you the idol of your own imagination. And so, whenever you turn from reasonable desires in anything, you only support some unreasonable temperament, some turn of mind that every Christian is called upon to renounce.

Our money and possessions are gifts from God, enabling us to do great good. However, if the gifts are idly spent, we bring great harm to ourselves. It is therefore absolutely necessary to make reason and religion the strict rule of using all our resources. Scripture exhorts us to be wise and reasonable, satisfying only such needs and desires as God would have satisfied. We are told to be spiritual and heavenly, pressing after a glorious change of our nature. (See 2 Peter 1:3–4.) And we have been commanded to love our neighbor as ourselves (Lev. 19:18), to love all mankind as God has loved them. We cannot do any of these things unless we are wise and reasonable, spiritual and heavenly, exercising a brotherly love and a godlike charity in the use of all our possessions.

This is seen so much in the Gospels, that you cannot read a chapter without reading something about it. I will give only one example from the Scriptures, which is sufficient to justify what I have written concerning this religious use of all our possessions.

When the Son of man shall come in his glory, and all the holy angels with him, then shall he sit upon the throne of his glory: and before him shall be gathered all nations: and he shall separate them one from another, as a shepherd divideth his sheep from the goats: and he shall set the sheep on his right hand, but the goats on the left. Then shall the King say unto them on his right hand, Come, ye blessed of my Father, inherit the kingdom prepared for you from the foundation of the world: for I was an hungered, and ye gave me meat: I was thirsty, and ye gave me drink: I was a stranger, and ye took me in: naked, and ye clothed me: I was sick, and ye visited me: I was in prison, and ye came unto me....Then shall he say also unto them on the left hand, Depart from me, ye cursed, into everlasting fire, prepared for the devil and his angels: for I was an hungered, and ye gave me no meat: I was thirsty, and ye gave me no drink: I was a stranger, and ye took me not in: naked, and ye clothed me not: sick, and in prison, and ye visited me not....These shall go away into everlasting punishment: but the righteous into life eternal.   (Matt. 25:31–36, 41–43, 46)

I have quoted this passage at length because, if one looks at the way of the world, one would hardly think that Christians had ever read this part of Scripture. Most Christians do not live as if their salvation depended upon these good works. And yet, the necessity of such works is here asserted in the highest manner, and pressed upon us by a lively description of the glory and terrors of the Day of Judgment. Some people, even those who may be considered virtuous Christians, look upon this text only as a general recommendation of occasional works of charity. They miss the point of the passage, which shows the necessity not only of occasional charities now and then, but of a life of continual charity—as much as we are able to perform.

If you have neglected these good works, you will confess that you have no right to go on claiming salvation, because people who have neglected them are, at the Last Day, to be placed on the left hand and banished with a "Depart from me, ye cursed." And who can be said to have performed these good works? Is it one who has assisted a prisoner or relieved the poor or sick once or twice? This would be as absurd as to say that one who had said his prayers once or twice had performed the duties of devotion. Then is it one who has done these works of charity several times? If so, then a man who had done acts of justice several times can be said to be a truly just man. What is the rule, then; what is the measure of performing these good works? How can a man know that he performs them as he should?

The rule is, actually, very clear and simple. It applies to every virtue and every right-minded disposition, including charity. Who is the humble or meek or devout or just or faithful man? Is it one who has done acts of humility, meekness, devotion, justice, or fidelity several times? No, but it is one who lives in the habitual exercise of these virtues. Only the person who exercises these works of charity to the utmost of his power can be said to have performed them. Only the man who loves God with all his heart, with all his mind, and with all his strength (Mark 12:30) has performed the duty of divine love. Only the man who has performed these good works with all his heart, with all his mind, and with all his strength has truly fulfilled his duty of them. For there is no other measure of our doing good, than our power of doing it.

Peter came to Jesus and asked,

> Lord, how oft shall my brother sin against me, and I forgive him? till seven times? Jesus saith unto him, I say not unto thee, Until seven times: but, Until seventy times seven.
> *(Matt. 18:21–22)*

It is not that we may cease to forgive after this number of offenses, but the expression of seventy times seven is meant to show us that we are not to limit our forgiveness by any number of offenses. Rather, we are to continue forgiving even the most repeated offenses against us. Christ also said,

> If he trespass against thee seven times in a day, and seven times in a day turn again to thee, saying, I repent; thou shalt forgive him.
> *(Luke 17:4)*

If, therefore, a man ceases to forgive his brother because he has forgiven him often enough already, or if he excuses himself from forgiving one man because he has forgiven several others, then he breaks this law of Christ about forgiving one's brother.

Now, the rule of forgiving is also the rule of giving. You are not to give or to do good works seven times, but seventy times seven. You are not to stop giving because you have given enough to the same person. No, you must see it as much your duty to continue relieving those who continue to live in need, as it was to relieve them once or twice. If it had not been in your power, you would have been excused from relieving any person once. On the other hand, if it is in your power to relieve people often, it is as much your duty to do it often as it is seldom the duty of others to do it because they are seldom able.

A person who is not ready to forgive every brother as often as he needs to be forgiven, does not forgive like a disciple of Christ. And a person who is not ready to give to every brother who needs to have something given him, does not give like a disciple of Christ. We are called to give to the point of seventy times seven as much as we are called to forgive to the point of seventy times seven. It is just as necessary to live in the continual exercise of all good works to the utmost of our power, as it is to live in the habitual exercise of this forgiving spirit toward all who need it.

The reason for this is very obvious. There is the same goodness, the same excellency, and the same necessity of being charitable at one time as at any other. That which is a reason for forgiving one offense, is the same reason for forgiving all offenses. No one could recommend charity today and not recommend it tomorrow. Likewise, neglecting it at one time is the same sin as if you neglected it at any other time.

Therefore, as evidence of our salvation, we will do these works of charity to the utmost of our power—not today, not tomorrow, but through the whole course of our lives. It is our duty to deny ourselves any needless expenses, to be moderate and frugal, so that we may give to those in need. It is our duty to do so at all times, so that we may be further able to do more good. For if it is at any time a sin to prefer needless, vain expense to works of charity, it is so at all times. Charity is better than all needless and vain expenses at one time as much as it is at another. See that you make yourself in some degree capable of doing these works of charity, and take care to make yourself as capable as you can be of performing them in all areas of your life.

As a result, you must either renounce your Christianity so far as to say that you need never perform any of these good works, or you must admit that you are to perform them all your life in as high a degree as you are able. There is no middle road to be taken. If you do not strive to fulfill all charitable works, if you neglect any of them that are in your power, and if you deny assistance to those who need what you can give, you number yourself among those who lack Christian charity. It is as much your duty to do good with all that you have, and to live in the continual exercise of good works, as it is your duty to be temperate in all that you eat and drink.

If it is necessary to do good works, as far as you are able, it must be necessary to renounce those needless ways of spending money—ways that render you unable to do works of charity. But, how are we to renounce all those foolish and unreasonable expenses that the pride and folly of mankind have made so common and fashionable in the world? Scripture tells us, "Be not conformed to this world: but be ye transformed by the renewing of your mind" (Rom. 12:2). We must conform no more to the ways of the world than we must conform to the vices of the world. We must avoid wasting our money on a whim as much as we must avoid drinking with the drunken or indulging ourselves in food. A course of such expenses is no more consistent with a life of charity than excess drinking is consistent with a life of sobriety.

Therefore, when anyone tells you of the lawfulness of expensive apparel, or the innocence of pleasing yourself with costly satisfactions, imagine that the same person tells you that you do not need to do works of charity, or that Christ does not require you to do good toward the poor and the needy, as unto Him. (See Matthew 25:40.) Then you will see the wickedness of such advice. For to tell you that you may live in the sort of expenses that make it impossible for you to live in the exercise of good works, is the same thing as telling you that you do not need to have any care about the good works themselves.

It has already been observed that prudent and religious care is to be used in the manner of spending our money or using our possessions, because the manner of spending comprises so great a part of our lives. The way in which we spend our money is so much the business of every day, that according to our wisdom or our imprudence in this respect, the whole course of our lives will be rendered either very wise or very foolish.

People who are well inclined to be religious, who receive instructions of piety with pleasure and satisfaction, often wonder why they make no great progress in the religion that they so much admire. The reason is because religion lives only in their heads, and something else has possession of their hearts. From year to year they continue to admire and praise piety itself, without ever living up to the reality and perfection of its precepts. If someone were to ask why religion does not get possession of their hearts, the answer is not because they live in gross sins or debaucheries, for their regard for religion preserves them from such disorders. However, it is because their hearts are constantly employed, perverted, and kept in a wrong state by the indiscreet use of things that are lawful to be used. (See 1 Corinthians 6:12.)

Indeed, it is lawful for them to use and enjoy what they have, but it never enters their minds to imagine any great danger in doing so. They never even think it possible for them to use their possessions imprudently or in sheer vanity. Although this does not destroy like gross sins, it still disorders their hearts and encourages them in sensuality and dullness, pride and vanity. Eventually, their hearts are rendered incapable of receiving the life and spirit of piety—merely by the use of innocent and lawful things.

What is more innocent than rest and retirement? And yet, what is more dangerous than sloth and idleness? What is more lawful than eating and drinking? And yet, what is more destructive to all virtue, more contributive to all vice, than sensuality and indulgence? The care of a family is certainly lawful and praiseworthy. And yet, many people are rendered incapable of all virtue because they have a worldly and irritable temper! It is because we fail to use these innocent and lawful things in compliance with the precepts of the Scriptures, that religion cannot get full possession of our hearts. If we would learn to rightly and prudently manage ourselves along these lines, we would learn the art of holy living, in which these things exist.

Gross sins are plainly seen and easily avoided by people who profess religion. Yet, it does not shock and offend our consciences to make use of innocent and lawful things. It can be done so indiscreetly that it is difficult to make people aware of the danger of it—and that makes it all the more dangerous.

A man who spends all his money on sports, or a woman who spends all her money on adorning herself, will hardly believe that the spirit of religion cannot subsist in such a way of life. These persons, as has been observed, may live free from debaucheries; they may be friends of religion, so far as to praise and speak well of it and admire it in their minds; but it cannot govern their hearts and be the spirit of their actions, until they change their ways of life and let religion give laws to the use and spending of their estate. They are drawn to a thousand other follies along with the one—follies that will render the whole course of their lives, businesses, conversations, hopes, fears, tastes, pleasures, and entertainments, all similar to it.

Perhaps the imperfections of your piety and the disorders of your passions are the result of your imprudent use and enjoyment of lawful and innocent things. More people are kept from a true sense and taste of religion by a regular kind of sensuality and indulgence than by gross drunkenness. More men live without regarding the great duties of piety because they have too great a concern for worldly goods, than because of direct injustice.

Perhaps one man would be devout if he were not so great an expert at what he does. Another may be deaf to all the motives of piety because he indulges an idle, slothful disposition. Perhaps one woman would not find it nearly so hard to be affected by religion if she would make fewer visits or if she would not always be talking. All these things are little when they are compared to great sins, yet they are not little because they are impediments and hindrances to a pious spirit.

Examination is the only eye of the soul, and the truths of religion can be seen by nothing else. Therefore, whatever makes a person more frivolous and trifling, also renders the soul incapable of seeing, understanding, and relishing the doctrines of piety. If you are going to make real progress in religion, you must not only abhor gross and notorious sins, but you must also regulate the innocent and lawful parts of your behavior and put the most common and allowed actions of life under the rules of discretion and piety.

Chapter Seven

AN EXAMPLE OF CHRISTIAN VIRTUE

When you are pious in even one part of your life, it is of great advantage to you. Through such piety, you grow accustomed to living by rule, and you are far more aware of how to govern yourself.

Think of a businessman who has brought one part of his affairs under certain rules. He is more likely to take the same care with the rest of his affairs. In the same manner, a man who has brought any one part of his life under the rules of religion, may thereafter be taught to extend the same order and regularity to all other parts of his life.

It would be wise for you to think your time too precious to be disposed of by chance and left to be devoured by anything that happens. If you would just observe how every day goes through your hands, and if you would strictly follow a certain order of time in your business, your times of rest, and your devotions, then your conduct will soon reform, improve, and perfect the whole course of your life. Once you know the value and reap the advantages of well-ordered time, you will not long be a stranger to the value of anything else that is of any real concern to you. Thus, a rule that relates even to the smallest part of our lives, is of great benefit to us, merely because it is a rule. The old proverb says, "Once begun, a task is easy; half the work is done." Similarly, one who has begun to live by a particular rule, has gone a great way toward the perfection of his whole life.

By *rule* I mean a religious rule observed through a principle of duty to God. For a man might oblige himself to be moderate in his meals only out of regard to his stomach; he might abstain from drinking only to avoid the headache; or he might be moderate in his sleep through fear of lethargy. He might be exact in all these rules without being at all the better man for them. On the other hand, when he is moderate and regular in any of these things out of a sense of Christian sobriety and self-denial—so that he may offer a more reasonable and holy life to God—then even the smallest rule of this kind is the beginning of great piety. Any rule in these matters is of great benefit, because it teaches us something about governing ourselves; it keeps up a tenderness of mind; it presents God often to our thoughts; and it brings a sense of religion into the ordinary actions of our everyday lives.

If a man were to make it a rule to himself, that, whenever he was in the company of anyone who swore, talked lewdly, or spoke evil of his neighbor, he would either reprove the man gently or leave the company as decently as he could, he would find that this little rule, like a little leaven hidden in a huge meal, would spread and extend itself through the whole form of his life. (See 1 Corinthians 5:6.)

If another were to abstain on the Sabbath from innocent and lawful things such as traveling, visiting, common conversation, and discoursing upon worldly matters; if he were to devote the day, besides the public worship, to resting, reading, devotion, instruction, and works of charity; he would thereby find a change made in his spirit, and a taste of piety raised in his mind to which he was previously an entire stranger.

It would be easy to show, in many other instances, how small matters are the first steps and natural beginnings of great perfection. Yet, the two things that out of all the rest most need to be under a strict rule are our time and our money. These, when they are rightly used, are the continual means of doing good and are the greatest blessings both to ourselves and others. One who is piously strict and exact in the wise management of either of these cannot be ignorant of the right use of the other for very long. Moreover, one who is happy in the religious care and disposal of them both, has already ascended several steps on the ladder of Christian perfection.

Miranda[3] is a sober, reasonable Christian. As soon as she had control of her time and fortune, her first thought was how she might best fulfill everything that God required of her in the use of them, and how she might make the best and happiest use of this short life. She depends on the truth of our blessed Lord, that "one thing is needful" (Luke 10:42). Therefore, she makes her whole life into one continual labor after it. She has one reason for doing or not doing, for liking or not liking anything, and that is the will of God. She

---

[3]Miranda: admirable, supposed to be a portrait of Miss Hester Gibbon, daughter of Mr. Edward Gibbon, who was grandfather of the great historian of the same name. Law was a tutor to Mr. Gibbon's son, and he was considered an honored friend of the Gibbon family.

does not claim to add any finery or ladylike manners to her Christianity; Miranda thinks too well to be taken with the sound of such silly words. Rather, she has renounced the world to follow Christ in the exercise of humility, charity, devotion, abstinence, and heavenly affections.

Miranda considers everything a duty to God and does everything in His name and for His sake. She considers her fortune the gift of God, to be used as she would use anything that belonged to Him, for the wise and reasonable ends of a holy life. Her fortune, therefore, is divided between herself and several other poor people. She does not indulge herself in needless, vain expenses, and she does not give to other people so that they can spend in that way. Therefore, as she will not give a poor man money to go see a puppet show, neither will she allow herself any to spend in the same manner.

Except for food, she never spends even ten pounds a year on herself. She has one rule that she observes in her dress: to be clean and wear the least expensive things. Everything about her resembles the purity of her soul, and she is always outwardly clean because she is always pure within.

Early every morning, she can be found praying. She rejoices in the beginning of every day because it begins all her pious rules of holy living and brings the fresh pleasure of repeating them. With her watchings and prayers, she seems to be as a guardian angel to those who dwell around her, blessing the place where she dwells and making intercession with God for those who are asleep. Her devotions have gone through several stages, and God has heard several of her private prayers, before the light even enters her sister's room. Miranda does not know what it means to have a dull morning. Her hours of prayer and her religious exercises are repeated too often to let any considerable part of the day lie heavy upon her hands.

When she is working, she has the same wisdom that governs all her other actions; she is either doing something that is necessary for herself or necessary for others. There is hardly a poor family in the neighborhood that does not wear something that has had the labor of her hands. When there is no useful or charitable work to be done, Miranda will work no more.

At her table she lives strictly by this rule of the Scriptures: "Whether therefore ye eat, or drink, or whatsoever ye do, do all to the glory of God" (1 Cor. 10:31). This makes her begin and end every meal as she begins and ends every day—with acts of devotion. She eats and drinks only for the sake of living and with so regular an abstinence that every meal is an exercise of self-denial, and she humbles her body every time that she is forced to feed it. She eats meat in order to give proper strength to her body, to render it able and willing to obey the soul, and to lift up eyes and hands toward heaven with greater readiness.

The Holy Scriptures, especially the New Testament, are her daily study. She reads with a watchful attention, constantly examining herself and trying herself by every doctrine that is there, to be ready for her trial at the Last Day. When she has the New Testament in her hand, she supposes herself at the feet of our Savior and turns all that she learns from Him into the laws of her life. She receives His sacred words with as much attention and reverence as if she saw Him in person and knew that He had just come from heaven to teach her the way that leads to it.

She is sometimes afraid that she spends too much money on books—practical books that enter into the heart of religion and describe the inward holiness of the Christian life. Yet, of all human writings, those concerning the lives of pious persons and eminent saints are her greatest delight. In these she searches as for hidden treasure, hoping to find some secret of holy living, some uncommon degree of piety that she may make her own. Miranda's head and heart are so filled with principles of wisdom and holiness—she is so full of the one main business of life—that she finds it difficult to talk about anything else; and if you were in her company when she found it proper to talk, you would be made wiser and better, whether you wanted it or not.

Because of Miranda's charity, there are several poor families that live in a comfortable manner and are from year to year blessing her in their prayers. She has saved nearly twenty poor tradesmen who failed in their businesses. She has educated several poor children who were picked up in the streets, and she has arranged honest employment for them. When a laborer is confined at home with sickness, she sends him twice his wages until he recovers—that he may have one part to give to his family as usual, and the other to aid in his recovery. If a family seems too large to be supported by the labor of those in it that can work, she pays their rent and gives them something yearly toward their clothing.

Miranda never lacks compassion, even for common beggars, and especially toward those who are old or sick or full of sores, or those lacking eyes or limbs. She imagines that our blessed Savior and His apostles were kind to beggars—that they spoke comfortably to them, healed their diseases, and restored eyes and limbs to the lame and blind. Peter said to the beggar who wanted alms from him,

> *Silver and gold have I none; but such as I have give I thee: In the name of Jesus Christ of Nazareth rise up and walk.*   (Acts 3:6)

Miranda, therefore, never treats beggars with disregard and aversion; but she imitates the kindness of our Savior and His apostles toward them. She may not be able to work miracles for them as Christ did, yet she relieves them with what power she has, that she may say with the apostle, "Such as I have give I thee."

If a poor traveler tells her that he has neither strength, nor food, nor money left, she never sends him away; she never tells him that she cannot relieve him because he may be lying about his condition or because she does not know him. Rather, she relieves him for that reason, because he is a stranger and unknown to her. It is the most noble part of her charity to be kind and tender to those whom she has never seen before, and perhaps may never see again in this life. "I was a stranger, and ye took me in" (Matt. 25:35), says our blessed Savior.

How can you perform this duty if you will not relieve people who are unknown to you? Besides, where has Scripture taught that merit is the measure of charity? The Scriptures say, "If thine enemy hunger, feed him; if he thirst, give him drink" (Rom. 12:20). We are to do acts of kindness to those who least of all deserve it. If I am to love and do good to my worst enemies (Matt. 5:44); if I am to be charitable to them, notwithstanding all their spite and malice; then surely merit is no measure of charity. If I am not to withhold my charity from bad people who are my enemies, surely I am not to deny alms to poor beggars, whom I neither know to be bad people, nor think of as my enemies.

Perhaps you will say that by this I am encouraging people to be beggars. Yet, the same thoughtless objection may be made against all kinds of charities, for they may encourage people to depend upon them. The same may be said against forgiving our enemies, for it may encourage people to do us harm. The same may be said even against the goodness of God, that by pouring His blessings on the just and the unjust, the evil and the good (Matt. 5:45), evil and unjust men are encouraged in their wicked ways. The same may be said against clothing the naked or giving medicines to the sick, for that may encourage people to neglect themselves and to be careless of their health. However, when the love of God dwells in you, when it has enlarged your heart and filled you with mercy and compassion, you will make no more objections such as these.

Every time you turn away the poor, the old, the sick, the helpless traveler, the lame, or the blind, ask yourself, "Do I sincerely wish that these poor creatures may be as happy as Lazarus, who was carried by angels into Abraham's bosom? (See Luke 16:23.) Do I sincerely desire that God would make them fellow heirs with me in eternal glory?" Now, if you search into your soul, you will find that you do not have these intentions. It is impossible for anyone to wish a poor creature so great a happiness, and yet not have the heart to give him a small donation.

For this reason, as far as you can, give to all, and pray to God to forgive all. You cannot refuse to give to those whom you pray God to bless, whom you wish to be partakers of eternal glory. Be glad to show some degree of love to people who are the objects of the infinite love of God. And if, as our Savior has assured us, "it is more blessed to give than to receive" (Acts 20:35), we ought to look upon those poor beggars as friends and benefactors who do us a greater good than they can receive, who come to exalt our virtue, to be witnesses of our charity, to be monuments of our love, to be our advocates with God, to appear for us in the Day of Judgment, and to help us to a blessedness greater than our alms can bestow on them.

This is the spirit, and this is the life, of the devout Miranda. If she lives ten years longer, she will have spent six thousand pounds in charity, for that which she allows herself may fairly be considered among her alms. When she dies, she will likely shine among apostles, saints, and martyrs; she will stand among the first servants of God and be glorious among those who have fought the good fight and finished their course with joy (2 Tim. 4:7).

Chapter Eight

THE APPLICATION OF CHRISTIAN VIRTUES

However contrary it may seem to the way of the world, this life of Miranda is yet suitable to the true spirit and founded upon the plainest doctrines of Christianity. To live as she does, is as truly suitable to the Gospel of Christ, as to be baptized or to receive the sacraments. Her spirit is the same as that which animated the saints of former ages, and it is because they lived as she does that we now celebrate their memories and praise God for their examples.

There is nothing in Miranda's character that is whimsical, trifling, or unreasonable, but everything is a right and proper instance of a solid and real piety. All Miranda's rules of living unto God, of spending her time and fortune, of eating, working, dressing, and conversing, are as essential to a reasonable and holy life as devotion and prayer.

Whatever can be said for the wisdom of sobriety, devotion, charity, or humility, is also a good argument for the wise and reasonable use of apparel. Whatever can be said against the folly of luxury, sensuality, extravagance, ambition, idleness, or indulgence, must also be said against the folly of dress. Religion is as deeply concerned with the one as with the other. If you may be vain in one thing, then you may be vain in everything, for one kind of vanity only differs from another as one kind of intemperance differs from another. If you spend your fortune in the needless, vain finery of dress, you cannot condemn prodigality, extravagance, or luxury without condemning yourself.

If you say it is your only folly, and that therefore there can be no great harm in it, you are like one who thinks he is only guilty of the folly of covetousness, or only the folly of ambition. Some people may live a life so believable that they appear guilty of no other fault than that of covetousness or ambition. Yet, the case is not as it appears, for covetousness or ambition cannot exist in the heart that is, in other respects, rightly devoted to God. In like manner, some people may spend almost all they have on needless, expensive clothing and jewelry, yet they seem to be in every other respect truly pious. Certainly, they are not, for it is impossible for a mind that is in a true state of religion to be vain in the use of clothes.

Suppose that the Virgin Mary or some other eminent saint was sent into the world to live again in this state of trial for a few years. Suppose, too, that you were going to her to be edified by her great piety. Would you expect to find her dressed and adorned in fine and expensive clothes? No. You would know this to be as impossible as finding her learning to dance. Simply add *saint* or *holy* to any person, either man or woman, and you will immediately imagine that such a character cannot allow himself or herself the vanity of fine apparel. It is as great nonsense as an apostle in an expensive suit; everyone's own natural sense convinces him of the inconsistency of these things.

Now, what is the reason that, when you think of a saint or an eminent servant of God, you cannot think of the vanity of apparel? Is it not because it is inconsistent with a right state of heart, with true and exalted piety? Is this not, therefore, a demonstration that a right state of heart, and true, exalted piety, must be missing where such vanity is allowed? As certainly as the Virgin Mary could not indulge herself or conform to the vanity of the world in dress and appearance, so it is certain that no one can indulge himself in this vanity except one who lacks piety of heart. Consequently, we must admit that all needless and expensive finery of dress is the effect of a disordered heart—one that is not governed by the true spirit of religion.

Covetousness is not a crime because there is any harm in gold or silver, but because it supposes a foolish and unreasonable state of mind, fallen from its true good and sunk into a poor and wretched satisfaction. In like manner, the expensive finery of dress is not a crime because there is anything good or evil in clothes, but because the expensive ornaments of clothing show a foolish and unreasonable state of heart, fallen from right notions of human nature. The purpose of clothing becomes perverted, and the necessities of life are turned into so many instances of pride and folly.

The whole world agrees on condemning those who think of nothing besides their appearance. Why is this? Is it because there is anything sinful in their particular dress or manners? No, but everyone will agree that the use and manner of clothes is a mark of the state of a man's mind, and that it is impossible for so ridiculous an outside to have anything wise, reasonable, or good within. Indeed, to suppose such a man to have great piety, is as much nonsense as to suppose that a coward has great courage. Everyone who transgresses the right and religious measures of eating and drinking is as guilty of intemperance as the glutton and the drunkard. Likewise, everyone who departs from the reasonable and religious ends of clothing is as guilty of the vanity of dress as the one who thinks of nothing else.

In the matter of apparel, there is no rule to be observed except the right use of clothes as is strictly according to the doctrines and spirit of our religion. If we attempt to make the way of the world our measure in these things, it is as weak and absurd as if we measured our sobriety, abstinence, or humility by the way of the world. This would be exceedingly absurd for Christians, who are to be so far from conforming to the fashions of this life that to have overcome the world (John 16:33) is an essential mark of Christianity.

Nothing is right in the use of clothes or in the use of anything in the world, except when it is used in the simplicity of the Gospel. Every other use of things (however polite and fashionable in the world) distracts and disorders the heart. It is inconsistent with that inward state of piety, that purity of heart, that wisdom of mind, and that regularity of affection that Christianity requires.

Therefore, judge the crime of vain apparel as an offense against the proper use of clothes, just as covetousness is an offense against the proper use of money. Consider it an indulgence of proud and unreasonable tempers, an offense against the humility and sobriety of the Christian spirit. Consider it an offense against all those doctrines that require you to "do all to the glory of God" (1 Cor. 10:31) and to make a right use of all your talents. (See Matthew 25:15–28.) Consider it as an offense against all those texts of Scripture that command you to love your neighbor as yourself (Matt. 19:19), to feed the hungry, to clothe the naked, and to do all works of charity that you are able.

You must not deceive yourself by saying, "What can be the harm in clothes?" for then the covetous man might as well say, "What can be the harm of gold or silver?" Rather, you must consider that it is a great deal of harm to lack a wise, reasonable, and humble state of heart, which is according to the spirit of religion, and which no one who indulges himself either in the vanity of dress or the desire of riches, can have in the manner that he ought to have it.

There is only one way for you to be a good Christian: you must live wholly unto God. And there is only one way for you to live wholly unto God: you must live according to the wisdom that comes from God. You must act according to right judgments of the nature and value of things; you must live in the exercise of holy and heavenly affections; and you must use all the gifts of God to His praise and glory.

Perhaps some people, who admire the purity and perfection of Miranda's life, may say, "How can such a life be set as an example to everyone? How can we who are married, or we who are under the direction of our parents, imitate such a life?" It is possible, because Miranda imitated the life of our blessed Savior, and you may do the same. The circumstances of our Savior's life, and His state and condition upon this earth, were more vastly different from yours than those of Miranda's; and yet, His life, the purity and perfection of His behavior, is the common example proposed to all Christians. It is His spirit, therefore, His piety, and His love that you are to imitate.

The same is true with the apostles. Their lives may have differed greatly from yours, but their behavior is still an example to you. It is their piety, their love for God, that you are to imitate, not the particular form of their lives. If you will act under God as they did, direct your actions to the purposes that they did, demonstrate the love of God through such charity to your neighbor, such humility and self-denial as they did—then, though you are only teaching your own children, while Paul converted whole nations, you are still following their steps and acting after their example.

Do not think, therefore, that you cannot or need not be like Miranda because you are not in her state of life. The same spirit and temperament would have made Miranda a saint in any place or condition. So, if you will simply aspire after her spirit and disposition, every form and condition of life will furnish you with sufficient means of employing it. Miranda is what she is because she does everything in the name of God and with regard to her duty to Him. When you do the same, you will be exactly like her, though you may be entirely different from her in the outward state of your life.

You say you are married and therefore do not have the time and money in your power that she has. However, Miranda's perfection is not comprised of the amount of time she spends or the amount of money she spends. Rather, she is careful to make the best use of all the time and money that God has put into her hands. If you, therefore, make the best use of all the time and money that are at your disposal, then you will be like Miranda. If she has two hundred pounds a year, and you have only two mites, do you not have more reason to be exact in the wisest use of them? If she has a great deal of time, and you have but a little, should you not be the more watchful and prudent, lest that little should be lost?

Suppose I had recommended a universal plainness of diet. Is this not a reasonable thing to recommend? Would it not logically follow that the nobleman and the laborer will live upon the same food? Suppose I had encouraged a universal dress code? Are not plainness and sobriety of dress recommended to all? Yet, would it not follow that all people are to be clothed in the same manner?

Let everyone guard against the vanity of dress; let them make their use of clothes a matter of conscience; let them desire to make the best use of their money; and then everyone will have a rule that is sufficient to direct them in every state of life. This rule will no more let people be vain in their dress than intemperate in their liquors; and yet, it will leave it as lawful to have some difference in their apparel as to have some difference in their drink.

But now, will you say that you may use the finest, richest wines whenever and however you please; that you may be as expensive in them as you desire, because different liquors are allowed? If not, how can you say that you may use clothes as you please and wear the richest things you can get, because the difference of clothes is lawful? Just as the lawfulness of different liquors leaves no room, nor any excuse, for the smallest degree of intemperance in drinking, so the lawfulness of different apparel leaves no room, nor any excuse, for the smallest degree of vanity in dress.

Although religion does not state the particular way in which all individuals should use these things, yet it gives general rules that are a sufficient direction in every state of life. Whoever lets religion teach him that the end of drinking is only to refresh our spirits, keep us in good health, and make soul and body fitter for all the offices of a holy and pious life—whoever lets religion teach him that he is to desire to glorify God by a right use of this liberty—will always know what intemperance is for his particular state. Likewise, whoever lets religion teach him that the end of clothing is only to hide our shame and nakedness and to secure our bodies from the injuries of weather—and that he is to desire to glorify God by a sober and wise use of this necessity—will always know what vanity of dress is for his particular state.

The only way to avoid luxury and indulgence is to make religion the strict measure of our allowance in both cases. And there is nothing in religion to excite a man to this pious exactness in one case, except what is as good a motive for the same exactness in the other. Furthermore, "all things are lawful...but all things are not expedient" (1 Cor. 6:12). There may be some things lawful in the use of liquors and apparel that, by abstaining from them for pious ends, may be made means of great perfection.

For instance, a man may deny himself the lawful use of liquors; he may refrain from such expense in his drink as might be allowed without sin. He may do this not only for the sake of a more pious self-denial, but also that he might be able to relieve and refresh the helpless, poor, and sick. Another may abstain from the use of that which is lawful in dress; he may be more frugal than the necessities of religion absolutely require. He does this not only as a means of a better humility, but that he may be more able to clothe other people.

Such persons might be said to do that which was highly suitable to the true spirit of, though not absolutely required by the letter of, the law of Christ.

> *And whosoever shall give to drink unto one of these...a cup of cold water only...verily I say unto you, he shall in no wise lose his reward.* (Matt. 10:42)

How dear must they be to Christ, who often give themselves water, that they may be able to give wine to the sick!

Let us now return to our earlier discussion. All that has been said here applies to both those who are married and those who are still under the direction of their parents. Although the obedience that is due to parents should not stop one from carrying his virtues higher than the parents require, yet his obedience requires him to submit to his parents' direction in all things not contrary to the laws of God. If, therefore, your parents require you to live more in the fashion and conversation of the world, or to be more expensive in your dress and person, or to dispose of your time in a way that does not suit your desires after greater perfection, you must submit and bear it as your cross until you are at liberty to follow the higher counsels of Christ, until you have it in your power to choose the best ways of raising your virtue to its greatest height.

While you are in this state, you may find it necessary at times to forego some means of improving your virtue. Yet, if you comply in all things lawful, out of a pious, tender sense of duty, then those things that you perform in this way, instead of being hindrances of your virtue, are turned into means of improving it. If you lose anything by being restrained from observing particular virtues, you gain humble compliance by that excellent virtue of obedience.

I have written this much to show how persons under the direction of parents may imitate the wise and pious life of Miranda. However, for those who are altogether in their own hands: if the liberty of their state carries them to choose the most excellent ways; if they, having all in their own power, turn the whole form of their lives into a regular exercise of the highest virtues; happy are they who have so learned Christ!

Not everyone can receive this saying. (See John 6:60.) "He that hath ears to hear, let him hear" (Matt. 11:15) and bless the Spirit of God, who has put such good inclinations into his heart. God may be served and glorified in every state of life. Some states of life are more desirable than others: they do more to purify our natures, more to improve our virtues, and more to dedicate us to God in a higher manner. Those who are at liberty to choose for themselves seem to be called by God to be more eminently devoted to His service.

Since the beginning of Christianity, there have been two types of people among good Christians. The one has feared and served God in the common offices and business of a secular, worldly life. The other has renounced the common business and common enjoyments of life, such as riches, marriage, honors, and pleasures, and has been wholly devoted to voluntary poverty, virginity, devotion, and seclusion, in order to live wholly unto God in the daily exercise of a divine and heavenly life.

Eusebius, the famous ecclesiastical historian, lived at the time of the first General Council, when the church was in its greatest glory and purity, when its bishops were holy fathers and eminent saints. The following is a testimony from his work entitled *Demanstratio Evangélico*.[4]

Therefore, two ways, or manners, of living have been instituted in the church of Christ. The one, raised above the ordinary state of nature and common ways of living, rejects wedlock, possessions, and worldly goods, and, being wholly separate and removed from the ordinary conversation of common life, is appropriated and devoted solely to the worship and service of God through an exceeding degree of heavenly love.

People of this order seem dead to the life of this world; although their bodies reside upon earth, they are forever dwelling in heaven in their minds and thoughts. As if they were actually inhabitants of heaven, they look down on human life, interceding to God Almighty for the whole race of mankind. They do not offer the blood of beasts or the burning of bodies, but they exercise the highest piety, with cleansed and purified hearts and with a whole form of life strictly devoted to virtue. These are their sacrifices, which they continually offer unto God, imploring His mercy and favor for themselves and their fellow creatures. Christianity receives this as the perfect manner of life.

The other is a lower form, suiting itself more to the condition of human nature. It permits chaste wedlock, the care of children and family, trade and business—all the employments of life are allowable under a sense of piety and fear of God. Those who have chosen this manner of life have their set

---

[4]Vol. 1, bk. 1, c. 8.

times for retirement and spiritual exercises, and particular days are set apart for their hearing and learning the Word of God. People of this order are considered in the second state of piety.

Those inspired by the life of Miranda and desirous of perfection, may unite themselves into little societies, professing voluntary poverty, virginity, seclusion, devotion, and living upon bare necessaries, so that some might be relieved by their charities and be blessed with their prayers and their example. Or, they may practice the same manner of life in as high a degree as they can by themselves. Such people would be so far from being chargeable with superstition or blind devotion, that they might be justly said to restore that piety that was the boast and glory of the church when its greatest saints were alive.

Now, as Eusebius observed, it was an exceedingly great degree of heavenly love that carried these persons above the common ways of life to such an eminent state of holiness. We should not marvel that the religion of Jesus Christ fills the hearts of many Christians with this high degree of love. Is it any wonder that a religion that opens such a scene of glory, that reveals things so infinitely above all the world, that so triumphs over death (Rom. 6:9), that assures us of mansions (John 14:2) of bliss where we shall so soon be "as the angels of God in heaven" (Matt. 22:30)—is it any wonder that such truths and expectations should, in some holy souls, destroy all earthly desires and make the ardent love of heavenly things the one continual passion of their hearts?

Christianity is founded upon the infinite humiliation, the cruel mockings and scourgings, the many sufferings, the poor, persecuted life, and the painful death of the crucified Son of God. (See Matthew 27:20–37.) Is it any wonder that many humble adorers of this profound mystery, many affectionate lovers of the crucified Lord, should renounce their share of worldly pleasures and give themselves up to a continual course of self-sacrifice and self-denial, that suffering here in this way with Christ, they may reign with Him hereafter (2 Tim. 2:12)? Truth itself has assured us that "one thing is needful" (Luke 10:42). Is it any wonder that some Christians are so full of faith that they believe this in the highest sense of the words? Should we marvel that they desire such a complete separation from the world that their care and attention to the one needful thing may not be interrupted?

Our Lord has said,

> *If thou wilt be perfect, go and sell that thou hast, and give to the poor, and thou shalt have treasure in heaven: and come and follow me.*   (Matt. 19:21)

What wonder is it that some Christians are such zealous followers of Christ, so intent upon heavenly treasure, so desirous of perfection, that they renounce the enjoyment of their estates, choose a voluntary poverty, and relieve all the poor that they are able? Paul said,

> *He that is unmarried careth for the things that belong to the Lord, how he may please the Lord...The unmarried woman careth for the things of the Lord, that she may be holy both in body and in spirit.*   (1 Cor. 7:32, 34)

What wonder is it if the purity and perfection of the virgin state has been the praise and glory of the church in its first and purest ages?

There have always been some so desirous of pleasing God, so zealous after every degree of purity and perfection, so glad of every means of improving their virtue, that they have renounced the comforts and enjoyments of wedlock, in order to trim their lamps (Matt. 25:1–13), to purify their souls, and to wait upon God in a state of perpetual virginity. If in these days we lack examples of these various degrees of perfection; if neither clergy nor laity are enough of this spirit; if we are so far departed from it that a man seems, like Paul at Athens, "a setter forth of strange gods" (Acts 17:18) when he recommends self-denial, renunciation of the world, regular devotion, seclusion, virginity, and voluntary poverty—it is because we have fallen into an age where the love not only of many, but of most, has grown cold (Matt. 24:12).

I have made this little appeal to antiquity and quoted these few passages of Scripture to support the life of Miranda, and to show that her highest rules of holy living, devotion, self-denial, renunciation of the world, charity, virginity, and voluntary poverty, are founded in the highest counsels of Christ and His apostles. They are suitable to the high expectations of another life and are the proper instances of a heavenly love, which were followed by the greatest saints of the best and purest ages of the church.

"He that hath ears to hear, let him hear" (Matt. 11:15).

Chapter Nine

A UNIVERSAL OBLIGATION

In the foregoing chapters, I have gone through several great instances of Christian devotion. I have shown that all the areas of our daily lives—our employments, our talents, and our money—are all to be made holy and acceptable unto God (Rom. 12:1) by a wise and religious use of everything, and by directing our actions and designs to the honor and glory of God. I will now show that this regular devotion, this holiness of everyday life, this religious use of everything that we have, is the duty of every Christian person, no matter what his state.

Fulvius[5] wishes to be free from the rules of life. He does not work, nor does he enter into any business, because he thinks that every employment or business calls people to carefully follow through on every duty. He will tell you that he did not enter into holy orders because he looks on it as a state that requires great holiness of life, and it does not suit his disposition to be so good. He will tell you that he never intends to marry because he cannot oblige himself to that regularity of life and good behavior, which he takes to be the duty of those who are at the head of a family.

---

[5]Fulvius: the name of a great patrician family in Rome. It suggests worldly power and pomp.

Fulvius lives by no rules and thinks all is very well because he is neither a priest, nor a father, nor a guardian, nor has any employment or family to look after. Yet, Fulvius is a rational creature, and, as such, he is as much obliged to live according to reason and order as a priest is obliged to attend to the altar, or a guardian is to be faithful to his trust. If he lives contrary to reason, he does not commit a small crime; he does not break a small trust. Rather, he breaks the law of his nature, he rebels against the God who gave him that nature, and he puts himself among those whom the God of reason and order will punish as apostates and deserters.

Although he has no employment, he is, as much as any man, obliged to be honest and faithful and to live according to the holiness of the Christian spirit. If he abuses this great calling, he is not false in a small matter, but he abuses the precious blood of Christ. He crucifies the Son of God afresh; he neglects the highest instances of divine goodness; he disgraces the church of God; he blemishes the body of Christ; and he abuses the means of grace and the promises of glory. "It shall be more tolerable for Tyre and Sidon at the day of judgment, than for [him]" (Matt. 11:22).

It is great folly for anyone to think himself at liberty to live as he pleases. For there is nothing more to be feared than the wrong use of our reason, nor anything more to be dreaded than the neglect of our Christian calling. That calling is not meant to serve the little uses of a short life, but to redeem souls unto God, to fill heaven with saints, and to finish a kingdom of eternal glory unto God. No man should think himself excused from the exactness of piety and morality, simply on the grounds that he has chosen to be idle and independent in the world.

The necessities of a reasonable and holy life are not founded in the conditions and employments of this life, but in the immutable nature of God and the nature of man. A man is not to be reasonable and holy because he is a priest or a father of a family; but he is to be a pious priest and a good father because piety and goodness are the laws of human nature. If a man could please God without living according to reason and order, there would be nothing displeasing to God in an idle priest or a reprobate father. Therefore, whoever abuses his reason is like one who abuses the priesthood, and whoever neglects the holiness of the Christian life is like one who disregards the most important trust.

Everyone would agree that a man who chooses to put out his eyes is a rebel against God, because he also chooses not to see and enjoy the light and the works of God. Everyone would think the same of a man who voluntarily kills himself by refusing to eat and drink. This man would deserve the highest indignation of God. Why is this behavior so sinful? Because a man who does these things abuses his nature and refuses to act the part for which God has created him. Therefore, everyone who abuses his reason, who acts a different part than that for which God created him, is like this man: a rebel against God and subject to His wrath.

Let us suppose that this man, instead of putting out his eyes, had only employed them in looking at ridiculous things, or had only shut them up in sleep. Or suppose that, instead of starving himself to death by not eating at all, he had turned every meal into a feast and had eaten and drank beyond reason. Could he be said to have lived more to the glory of God? Could he be said to have acted any more the part for which God had created him, than if he had put out his eyes or starved himself to death?

Now, suppose that a man acts unreasonably to the point of extinguishing his reason, instead of putting out his eyes or living in a course of folly and impertinence or starving himself to death. This man is as great a rebel against God as the others, because one who puts out his eyes or murders himself is just as guilty of abusing the powers God has given him, of refusing to act that part for which he was created, and of putting himself into a state contrary to the divine will. Surely this is the guilt of everyone who lives an unreasonable, unholy, and foolish life.

No particular state or lifestyle is an excuse for the abuse of our bodies or for suicide, nor is it an excuse for the abuse of our reason or the neglect of the holiness of the Christian religion. It is as much the will of God that we should make the best use of our rational faculties, that we should conform to the purity and holiness of Christianity, as it is His will that we should use our eyes, and eat and drink for the preservation of our lives. Until a man can show that he sincerely endeavors to live according to the will of God; until he can show that he is striving to live according to the holiness of the Christian religion—whoever or wherever he may be—then he must answer for everything as if he has refused to live, has abused the greatest trusts, and has neglected the highest calling in the world.

Everyone can see that all classes of men are to be equally and exactly honest and faithful. There is no exception made to this duty, for any particular state of life, whether public or private. According to the reason and nature of things, the nature of God, and the nature of man, we should find it necessary to use our reason for every grace or religious quality of the Christian life—not only piety, but also humility, sobriety, justice, devotion, and honesty. On the other hand, pride, sensuality, and covetousness are great disorders of the soul, and they are as great an abuse of our reason, and as contrary to God, as cheating and dishonesty.

Theft and dishonesty, indeed, appear to be greater sins in vulgar eyes because they are so hurtful to civil society and are so severely punished by human laws. However, we ought to consider mankind in a higher view, as God's order of rational beings who are to glorify Him by the right use of their reason and by conforming to the order of their nature. Thereby we will find that every temperament that is equally contrary to reason and order—every disposition that opposes God's purposes and plans, and disorders the beauty and glory of the rational world—is equally sinful in man and equally repulsive to God. The sin of sensuality is like the sin of dishonesty because both render us the objects of God's displeasure.

Again, let us consider mankind as an order of fallen spirits that are redeemed and baptized into a fellowship with the Son of God to be temples of the Holy Spirit (1 Cor. 6:19); to live according to His holy inspirations; to offer to God the reasonable sacrifice of a humble, pious, and thankful life (Rom. 12:1); to purify themselves from the disorders of their fall (James 4:8); and to make a right use of the means of grace, in order to be sons of eternal glory (Heb. 2:10).

If we look at mankind in this true light, then anything that abuses this infinite mercy—any action that makes us less like Christ, that disgraces His body, that abuses the means of grace, and that opposes our hopes of glory—can make us forever abhorrent to God. Pride and sensuality and other such vices do not hurt civil society as cheating and dishonesty do; yet they hurt the society that is greater and more glorious in the eyes of God than all the societies that relate to this world.

Nothing, therefore, can be more false than to imagine that, because we are private persons who have taken upon ourselves no employment of life, we may indulge our appetites and be less careful of the duties of piety and holiness. This would be just as good an excuse for cheating and dishonesty. One who abuses his reason, who indulges himself in lust and sensuality and neglects to act the wise and reasonable part of a true Christian, has everything in his life to render him hateful to God that is found in cheating and dishonesty. As a result, if you choose to be an idle glutton, rather than to be unfaithful; if you choose to live in lust and sensuality rather than to harm your neighbor's personal property; you have made no better a provision for the favor of God than one who chooses to rob a house instead of a church.

For the abusing of our own nature is as great a disobedience against God, as the injuring of our neighbor; and one who lacks piety toward God has done as much to damn himself, as one who lacks honesty toward men. Every argument, therefore, that proves it necessary for all men in all stations of life to be truly honest, proves it equally necessary for all men in all stations of life to be truly holy and pious, and to do all things in a manner suitable to the glory of God. All men are obliged to be holy and devout in the common course of their lives, in the use of everything that they enjoy.

Let us take another example, this one concerning our obligation to pray. Prayer is a duty that belongs to all states and conditions of men; this much is agreed upon. No state of life is to be excused from prayer, just as no state of life is to be excused from piety and holiness. The reason why we are to pray to God and to glorify Him with hymns and psalms of thanksgiving (Ps. 95:2), is because we are to live wholly unto God and to glorify Him in all possible ways. It is not because the words of praise or the forms of thanksgiving are more particularly parts of piety, or more the worship of God than other things. Rather, it is because they are ways of expressing our dependence, obedience, and devotion to God.

It plainly follows that we are equally obliged to worship and glorify God in all other actions that can be turned into acts of piety and obedience to Him. And, since actions are much more significant than words, it must be a much more acceptable worship of God to glorify Him in all the actions of our everyday lives, than with any form of words at any particular times. We are to worship God with all forms of thanksgiving, yet whoever can say, "I have learned, in whatsoever state I am, therewith to be content" (Phil. 4:11), praises God in a much higher manner than one who has a set time every day for the singing of psalms.

To live in the world as a stranger and a pilgrim (1 Pet. 2:11), using all its enjoyments as not abusing them (1 Cor. 7:31) and making all our actions into steps toward a better life, is to offer a better sacrifice to God than any form of prayer. To be humble in all our actions; to avoid every appearance of pride and vanity; to be meek and lowly in our words, dress, behavior, and designs; is to imitate Christ and to worship God in a higher manner than they who have only certain times to fall low on their knees in devotions.

One who dares not say an ill-natured word or do an unreasonable thing because he considers God as omnipresent, performs a better devotion than one who dares not miss a church service. One who contents himself with necessities, that he may give the remainder to those who need it—or one who dares not spend any money foolishly, because he considers it a gift from God that must be used according to His will—praises God with something that is more glorious than songs of praise.

Setting aside a time for prayer is a proper instance of devotion. Even so, one who avoids all times, places, and actions that are not strictly conformable to wisdom and holiness, worships the divine nature with the most true and substantial devotion. For who does not know that it is better to be pure and holy than to talk about purity and holiness? Yet, we must remember that prayers are far from being a sufficient devotion in themselves. We are to praise God with words and prayers, because it is one way of glorifying the God who has given us such faculties. However, words are such small things in themselves, and times of prayer are so little if compared with the rest of our lives, that devotion that consists of times and forms of prayer is but a very small thing if compared to the devotion that is to appear in every other area and circumstance of our lives.

It is an easy thing to worship God with forms of words and to observe times of offering them unto Him. It is the same with the smallest kind of piety. On the other hand, it is more difficult to worship God with our substance, to honor Him with the right use of our time, and to offer to Him the continual sacrifices of self-denial. It requires more piety to eat and drink only for such ends as may glorify God, to undertake no labor nor allow any diversion except where we can act in the name of God. It is more difficult to sacrifice all our corrupt tempers, correct all our passions, and make piety to God the rule and measure of all the actions of our everyday lives. Devotion of this kind is a much more acceptable service unto God, than those words of devotion that we offer to Him either in the church or in our prayer closet.

I do not intend to lessen the true and great value of prayers, either public or private; but you must realize that they are certainly a very small part of devotion when compared to a devout life. To see this in yet a clearer light, suppose that a man has appointed times, which he strictly observes, for praising God with psalms and hymns. Suppose, also, that he is restless and uneasy in his daily life, full of murmurings and complaints about everything, including the seasons, pleased only when it is not a problem to be so, and having something to dislike in everything that happens to him.

Can you imagine anything more absurd and unreasonable than this kind of character? Is this man to be considered thankful to God, because he has forms of praise, which he offers to Him? No, such forms of praise are so far from being an acceptable devotion to God that they must be abhorred as an abomination. The absurdity of this instance has the same application in any other part of our lives; if our daily lives are contrary in any way to our prayers, it is the same abomination as songs of thanksgiving in the mouths of murmurers. Bending your knees while clothed with pride; making heavenly petitions while hoarding up treasures on earth; having holy devotions while living in the follies of the world; saying prayers of meekness and charity while your heart is the seat of pride and resentment; and spending hours in prayer while giving up days and years to idle and foolish diversions—these are as absurd and unacceptable to God as thanksgiving from a person who lives in complaints and discontentment.

Unless our lives are lived according to the common spirit of our prayers, our prayers are so far from being a real or sufficient part of devotion that they become empty lip service or, what is worse, a notorious hypocrisy. This may serve to convince us that all orders of people are to labor and aspire after the same utmost perfection of the Christian life. We are to make the spirit and quality of our prayers the common spirit and quality of our lives. Because the same holiness of prayers requires the same holiness of life, all Christians are called to be holy. A soldier or businessman is not called to minister at the altar or preach the Gospel, but every soldier or businessman is obliged to be as devout, humble, holy, and heavenly minded in every area of his life, as a clergyman is obliged to be zealous, faithful, and laborious in all areas of his profession.

All men, therefore, have one and the same important business: to live up to the excellency of their rational nature and to make reason and order the law of all their designs and actions. Likewise, all Christians have one and the same calling: to live according to the excellency of the Christian spirit and to make the sublime precepts of the Gospel the rule and measure of their entire lives. The reason for this is because all people are to pray for the same holiness, wisdom, and divine qualities, and to make themselves as fit as they can for the same heaven. The one thing needful to one, is the one thing needful to all. The merchant is no longer to hoard up treasures on earth; the soldier is no longer to fight for glory; the great scholar is no longer to pride himself in the depths of science; instead, they must all with one spirit "count all things but loss for the excellency of the knowledge of Christ Jesus" (Phil. 3:8).

The fine lady must teach her eyes to weep and be clothed with humility. The polite gentleman must exchange the carefree thoughts of wit and fancy for "a broken and a contrite heart" (Ps. 51:17). The man of quality must so far renounce the dignity of his birth, that he thinks himself miserable until he is born again. Servants must consider their service as done unto God (Eph. 6:5–6). Masters must consider their servants as their brothers and sisters in Christ (1 Tim. 6:2), to be treated as their fellow members of the body of Christ.

Young ladies must either devote themselves as virgins to piety, prayer, self-denial, and all good works; or else marry, to be holy, sober, and prudent in the care of a family, bringing up their children in piety, humility, and devotion, and abounding in all other good works, to the utmost of their state and capacity. They may choose a married life or a single life, but it is not left to them to choose whether they will live lives of holiness, humility, devotion, and all other duties of the Christian life. Even if they have fortunes or are born of rich parents, it is not up to them to divide themselves between God and the world, or to take such pleasures as their fortunes will afford them—just as it is not allowable for them to be sometimes chaste and modest and sometimes not.

They are not to consider how much religion may secure them a fair character, or how they may add devotion to an impertinent, vain, and giddy life. Instead, they must look into the spirit and quality of their prayers, into the nature and end of Christianity, and then they will find that, whether married or unmarried, they have but one business upon their hands: to be wise and pious and holy, not in little modes and forms of worship, but in the whole turn of their minds, in the whole form of all their behavior, and in the daily course of their lives.

Young gentlemen must consider what our blessed Savior said to the young man in Luke's gospel. He bid him, "Sell all that thou hast, and distribute unto the poor" (Luke 18:22). Although this text does not require everyone to sell all he owns, it certainly obliges all kinds of people to use what they own in wise and reasonable and charitable ways. One may sufficiently show that all that he has is devoted to God when no part of it is kept from the poor to be spent in needless, vain, and foolish expenses. If young men plan to live a life of pleasure and indulgence; if they spend their estates in high living, in luxury and intemperance, in pleasures and entertainment, in sports and gaming and such extravagant gratifications of their foolish passions; they have as much reason to think themselves angels, as to think themselves disciples of Christ.

Let them be assured that the only business of a Christian gentleman is to distinguish himself by good works, to be eminent in the most sublime virtues of the Gospel, to bear with the ignorance and weakness of the vulgar, to be a friend and patron to everyone who resides near him, to live in the utmost heights of wisdom and holiness, and to show through the whole course of his life a true religious greatness of mind. Young gentlemen must aspire after the kind of gentility they might have learned from seeing Jesus. They must show no other spirit of a gentleman except what they might have received by living with the holy apostles. They must learn to love God with all their heart, all their soul, and all their strength (Mark 12:30), and their neighbor as themselves (Matt. 19:19). Only then can they have all the greatness and distinction that they will have here, and they will be fit for an eternal happiness in heaven thereafter.

It is the same in all groups and conditions, for both men and women. This is to be the common holiness, the common life of all Christians. The merchant is not to leave devotion to the clergyman, nor the clergyman to leave humility to the laborer. Women of fortune are not to leave it to poor women to be discreet and chaste, to keep the home, and to adorn themselves in modest apparel, with decency and sobriety (see 1 Timothy 2:9); nor are poor women to leave it to the rich to attend to the worship and service of God. Great men must be eminent for true poverty of spirit, and people of a low and afflicted state must greatly rejoice in God. The man of strength and power is to forgive and pray for his enemies, and the innocent sufferer who is chained in prison must, with Paul and Silas, at midnight sing praises to God (Acts 16:25). God is to be glorified, holiness is to be practiced, and the spirit of religion is to be the common spirit of every Christian, in every state and condition of life.

For the Son of God did not come from above to add an external form of worship to the various ways of life that are in the world. That would have left people to live as they did before, in whatever fashion and spirit the world approved of. Instead, He came down from heaven, altogether divine and heavenly in His own nature, to call mankind to a divine and heavenly life, to the highest change of their own natural temperaments—that they might be born again of the Holy Spirit, walk in the wisdom and light and love of God (Eph. 5:2, 8), and be like Him to the utmost of their power. Christ came that men might renounce all the ways of the world, whether of greatness, business, or pleasure; He calls every person to a denial of all his most agreeable passions and to a life of such wisdom, purity, and holiness, as might befit a glorious enjoyment of God to all eternity.

Therefore, whatever is foolish, ridiculous, vain, earthly, or sensual in the life of a Christian, is something that should not be there; it is a spot and a defilement that must be washed away with tears of repentance. If anything of this kind runs through the course of our lives, if we allow ourselves things that are either vain, foolish, or sensual, then we renounce our claim to faith in Jesus Christ.

It is true that He is wisdom and holiness, and that He came to make us like Himself and to baptize us into His Spirit. Even more so, it is true that no one can keep his Christian faith except one who, to the utmost of his power, lives a wise and holy and heavenly life. This, and this alone, is Christianity: a universal holiness in every part of life, a heavenly wisdom in all our actions, not conforming to the spirit of the world, but turning all worldly enjoyments into means of piety and devotion to God.

But, now, if this devout state of heart, if these habits of inward holiness, are true religion, then true religion is equally the duty and happiness of all classes of men. There is no sense in recommending it to one and not recommending it to all. If it is the happiness and glory of a bishop to live in a devout spirit, full of these holy qualities, doing everything as unto God, it is as much the glory and happiness of all men and women, whether young or old, to live in the same spirit. Whoever can find any reasons why an ancient bishop should be intent upon divine things, turning all his life into the highest exercises of piety, wisdom, and devotion, will find himself many, many reasons why he should, to the utmost of his power, do the same himself.

If you say that a bishop must be an eminent example of Christian holiness because of his high and sacred calling, you are right. However, if you say that it is more proper for him than for you to be such an example, you are greatly mistaken; for there is nothing to make the highest degrees of holiness desirable to a bishop, but what makes them equally desirable to every other person. For an exalted piety, high devotion, and the religious use of everything, are as much the glory and happiness of one state of life as they are of another.

If you can imagine the best bishop in the world, what sort of piety would he have? How would you have him love God, and how would you have him imitate the life of our Savior and His apostles? How would you have him live above the world, shining in all the instances of a heavenly life? When you have answered all these questions, then you have discovered the spirit that you ought to make the spirit of your own life.

If you will think about this for a while, perhaps you will find more conviction from it than you might have thought. Every person knows how good and pious he would have some people be; everyone knows how wise and reasonable it is for a bishop to be entirely above the world and to be an eminent example of Christian perfection. As soon as you think of a wise and ancient bishop, you imagine some exalted degree of piety, a living example of all those holy qualities that you find described in the Gospel.

Now, if you ask yourself, "What is the happiest thing for a young clergyman to do?" you will be forced to answer that nothing can be so glorious for him than to be like that holy and excellent bishop. If you go on and ask, "What is the happiest thing for any young man or woman to do?" the answer must be the same: nothing can be so glorious for them than to live in such habits of piety, in such exercises of a divine life, as this good old bishop does. For everything that is great and glorious in religion is as much the true glory of every man or woman as it is the glory of any bishop. If high degrees of divine love, fervent charity, spotless purity, heavenly affection, constant self-denial, or frequent devotion, is the best and happiest way of life for any Christian, it is so for every Christian.

If you were to see a bishop living below his character in the whole course of his life, conforming to all the foolish passions of the world, and being governed by the same cares and fears that govern vain and worldly men, what would you think of him? Would you think that he was only guilty of a small mistake? No, you would condemn him as erring in that which is not only the most, but the only, important matter that relates to him. Think about this again and again, until your mind is fully convinced how miserable a mistake it is for a bishop to live a careless, worldly life.

While you are thinking in this manner, turn your thoughts toward one of your acquaintances, your brother or sister, or any young person. Now, if you see that his life is straying from the doctrines of the Gospel, if you see that his way of life cannot be said to be a sincere endeavor to "enter...at the strait gate" (Matt. 7:13), you see something that you are to condemn, in the same degree and for the same reasons as you condemned the bishop. He does not commit a small mistake, but a large one, and he mistakes his true happiness as much as that bishop who neglects the high duties of his calling.

Now, apply this reasoning to yourself. If you find yourself living an idle, indulgent, vain life, choosing rather to gratify your passions than to live up to the doctrines of Christianity and to practice the plain precepts of our blessed Lord, you can convict yourself of all the blindness and unreasonableness that you can charge upon any irregular bishop.

All the virtues of the Christian life, its perfect purity and its heavenly qualities, are as much the sole rule of your life as they are of a bishop's. If you neglect these holy tempers, if you do not eagerly aspire to them, if you do not show yourself a visible example of them, then you are as much fallen from your true happiness, you are as great an enemy to yourself and have made as bad a choice, as that bishop who chooses to enrich his family rather than to be like an apostle. The highest holiness and the most heavenly dispositions are the duty and happiness of a bishop as much as they are the duty and happiness of all Christians. The wisest bishop in the world lives in the greatest heights of holiness and is most exemplary in all the exercises of a divine life.

Likewise, the wisest youth, the wisest businessman or soldier, the wisest woman, whether married or unmarried, is one who lives in the highest degrees of Christian holiness, and in all the exercises of a divine and heavenly life.

Chapter Ten

THE HAPPINESS OF TRUE PIETY

Some people may object that all these rules of holy living are too great a restraint upon human life. They may object that introducing a regard to God in all their actions will make them too anxious. They may even say that by depriving ourselves of so many seemingly innocent pleasures, we will render our lives dull, uneasy, and melancholy.

In response to these concerns, I will present three points. First, these rules are prescribed for, and will certainly procure, quite a contrary end. Instead of making our lives dull and melancholy, they will render them full of contentment and strong satisfaction. By these rules we only exchange the childish satisfactions of our vain and sickly passions for the solid enjoyments and real happiness of a sound mind.

Secondly, there is no foundation for comfort in the enjoyments of this life, except in the assurance that a wise and good God governs the world. Therefore, the more we find God in everything and every place, and the more we look up to Him in all our actions, then the more we will conform to His will, act according to His wisdom, and imitate His goodness. By so doing, we can enjoy God, partake of the divine nature, and heighten and increase all that is happy and comfortable in human life.

Thirdly, whoever is attempting to subdue and root out of his mind all those passions of pride, envy, and ambition that religion opposes, is doing more to make himself happy, even in this life, than one who is indulging in them. These passions are the causes of all the anxieties and vexations of human life: they are the fevers of our minds, vexing them with false appetites and restless cravings after things we do not really want, and spoiling our taste for those things that are our proper good.

Imagine that you saw a man somewhere who proposed reason as the rule of all his actions. He only desired things that nature and religion approve. He was as pure from pride, envy, and covetousness as from thoughts of murder. And, in this freedom from worldly passions, he had a soul full of divine love, wishing and praying that all men may have all the worldly things they need and be partakers of eternal glory in the life to come.

As you imagine a man living in this manner, your own conscience will immediately tell you that he is the happiest man in the world, and that it is not possible to imagine any higher happiness in the present state of life. On the other hand, if you suppose him to be in any degree less perfect, if you suppose him to be subject to even one foolish or vain passion, your own conscience will again tell you that he lessens his own happiness and robs himself of the true enjoyment of his other virtues. The more we live by the rules of religion, the more peaceful and happy we render our lives.

Real happiness is only to be had from the greatest degrees of piety, the greatest denials of our passions, and the strictest rules of religion. If we look into the world and see the anxieties and troubles of human life and human misery, we will find that they are all caused by our violent and irreligious passions. Trouble and uneasiness are founded in the lack of something in our lives. If we, therefore, are to know the true cause of our troubles and worries, we must find out the cause of our needs. Whatever creates and increases our needs, does, in the same degree, create and increase our troubles and anxieties.

God Almighty has sent us into the world with very few needs: food, clothing, and shelter are the only things necessary in life. As these are only our present needs, the present world is well furnished to supply these needs. This is the state of man—born with few needs into a large world very capable of supplying them. One would reasonably suppose that men should pass their lives in contentment and thankfulness to God—or at least that they should be free from cares and concerns—because they live in a world that has more than enough to supply all their needs. Furthermore, this short life, furnished with all that we need in it, is only a short passage to eternal glory, where we will be clothed with the brightness of angels and enter into the joys of God.

From this we might reasonably expect that human life should be a state of peace, joy, and delight in God. It would certainly be this way if reason had its full power over us. However, though God, nature, and reason make human life thus free from needs and so full of happiness, yet our passions, in rebellion against God and nature and reason, create a new world of evils and fill human life with imaginary needs and vain anxieties. The man of pride has a thousand needs that have been created by his own pride; these render him as full of trouble as if God had created him with a thousand appetites, without creating anything that was proper to satisfy them. Envy and ambition also have their endless desires, which trouble the souls of men and, by their contradictory motions, render them as foolishly miserable as those who want to fly and crawl at the same time.

If any complaining, disquieted man were to tell you the ground of his uneasiness, you would plainly see that he is the author of his own torment—that he is vexing himself over some imaginary evil that will cease to torment him as soon as he is content to be what God and nature and reason require him to be. If you were to see a man passing his days in worry because he could not walk on the water or catch birds as they flew by him, you would readily confess that his uneasiness is his own doing. However, if you were to look into the most tormenting disquiets of life, you would find them all just as absurd. People are only tormented by their own folly, and they worry themselves with things that should concern them no more than walking on the water or catching birds.

Can you imagine anything more extravagant and silly than a man racking his brains and studying night and day how to fly? He wanders from his own house and home, wearying himself with climbing upon every ascent, asking everybody he meets to lift him up from the ground, bruising himself with continual falls, until at last he breaks his neck—and all this because he thought it would be glorious to have people gazing up at him, and because he would be happy to eat, drink, and sleep at the top of the highest trees in the land. Would you not readily admit that such a man was only troubled by his own foolishness? Of course, such a silly creature is very rare, if he exists at all, yet we may just as easily consider an ambitious man a vain and senseless flyer.

Imagine, again, a man who has a large pond of water, yet lives in continual thirst, never taking even a small drink for fear of lessening his pond. He wastes his time and strength fetching more water to his pond—always thirsty, yet always carrying a bucket of water in his hand. He watches early and late to catch the drops of rain, gaping after every cloud and running greedily into every mire and mud in hopes of water. In addition, he is always studying how to make every ditch empty itself into his pond. He grows old and gray in these anxious labors, and he ends his careful, thirsty life by falling into his own pond. Would you not say that this man was not only the author of all his own anxieties, but was foolish enough to be considered among idiots and madmen? Yet, however foolish and absurd this character is, he does not represent half the follies and absurdities of the covetous man.

I could easily proceed to show the same effects of all our other worldly passions, and make it clear that all our troubles, anxieties, and complaints are entirely of our own making, in the same absurd manner as the covetous and the ambitious man. Wherever you look, you will see worldly concerns, but they are like the worries of the man who was always in search of water to drink when he had more than enough at home for a hundred horses.

The strictest rules of religion are far from making anyone's life dull, anxious, and uncomfortable. On the contrary, all the miseries, vexations, and complaints of the world, are caused by a lack of religion. Religion teaches us to deny all the desires that disturb human life, that make us a bother to ourselves, quarrelsome with others, and unthankful to God. All those absurd passions that weary us in vain labors and foolish anxieties, carrying us from project to project and place to place in pursuit of we know not what, are solely infused into us by pride, envy, ambition, and covetousness. Unless we deny these selfish and worldly attitudes, then all the wants that neither God, nor nature, nor reason has subjected us to, will remain.

If you reduce your desires to such things as nature and reason require, if you regulate all the motions of your heart by the strict rules of religion, you will remove yourself from that infinity of needs and anxieties that torments every heart that is left to itself. Indeed, religion preserves us from a great many evils and helps us in many respects to a more happy enjoyment of ourselves. However, many people imagine that this is only true of a moderate share of religion, where the excesses of our passions are only gently restrained. They suppose that the strict rules and restraints of piety are such contradictions to our nature that they must make our lives dull and uncomfortable.

This objection supposes that religion, moderately practiced, adds much to the happiness of life; yet the heights of piety, required by the perfection of religion, are thought to have a contrary effect. It supposes, therefore, that a person is happy to be kept from the excesses of envy, but unhappy to be kept from other degrees of envy. One is happy to be delivered from a boundless ambition, but unhappy to be without a more moderate ambition. It supposes, also, that the happiness of life consists of a mixture of virtue and vice, a mixture of ambition and humility, charity and envy, heavenly affection and covetousness. In this manner, a person would be happy to be free from excessive pains, but unhappy to be without more moderate pains. This is as absurd as saying that the happiness of health consists of being partly sick and partly well.

If humility is the peace and rest of the soul, then no one has so much happiness from humility as one who is the most humble. If excessive envy is a torment of the soul, the one who most perfectly extinguishes every spark of envy, most perfectly delivers himself from torment. If there is any peace and joy in doing any action according to the will of God, one who brings most of his actions under this rule, increases the peace and joy of his life most of all. It is the same way for every virtue: if you live up to every degree of it, you will have more happiness from it. And the same is true of every vice: if you only negate its excesses, you do very little for yourself; but if you reject it in all degrees, then you feel the true ease and joy of a reformed mind.

For example, if religion only restrains the excesses of revenge but lets the spirit of revenge remain in you for lesser instances, then your religion may have made your life a little more outwardly decent, but you are not at all happier or easier in yourself. However, if you have sacrificed all thoughts of revenge in obedience to God and are resolved to return good for evil at all times (1 Thess. 5:15)—that you may render yourself more like God and fitter for His mercy in the kingdom of love and glory—this is a height of virtue that will make you feel its happiness. And, to deny ourselves those enjoyments that true piety requires us to deny, actually deprives us of no real comfort of life.

Piety does not require us to renounce any way of life in which we can act reasonably and offer what we do to the glory of God. All ways of life, all satisfactions and enjoyments that are within these bounds, are in no way denied us by even the strictest rules of piety. Whatever you can do or enjoy as the servant of God, as His rational creature that has received reason and knowledge from Him—all that you can perform so as to conform to a rational nature and the will of God—all this is allowed by the laws of piety. Will you insist that your life will be continually uncomfortable unless you are free to displease God and act contrary to that reason and wisdom that He has implanted in you? Surely it cannot be uncomfortable to be rescued by religion from such self-murder, and to be rendered capable of eternal happiness.

Imagine a person who is destitute of the knowledge we have from our senses. He is placed somewhere by himself, in the midst of a variety of things that he does not know how to use. Next to him are bread, wine, water, sand, iron chains, gravel, garments, and fire. He has no knowledge of how to use these things, nor any direction from his senses concerning how to quench his thirst or satisfy his hunger. Suppose that in his thirst, he puts sand into his eyes; when his eyes begin to sting, he puts wine into his ears; in his hunger, he puts gravel into his mouth; in his pain, he loads himself with the iron chains; when he feels cold, he puts his feet in the water; when he feels the heat of the fire, he runs away from it; when he is weary, he makes a seat of his bread.

Through his ignorance, this man will vainly torment himself while he lives, and he will die blinded with dust, choked with gravel, and loaded with irons. However, if some good being came to him and showed him how and why to use all the things that were around him, this man would certainly be happier for all that he had. By knowing the strict rules of using each item, he could deliver himself from the pains of hunger, thirst, and cold. Now, could you reasonably affirm that those strict rules of using those things, would render that poor man's life dull and uncomfortable? This is in some measure a representation of the strict rules of religion: they only relieve our ignorance, save us from tormenting ourselves, and teach us to use everything around us to our proper advantage.

Man is placed in a world full of many things; his ignorance makes him use many of them as absurdly as the man who put sand into his eyes to relieve his thirst, or put on chains to remove pain. Religion comes to relieve him by giving him strict rules of using everything that is around him. By using everything according to his own rational nature and the nature of the things, man may always have the pleasure of receiving a right benefit from them. Religion shows him what is right in food and drink and clothing; he may expect nothing from the things of this world except the satisfaction of such needs. Then, extending his assistance as far as he is able, he may help all his fellow creatures to the same benefit from the world that he has.

Religion tells a man that this world is incapable of giving him any other happiness; that all endeavors to be happy in piles of money, acres of land, fine clothes, rich beds, or show and splendor, are only vain endeavors, ignorant attempts after impossibilities. These things are no more able to give the least degree of happiness than sand in the eyes can cure thirst or gravel in the mouth can satisfy hunger. Like dust and gravel misapplied, they will only serve to render a man more unhappy by an ignorant misuse of them.

Although this world can do no more for a man than satisfy these needs of the body, there is yet a much greater good prepared for man than eating, drinking, and dressing. It is invisible to his eyes, being too glorious to be perceived by flesh and blood, but it is reserved for him as soon as this short life is over. In a new body formed to an angelic likeness, he will dwell in the light and glory of God to all eternity.

Religion also tells him that this state of glory will be given to all those who make a right use of the things of this present world, who do not blind themselves with sand or eat gravel or groan under loads of iron that they put on themselves. It will be given to those who, with faith and thankfulness, worship the One who gives all that they enjoy here, and all that they hope for hereafter.

Now, can anyone say that the strictest rules of such a religion as this exclude us from any of the comforts of life? Might we not say the same of those rules that only hinder a man from choking himself with gravel? These rules are strict because they are for our good. Who would complain of the severe strictness of a law that, without any exception, forbade putting sand into our eyes? Who could think it too rigid, that there was no allowance or leeway? The strictness of religion requires something of us only where every degree of the thing is wrong, where every indulgence does us some hurt.

If religion forbids all instances of revenge, without any exception, it is because all revenge has the nature of poison. We do not always take revenge in order to end someone's life, yet if we take any revenge at all, it corrupts our entire lives and makes it difficult to be restored to our former health.

If religion commands us to universal charity, to love our neighbor as ourselves (Matt. 19:19), to forgive and pray for all our enemies without any reserve (Matt. 5:44), it is because all degrees of love are degrees of happiness that strengthen and support the divine life of the soul. They are as necessary to its health and happiness as proper food is necessary to the health and happiness of the body.

If religion has laws against laying up treasures upon earth (Matt. 6:19), and commands us to be content with food and clothing (1 Tim. 6:8), it is because the world is being abused to our own vexation, and all its conveniences are being turned into snares and traps to destroy us. This plainness and simplicity of life secures us from the cares and pains of restless pride and envy, and makes it easier to keep that straight road that will carry us to eternal life.

If religion says, "Sell that thou hast, and give to the poor" (Matt. 19:21), it is because there is no other natural or reasonable use of our riches, no other way of making ourselves happier in them. It is as strictly right to give to others what we do not need ourselves, as it is right to use as much as our own needs require. However, if a man has more food than his own nature requires, how base and unreasonable it is to invent foolish ways of wasting it, filling his own belly rather than letting his fellow creatures have the same comfort from food that he has had!

Therefore, this use of our riches is so far from being a difficult law, that a reasonable man would rejoice in the religion that teaches him to be happier in whatever he gives away than in the things he keeps for himself. Religion also teaches him to make spare food and clothing into greater blessings to him than that which feeds and clothes his own body.

If religion requires us sometimes to fast and deny our natural appetites, it is to lessen the struggle and war that is in our nature; it is to render our bodies fitter instruments of purity and more obedient to the good motions of divine grace; it is to dry up the springs of our passions that war against the soul, to cool the flame of our blood, and to render the mind more capable of divine meditations. Although these abstinences give some pain to the body, yet they so lessen the power of bodily appetites and passions and so increase our taste of spiritual joys, that even these severities of religion, when practiced with discretion, add much to the comfortable enjoyment of our lives.

If religion calls us to a life of watching and prayer (Matt. 26:41), it is because we live among a crowd of enemies, and are always in need of the assistance of God. If we are to confess and bewail our sins (1 John 1:9), it is because such confessions relieve the mind—as burdens and weights taken off the shoulders relieve the body—and restore it to ease. If we are to be frequent and fervent in holy petitions, it is to keep us steady in the sight of our true God, that we may never lack the happiness of a lively faith, a joyful hope, and well-grounded trust in God. If we are to pray often, it is so that we may be happy in the secret joys that only prayer can give, that we may be filled with all the happiness that we are capable of having here on earth.

If there were anything in the world more worth our care, any exercise of the mind or conversation with others that turned more to our advantage than this intercourse with God, we would not be called to such a continuance in prayer.

However, if a man considers the activities he leaves when he retires to devotion, he will find that he is often relieved from doing nothing, from dull idleness, unprofitable labor, or vain conversation. If he considers that all that is happening in the world is only for the body and bodily enjoyments, he will have reason to rejoice at his hours of prayer, which carry him to higher consolations, which raise him above these poor concerns, which open to his mind a scene of greater things, and which accustom his soul to the hope and expectation of them.

If religion commands us to live wholly unto God and to do all to His glory (1 Cor. 10:31), it is because every other way goes wholly against ourselves and will end in our own shame and confusion. There is no glory or greatness except what is of the glory and greatness of God. We may talk of human glory as we may talk of human life or human knowledge; but human glory, whenever we find it, must be only as much glory as we enjoy in the glory of God.

This is the state of all creatures, whether men or angels: they do not make themselves, so they enjoy nothing from themselves; they may be great, but only as great receivers of the gifts of God; their power can only be a portion of the divine power acting in them; their wisdom can be only part of the divine wisdom shining within them; and their light and glory, only a share of the light and glory of God shining upon them. They are not men or angels because they had a mind to be so, but because the will of God formed them to be what they are. Therefore, they cannot enjoy this or that happiness of men or angels just because they have a mind to do so, but only because it is the will of God that such things be the happiness of men, and such things the happiness of angels.

If God is all in all and His will is the measure of all things; if nothing can be done except by His power; if nothing can be seen except by a light from Him; if we have nothing to fear except His justice; if we have nothing to hope for except His goodness; if the nature of man is to be helpless in himself; if this is the state of all creatures, including those in heaven and those on earth; if they are nothing, can do nothing, can suffer no pain, nor feel any happiness, except insofar as the power of God does all this; if this is the state of things, then how can we have the least glimpse of joy or comfort? How can we have any peaceful enjoyment of ourselves except by living wholly unto that God, using and doing everything according to His will?

A life thus devoted to God, looking to Him in all our actions and doing all things suitably to His glory, is so far from being dull and uncomfortable that it creates new comforts in everything that we do. Those who live according to their own wills, who cannot submit to the dull and melancholy business of a life devoted unto God, are like the man in the parable, to whom his lord had given one talent. (See Matthew 25:14–29.) He could not bear the thought of using his talent according to the will of the one who had given it to him, so he chose to make himself happier in a way of his own. He said,

> Lord, I knew thee that thou art an hard man, reaping where thou hast not sown, and gathering where thou hast not strowed: and I was afraid, and went and hid thy talent in the earth: lo, there thou hast that is thine.
> (Matt. 25:24–25)

His lord, having convicted the man by his own words, dispatched him with this sentence:

> *Cast ye the unprofitable servant into outer darkness: there shall be weeping and gnashing of teeth.* (Matt. 25:30)

Here you see how happy this man made himself by not acting wholly according to his lord's will. It was, according to his own account, a happiness of murmuring and discontent: "I knew," he said, "that you are a hard man." It was a happiness of fears and apprehensions: he said, "I was afraid." It was a happiness of vain labors and fruitless travels: he said, "I went and hid the money." And after all his foolish passions, tormenting fears, and fruitless labor, he was rewarded with darkness, eternal weeping, and gnashing of teeth.

This is the happiness of those who look upon a strict and true piety, that is, a right use of their talent, as a dull and melancholy way of life. They may live free from the restraints and directions of religion for a while, but they live under the absurd government of their passions for their entire lives. Like the man in the parable, they live in murmurings and discontents, in fears and apprehensions. They may avoid doing good (Gal. 6:10), spending their time devoutly (Eph. 5:16), laying up treasures in heaven (Matt. 6:20), clothing the naked, and visiting the sick (Matt. 25:36); but then they, like this man, must travel, labor, work, and dig to hide their talent in the earth—all in vain. At their Lord's coming, like him, they will be convicted with their own words and accused by their own hearts, and everything that they have said and thought of religion will show the justice of their condemnation to eternal darkness, weeping, and gnashing of teeth. This is the price of avoiding the strictness and perfection of religion, in order to live happily.

On the other hand, if you wish to see a brief description of the happiness of being rightly employed and wholly devoted to God, you must look at the man in the parable to whom his lord had given five talents. He said,

> *Lord, thou deliveredst unto me five talents: behold, I have gained beside them five talents more. His lord said unto him, Well done, thou good and faithful servant: thou hast been faithful over a few things, I will make thee ruler over many things: enter thou into the joy of thy lord.*
>
> *(Matt. 25:20–21)*

Here you see a life that is wholly intent upon the improvement of the talents, that is wholly devoted to God, and that is in a state of happiness, prosperous labors, and glorious success. There are no uneasy passions, murmurings, vain fears, or fruitless labors, as in the former case. The man is not toiling and digging in the earth for no reason or benefit. Rather, his pious labors prosper in his hands; his happiness increases upon him; the blessing of five becomes the blessing of ten talents; and he is received with a "Well done, good and faithful servant: enter into the joy of the Lord."

These men in the parable had either to be happy in using their gifts to the glory of the Lord, or miserable by using them according to their own humors and fancies. Likewise, the state of Christianity leaves us no other choice. All that we have, all that we are, and all that we enjoy, are only talents from God. If we use them to live pious and holy lives, our five talents will become ten, and our efforts will carry us into the joy of our Lord. However, if we abuse them to the gratification of our own passions, sacrificing the gifts of God to our own pride and vanity, we will live here in vain labors and foolish anxieties—shunning religion as a melancholy thing and accusing our Lord of being a hard master—and fall into everlasting misery.

We may amuse ourselves for a while with names and sounds and shadows of happiness; we may talk of this or that greatness and dignity; yet, if we desire real happiness, we have no other possible way to reach it except by improving our talents. We must use the powers and faculties of men in this present state in such pious and holy ways that we may be happy and glorious in the powers and faculties of angels in the world to come.

Therefore, anyone who thinks that a life of strict piety and devotion to God is a dull, uncomfortable state, is ignorant of the nature of religion, the nature of man, and the nature of God. Certainly, there is neither comfort nor joy to be found in anything else!

Chapter Eleven

WHOLLY DEVOTED TO GOD

We may see even more of the happiness of a life devoted to God, by considering the poor contrivances for happiness and the contemptible ways of life of those who are not under the directions of a strict piety. If you look at their lives, you will see that they are desperately seeking happiness by other methods; they live by no rule but their own whims and fancies. If you see what they call joy, greatness, and happiness—if you see how they rejoice, repent, change, and fly from one delusion to another—you will find great reason to rejoice that God has appointed a narrow way that leads to life (Matt. 7:14), and that we are not left to the folly of our own minds or forced to take up the shadows of joy and happiness that the world has invented.

I use the word *invented* because the joy and happiness of the world are contrived, with no foundation in nature and reason. Such is not the proper good or happiness of man; they cannot perfect body or mind, or carry him to his true end.

For instance, when a man sets out to be happy in ways of ambition by raising himself to some imaginary heights above other people, this is truly an invention of happiness. It has no foundation in nature; otherwise, a man would be able to make himself happy by climbing up a ladder. If a woman seeks happiness in fine makeup, jewels, and rich clothes, this is merely an invention of happiness, just as contrary to nature and reason as if she thought to make herself happy by painting a post and putting the same finery upon it.

It is in this respect that I call these joys and happinesses of the world mere inventions of happiness, because neither God, nor nature, nor reason, has appointed them as such. Whatever appears joyful or great or happy in them is entirely created or invented by the blindness and vanity of our own minds. Study these inventions of happiness, that you may learn how great a religion is that delivers you from a multitude of follies and vain pursuits that are the torment and vexation of minds that wander from their true happiness in God. Look at Erraticus,[6] and learn how miserable they are, who are left to the folly of their own passions.

Erraticus is rich and in good health, yet always uneasy and always searching after happiness. Every time you visit him, you find some new project in his head; he is preoccupied with it as something that is more worthwhile and more beneficial to him than anything that is already past. Every new thing so seizes him, that if you were to take him from it, he would think himself ruined. His optimism and strong passions promise him so much happiness in everything, that he is always cheated, and he is satisfied with nothing.

When he first set out on his own, fine clothes were his delight; he had only the best tailors and barbers; and he had no thoughts of excelling in anything but dress. Yet, when this happiness did

---

[6]Erraticus: the Latin root of our word *erratic*.

not fulfill his expectations, he gave up his fine fabrics, put on a plain coat, railed at fancy dressers, and gave himself up to gambling with great eagerness. This new pleasure satisfied him for some time: he wanted no other way of life. Yet, when he was drawn into a duel, where he narrowly escaped his death, he gave up the dice and sought happiness no longer among the gamblers.

His subsequent attempts at happiness led him from the diversions and merrymaking of the town to hunting and horseback riding, to traveling and studying—each thing providing him with a few months or years of enjoyment, yet always with disappointment in the end. If you happen to meet Erraticus when he has just entered upon a new pursuit, you will be saluted with great civility. On the other hand, if you find him when some project is almost worn out, you will find a peevish, ill-bred man.

Yet, he is now at a standstill and is doing what he never did in his life before: he is reasoning with himself and reflecting upon his life. He loses several days in considering which of his cast-off ways of life he will try again. But, suddenly, a new project comes to mind to relieve him. He is now living upon herbs, and he has taken up running to get himself as fit as any runner in the country.

I have made this kind of life seem so circumstantial because every particular folly that you see here will naturally turn itself into an argument for the wisdom and happiness of a religious life. For instance, if I were to detail the circumstances of terror and distress that daily attend a life at sea, the more particular I was in the account, the more you would feel and rejoice in the happiness of living upon the land. In like manner, the more I

129

enumerate the follies, anxieties, delusions, and restless desires that go through every part of a life devoted to human passions and worldly enjoyments, the more you must be affected with that peace, rest, and solid contentment that religion gives to the souls of men.

We often learn the nature of things by looking at that which is contrary to them; so perhaps we best comprehend the excellency of wisdom by contemplating the wild extravagances of folly. If you were told very generally about the folly and madness of a life devoted to the world, it would make little or no impression upon you; but if you were shown how such people live every day, if you were to see the continual folly and madness of all their particular actions and designs, this would be an affecting sight, and you would bless God for having given you a greater happiness to aspire to.

Perhaps you will say that the ridiculous, restless life of Erraticus is not the usual state of those who live by their own caprices and who neglect the strict rules of religion, and that therefore it is not so great an argument of the happiness of a religious life as I would make it. Yet, I am afraid the example of Erraticus is one of the most common in life, and I think few people could read it without seeing something in it that belongs to themselves. For where will we find that wise and happy man who has not been eagerly pursuing different appearances of happiness, sometimes thinking it was here, and sometimes there?

If people were to divide their lives into particular stages, and ask themselves what they were pursuing or what was their chief end when they were twenty years old, twenty-five, thirty, forty, fifty, and so on, until they were brought to their end, numbers of people would find that they had liked and disliked and pursued as many different appearances of happiness as Erraticus did. That is what happens with all who think that true happiness is in anything but a strict and regular piety.

But, assuming that most people are not as restless and fickle as Erraticus, the difference then is only this: Erraticus is continually changing and trying something new, but others are content with some one state. They do not leave gambling to begin hunting, but they have such steady spirits that they seek after no other happiness except that of getting rich; others grow old in playing and watching sports; others are content to drink themselves to death, without the least inquiry after any other happiness.

If you want to know what sort of happiness comes from being governed by the wisdom of religion and being devoted to the joys and hopes of a pious life, look at the poor condition of Succus,[7] whose greatest happiness is a good night's rest in bed and a good meal when he is up. When he talks of happiness, it is always in expressions that show you that he has only his bed and his dinner in his thoughts. This regard to his meals and repose makes Succus order all the rest of his time in relation to them.

All the hours that are not devoted either to repose or nourishment, are looked upon by Succus as wasted time. For this reason, he lodges near a coffeehouse and a tavern, so that, when he rises in the morning, he may be near the news, and when he parts at night, he may not have far to go to bed. In the morning you always see him in the same place in the coffee room; and if he seems more attentively

---

[7]Succus: the suggestion is of juicy and appetizing meat.

engaged than usual, it is because some criminal has broken out of prison, or some lady was robbed last night, but they cannot tell where. When he has learned all that he can, he goes home to settle the matter with the barber who comes to shave him.

The time between dinner and supper is wasted time to Succus. If melancholy thoughts ever come into his head, it is at this time, when he is often left to himself for an hour or more. He is afraid to sleep, because he has heard it is not healthful at that time. Yet, he is soon relieved by a settled method of playing cards until it is time to think of what he will eat for supper. After this, Succus takes his glass, talks on the excellency of the English constitution, and gives high praises to that minister who keeps the best table.

On a Sunday night you may sometimes hear him condemning the iniquity of the town rakes; and the bitterest thing that he says against them, is that he truly believes some of them are so degraded that they have not had a regular meal or a sound night's sleep in a week. At eleven, Succus bids all good night, and parts in great friendship. He sleeps until it is time to go to the coffeehouse next morning.

Now, can we see religion as a burden, a dull and melancholy state, because it calls men from such happiness as this, to live according to the laws of God, to labor after the perfection of their nature, and to prepare themselves for an endless state of joy and glory in the presence of God? Consider how unreasonable it is to think that a life of strict piety must be a dull and anxious state. For how can the duties and restraints of religion render our lives heavy and melancholy, when they only deprive us of the so-called happiness of worldly men and women?

Must it be tedious and tiresome to live in the continual exercise of charity, devotion, and temperance; to act wisely and virtuously; to do good to the utmost of your power; to imitate the divine perfections; and to prepare yourself for the enjoyment of God? Must it be dull and tiresome to be delivered from blindness and vanity, from false hopes and vain fears; to improve in holiness and feel the comforts of conscience in all your actions; to know that God is your friend, and that all things must work together for your good (Rom. 8:28)? Must it be boring and wearisome to know that neither life nor death, neither men nor devils (Rom. 8:38–39) can do you any harm, but that all your sufferings and labors that are offered to God, all your prayers and works of love and charity, all your improvements will in a short time be rewarded with everlasting glory in the presence of God? Must such a state as this be dull and tiresome?

If this cannot be said, then there is no happiness or pleasure lost in being strictly pious; nor does the devout man have anything to envy in any other state of life. For all the art and contrivance in the world, without religion, cannot make more of human life, or carry its happiness to any greater height. The finest wit, the greatest genius upon earth, if not governed by religion, must be as foolish, low, and vain in his methods of happiness as the poor Succus.

If you were to see a man endeavoring all his life to satisfy his thirst by holding up the same empty cup to his mouth, you would certainly despise his ignorance. On the other hand, if you were to see others, with finer taste, ridiculing the dull satisfaction of one cup and thinking to satisfy their own thirst by a variety of gilt and golden empty cups, would you think that these were wiser or happier or better employed for their finer tastes? This is the difference that can be seen in the happiness of this life.

A dull and heavy soul may be content with one empty appearance of happiness, continually trying to hold the same empty cup to his mouth all his life. Yet, when the thinker, the scholar, the genius, the statesman, and the gentleman put all their heads together, they can only show you a greater number of empty appearances of happiness. If they had the world in their hands, they could cut and carve as they please, but would only make a greater variety of empty cups.

If you will accustom yourself to such meditations as these, reflect upon the vanity of all orders of life without piety, and consider how all the ways of the world are only so many different ways of error, blindness, and mistake, you will soon find your heart made wiser and better by it. These meditations will awaken your soul into a zealous desire of that solid happiness that is only to be found in turning to God.

Examples of great piety are not now common in the world; you might not have the privilege of living within sight of any, or of having your virtue excited by their light and fervor. Yet, the misery and folly of worldly men meets your eyes in every place, and you need not look far to see how poorly, how vainly, men dream away their lives because they lack religious wisdom. This is why I have detailed the lives of so many vain and worldly characters. I hope that the corruption of the age has taught you that you may be made wise by seeing the misery and folly that reigns where piety is not.

If you will ponder these things, your own reflections will carry this instruction much farther, and all your dealings with the world will be a daily reminder to you to seek a greater happiness than all the enjoyments of this world can give.

To meditate upon the perfection of the divine attributes; to contemplate the glories of heaven; to consider the joys of saints and angels, living forever in the brightness and glory of the divine presence—these are the meditations of souls advanced in piety, and they are not suited for every capacity. However, to see and consider the emptiness and error of all worldly happiness; to see the grossness of sensuality, the poorness of pride, the stupidity of covetousness, the vanity of dress, the delusion of honor, the blindness of our passions, the uncertainty of our lives, and the shortness of all worldly projects—these are meditations suited to all capacities, fitted to strike all minds. They require no depth of thought or sublime speculation, but they are forced upon us by all our senses and taught us by almost everything that we see and hear.

This is the wisdom that cries and "put[s] forth her voice" (Prov. 8:1) in the streets, that stands at all our doors, that appeals to all our senses. It teaches us in every thing and every place, by all that we see and all that we hear, by births and burials, by sickness and health, by life and death, by pains and poverty, by misery and vanity, and by all the changes and chances of life, that there is nothing else for man to look after, no other end in nature for him to drive at, except a happiness that is only to be found in the hopes and expectations of religion.

Chapter Twelve

A LIFE WITHOUT PIETY

Our Lord and Savior said a very blessed thing to His disciples in these words: "Blessed are your eyes, for they see: and your ears, for they hear" (Matt. 13:16). These words teach us two things: first, that the dullness and heaviness of men's minds, with regard to spiritual matters, is so great that it may justly be compared to the lack of eyes and ears. Secondly, that God has so filled every thing and every place with motives and arguments for a godly life, that those who are so blessed as to use their eyes and their ears must be affected through them. (See Romans 1:20.)

This was especially the case of those who witnessed firsthand the life, miracles, and doctrines of Christ, yet it is as truly the case of all Christians, at any time. The reasonings of religion, the calls to piety, are so written and engraved upon everything, and present themselves so strongly and so constantly to our senses in everything we meet, that they can only be disregarded by eyes that do not see, and ears that do not hear. (See Jeremiah 5:21.)

Is there a greater motive for a religious life than the vanity, the poorness, of all worldly enjoyments? Who can help seeing and feeling this every day of his life? Is there a greater call to look toward God than the pains, the sickness, the crosses, and the anxieties of this life? Whose eyes and ears are not daily witnesses of them? What miracles could more strongly appeal to our senses, or what message from heaven could speak louder to us, than the daily dying and departure of our fellow creatures? The great purpose of life is not left to be discovered by fine reasoning and deep reflections, but it is pressed upon us in the plainest manner by the experience of all our senses, by everything that we meet with in life.

If we would only intend to see and hear, then the whole world would become a book of wisdom and instruction to us. All that is regular in the order of nature, all that is accidental in the course of things, all the mistakes and disappointments that happen to ourselves, all the miseries and errors that we see in other people, would become lessons of advice to us—teaching us, with as much assurance as an angel from heaven, that we cannot raise ourselves to any true happiness unless we turn all our thoughts, wishes, and endeavors to the happiness of another life.

It is this right use of the world that I would lead you into by drawing, out of every shape of human folly, fresh arguments and motives for living up to the highest purposes of your creation. If you would simply carry this intention of profiting by the follies of the world, and of learning the greatness of religion from the littleness and vanity of every other way of life—if you would carry this intention in your mind, you would find every day, every place, and every person a fresh proof of the wisdom of living wholly unto God. You would then often return home the wiser, the better, and the more strengthened in religion by everything that has fallen your way.

Octavius[8] is a learned man, well versed in most genres of literature, and no stranger to any country in Europe. The other day, having just recovered from a lingering fever, he told his friends that he fully believed he had only one more year to live. Such a declaration piqued the interest of his friends, who were expecting to hear something truly excellent from so learned a man. Then Octavius proceeded in this manner:

> My friends, I have left off all taverns; the wine of those places is not good enough for me in this decay of nature. I must now be nice in what I drink; I cannot pretend to do as I have done; and therefore am resolved to furnish my own cellar with a little of the very best, though it cost me ever so much.
>
> I must also tell you, my friends, that age forces a man to be wise in many other respects, and makes him change many of his opinions and practices. You know how much I have liked to have many acquaintances; I now condemn it as an error. Three or four cheerful, diverting companions are all that I now desire; because I find that, in my present infirmities, if I am left alone or to grave company, I am not so easy to myself.

A few days after Octavius had made this declaration to his friends, he relapsed into his former illness and was committed to a nurse, who closed his eyes before his fresh parcel of wine came in. Young Eugenius,[9] who was present at this

---

[8]Octavius: suggested by the name of the Emperor Augustus, who asked his friends to applaud him on his deathbed as they would applaud a good pantomime leaving the stage.

[9]Eugenius: noble (Acts 17:11).

discourse, went home a new man, with full resolutions of devoting himself wholly unto God. Said Eugenius,

> I never was so deeply affected with the wisdom and importance of religion, as when I saw how poorly and meanly the learned Octavius was to leave the world. How often had I envied his great learning, his skill in languages, his knowledge of antiquity, his cleverness, and his fine manner of expressing himself upon all subjects! But, when I saw how poorly it all ended, what was to be the last year of such a life, and how foolishly the master of all these accomplishments was then forced to talk, for failing to acquaint himself with the joys and expectations of piety, I was thoroughly convinced that there was nothing to be envied or desired, but a life of true piety; nor anything so poor and comfortless as a death without it.

If you are fortunate enough to have any part of Eugenius's thoughtful disposition, you will find a variety of this kind of instruction; you will find that arguments for the wisdom and happiness of a strict piety offer themselves in all places, and appeal to all your senses in the plainest manner. You will find that the whole world preaches to an attentive mind, and that if you have ears to hear, almost everything you meet teaches you some lesson of wisdom.

But, if to these instructions, which we receive from our senses, we add the great truths that the Son of God has taught us, it will be as much beyond all doubt that there is only one way to happiness for man as that there is only one God. Religion teaches us that our souls are immortal;

that piety and devotion will carry them to an eternal enjoyment of God; and that carnal, worldly tempers will sink them into an everlasting misery with damned spirits. With that in mind, what gross nonsense and stupidity it is, to give the name of joy or happiness to anything but that which carries us to this joy and happiness in God!

If our souls were to die with our bodies, there might be some reason for all the different kinds of happiness that are now talked about so much. However, since the afterlife begins at the death of our bodies; since all men are to be immortal, either in misery or happiness, in a world entirely different from this; since men are all hurrying toward all uncertainties as fast as death can cut them down—some in sickness, some in health, some sleeping, some waking, some at midnight, others at dawn, and all at hours that they do not even know of—how can any man exceed another in joy and happiness unless he exceeds him in those virtues that prepare him for a happy death?

Cognatus[10] is a sober, regular clergyman of good repute in the world, and he is well esteemed in his parish. All his parishioners say he is an honest man and very notable at making a bargain. The farmers listen to him with great attention when he talks of the most proper time for selling corn. He has been, for twenty years, a diligent observer of markets, and has raised a considerable fortune by good management.

Cognatus has been very prosperous all his life, yet he has always had the uneasiness and anxieties of those who are deep in worldly business. Taxes, losses, bad mortgages, bad tenants, and the

---

[10]Cognatus: relation, suggestive of nepotism.

hardness of the times are frequent subjects of his conversation; and a good or bad season has a great effect on his spirits. Cognatus has no other purpose for growing rich except that he may leave a considerable fortune to his niece, whom he has politely educated in expensive finery by what he has saved out of two livings, for he has hired a curate who does most of his work at the church. The neighbors look upon Cognatus as a happy clergyman, because they see him (as they call it) in good circumstances; and some of them intend to dedicate their own sons to the church because they see the success of Cognatus, whose father was but an ordinary man.

But, if Cognatus, when he first entered into holy orders, had perceived how absurd it is to grow rich by the Gospel; if he had had the piety of the great St. Austin, who did not dare to enrich any of his relations with the revenue of the church; if, instead of twenty years' care to lay up treasures upon earth (Matt. 6:19), he had distributed the income of every year in the most Christian acts of charity and compassion; if, instead of tempting his niece to be proud and providing her with such ornaments as the apostle forbids (1 Tim. 2:9), he had clothed, comforted, and assisted numbers of widows, orphans, and distressed who would all appear for him at the Last Day; if, instead of the cares and anxieties of bad bonds, troublesome mortgages, and ill bargains, he had had the constant comfort of knowing that his treasure was securely laid up "in heaven, where neither moth nor rust doth corrupt, and where thieves do not break through nor steal" (Matt. 6:20)—if he had done these things, he would not have mistaken the spirit and dignity of his position, or lessened any of that happiness that is to be found in his sacred employment.

If, instead of rejoicing in the happiness of a second living, he had thought it unbecoming for a clergyman to open a business; if he had thought it better to recommend some honest labor to his niece, rather than to support her in idleness by the labors of a curate—if this had been the spirit of Cognatus, could it, with any reason, be said that these rules of religion, this strictness of piety, had robbed Cognatus of any real happiness? Could it be said that a life governed by the spirit of the Gospel must be dull and melancholy, if compared to that of raising a fortune for a niece? No, this cannot be said in the present case, and if you enter into the particulars of every other kind of life, you will find that, however easy and prosperous it may seem, you cannot add piety to any part of it without adding a better joy and happiness to it.

Most people, when they think of happiness, think of being sober, prudent, rich, prosperous, generous, and charitable. Yet, if the purpose of life is to die as free from sin and as exalted in virtue as we can, if we are to stand trial before Christ and His holy angels for everlasting happiness or misery, what can it possibly matter what a man had or did not have in this world? What can it matter what you call the things a man has left behind, whether you call them his or anyone else's; whether you call them trees or fields, birds or feathers; whether you call them a hundred thousand pounds or a hundred thousand pairs of boots and spurs? The things mean no more to him than the names.

It is easy to see the folly of a life spent to furnish a man with a hundred thousand pairs of boots and spurs. Likewise, one does not need any better mind or any finer understanding, to see the folly of a life spent in making a man a possessor of ten towns before he dies. When he has all his towns or all his boots, his soul will still go to its own place among separate spirits, and his body will still be laid in a coffin until the last trumpet calls him to judgment. Therefore, how can we say that one who has worn out his life in raising a hundred thousand pounds, has acted more wisely than one who has taken the same care to procure a hundred thousand of anything else?

Our souls ought to mean more to us than our bodies. It is better to grow in the virtues of the soul than to have a fit body or a full purse; better to be ready for heaven than to have a variety of fine houses upon the earth; better to secure an everlasting happiness than to have plenty of things that we cannot keep; better to live in habits of humility, piety, devotion, charity, and self-denial than to die unprepared for judgment; better to be most like our Savior, or some eminent saint, than to excel all the tradesmen in the world in business and bulk of fortune. How little is lost and how much is gained by introducing a strict and exact piety into every condition of human life! A true and exalted piety is so far from rendering any life dull and tiresome, that it is the only joy and happiness of every condition in the world.

Imagine some person who has an incurable disease or condition. If you were to see such a man wholly intent upon doing everything in the spirit of religion, making the wisest use of all his time, fortune, and abilities; if he were for carrying every duty of piety to its greatest height, and striving to have all the advantages that could be had from the remainder of his life; if he avoided all business except what was necessary; if he were averse to all the follies and vanities of the world, had no taste for finery and show, but sought all his comfort in the hopes and expectations of religion; you would certainly commend his prudence. In fact, you would say that he had taken the right steps to make himself as joyful and happy as anyone can be in a state of such illness.

On the other hand, if you were to see the same man with trembling hands, short breath, thin jaws, and hollow eyes, wholly intent upon business and bargains as long as he could speak; if you were to see him pleased with fine clothes when he could hardly stand up to get dressed, and wasting his money on horses and dogs rather than purchasing the prayers of the poor for his soul (which was so soon to be separated from his body); you would certainly condemn him as a weak, silly man.

The reasonableness, wisdom, and happiness of a religious spirit in the sick man, is the same wisdom and happiness of a pious spirit in every other man, no matter what his state of life. How do we know that a healthy man will not soon be in the state of the sick man? How soon he will want all the same comforts and satisfactions of religion that every dying man wants!

If it is wise to live piously when we have only a year to live, is it not even more wise to live piously because we may have more years to come? If one year of piety before we die is so desirable, are not more years of piety much more desirable? Likewise, if a man knows he has only five years to live, he must not be able to think at all if he does not intend to make the best use of them all. When he sees that his stay in this world is so short, he must know that this is not a world for him; and when he sees how near he is to another world that is eternal, he must surely think it necessary to diligently prepare himself for it.

Piety appears to be very reasonable in such circumstances, yet is it not more reasonable for everyone to live piously, in every circumstance of life? It is very rare that a man knows he has only five years left. So, if it is reasonable and necessary to deny our worldly attitudes and live wholly unto God because we are certain that we will die at the end of five years, surely it must be much more reasonable and necessary for us to live in the same spirit because we have no guarantee that we will live even five weeks.

Even if we were to add twenty years to the five, how small a difference there is between five and twenty-five years! It is written, "One day is with the Lord as a thousand years, and a thousand years as one day" (2 Pet. 3:8), because, in regard to His eternity, this difference is nothing. We are all created to be eternal, to live in an endless succession of ages upon ages, where thousands and millions of years will have no proportion to our everlasting life in God. With regard to this eternal state, which is our real state, twenty-five years is as poor a pittance as twenty-five days. We can never make any true judgment of time as it relates to us, without considering the true state of our duration. If we are temporary beings, then a little time may justly be called a great deal in relation to us; but if we are eternal beings, then the difference of a few years is as nothing.

Suppose there are three different kinds of rational beings, all of fixed but different duration.

One lives certainly only a month, the other a year, and the third a hundred years. Now, if these beings were to meet together and talk about time, they would talk in very different languages: half an hour to those who are to live only a month, must be a very different thing than what it is to those who are to live a hundred years. Therefore, if we wish to know the nature of time in regard to ourselves, we must consider our state. We cannot judge the value of any particular time to ourselves, except by comparing it to that eternal duration for which we are created.

If you wish to know what five years signify to a being that is to live a hundred, you must note the proportion of five to one hundred; and then you will judge right. However, if you wish to know what twenty years signify to a son of Adam, you must compare it to an eternal duration, to which no number of millions bears any proportion; and then you will judge right by finding it nothing. Consider, therefore, how you would condemn the folly of a man who gives up his share of future glory for the sake of being rich or great or praised or delighted in any enjoyment, only one day before he was to die! If the time comes when many years seem to be less than a day does now, what a condemnation it will then be if eternal happiness was lost for something less than the enjoyment of a day!

Why does a day seem a trifle to us now? It is because we have years to set against it. It is the duration of years that makes it appear as nothing. What a trifle, therefore, must the years of a man's life appear to be, when they are set against eternity, when there is nothing but eternity to compare them with! This will be the case of every man as soon as he is out of the body; he will be forced to forget the distinctions of days and years, and to measure time, not by the course of the sun, but by setting it against eternity.

Just as the stars look like tiny points because they are placed at such a distance from us, so will all our time appear as but a moment when we are placed in eternity. At that time, a luxury, an indulgence, a condition of prosperity, or a greatness of fifty years will seem, to everyone who looks back upon it, as short an enjoyment as if he had been snatched away in his first sin.

These reflections upon time are only to show that those who are less careful of an eternal state because they may be at some years' distance from it, judge their lives far more miserably than if they knew they were within a few weeks of it.

Chapter Thirteen

THE PRAYER HABITS OF A
DEVOTED CHRISTIAN

In the foregoing chapters, I have pointed out the
necessity of a devout spirit in every part of our
lives, in all our business, and in the use of all
the gifts of God. I come now to considering that
part of devotion that relates to times and hours of
prayer.

I must take it for granted that every Christian
in good health is up early in the morning. Indeed,
in my mind, it is much more reasonable to suppose
that a person gets up early because he is a Christian, than because he is a laborer, a tradesman, or
a servant, or has some business that requires his
skills.

We naturally scorn a man who is in bed when
he should be at work in his shop or his business,
and we cannot think anything good about a man
who is such a slave to drowsiness that he neglects
his business for it. How repulsive, therefore, we
must appear in the sight of heaven, if we are in
bed, shut up in sleep and darkness, when we
should be praising God! How hateful if we are such
slaves to drowsiness that we neglect our devotions
for it! For if he is to blame who chooses the lazy
indulgence of sleep rather than to perform his
proper share of worldly business, how much more
is he to be reproached who would rather lie in bed

than be raising up his heart to God in acts of praise and adoration!

Prayer is the nearest approach to God, and the highest enjoyment of Him, that we are capable of in this life. It is the noblest exercise of the soul, the most exalted use of our best faculties, and the highest imitation of the blessed inhabitants of heaven. When our hearts are full of God, sending up holy desires to the throne of grace, we are then in our highest state; we are on the heights of human greatness. We are not before kings and princes, but we are in the presence of the Lord; and we can be no higher until death is swallowed up in glory. (See 1 Corinthians 15:54.)

On the other hand, sleep is meant for refreshment of the body, not for enjoyment; we are forced to receive it either in a state of insensibleness or in the folly of dreams. Sleep is such a dull, stupid state of existence, that we even despise among mere animals those that are most drowsy. Therefore, whoever chooses to increase the slothful indulgence of sleep rather than to be early at his devotions to God, chooses the dullest refreshment of the body before the highest, noblest employment of the soul; he chooses the state that is a reproach to mere animals, rather than the exercise that is the glory of angels.

Perhaps you will say that you are always careful of your devotions when you get up, even though you rise late. It may be so, but what then? Is it good that you rise late because you pray once you are up? Is it right that you waste a great part of the day in bed because some time after you say your prayers? No, it is as much your duty to rise to pray, as to pray when you are risen. And if you are late at your prayers, you offer to God the prayers

149

of an idle, slothful worshipper, who rises to prayers as idle servants rise to their labor.

Furthermore, if you still think that you are careful about your devotions even though you rise late, you deceive yourself, for you cannot perform your devotions as you should. Think about it. If you must waste a good part of the morning because you must indulge in sleep, how can you be any more prepared for prayer than for fasting, abstinence, or any other self-denial once you are awake? You may be more able to say a quick prayer than to fast, but do you expect to enter into the true spirit of prayer?

When we rise late, our drowsiness makes us unable to enjoy anything that is not idle, indulgent, or sensual—because these things please us for the same reason that sleep pleases us. On the other hand, everything that requires care, trouble, or self-denial, is hateful to us for the same reason that we hate to rise from our beds. One who loves to sleep through his mornings would be glad to have the whole day spent in the same manner—perhaps not with sleep, but with enjoyments that gratify and indulge the body in the same manner as sleep does. The memory of a warm bed is in his mind all day long, and he takes pleasure in the fact that he is not one of those who sit starving in church.

Do you think that such a one can truly mortify the body that he indulges in this manner? Do you think that he can truly perform his devotions or relish the joys of a spiritual life when he lives in such a drowsy state of indulgence? Surely, you will not pretend that he knows and feels the true happiness of prayer, when he does not even think it worth his while to be early at it. One who turns sleep into an idle indulgence does as much to corrupt and disorder his soul, to make it a slave to bodily appetites, and to keep it incapable of all devout and heavenly inclinations, as the glutton turns the necessities of eating into a course of indulgence.

A person who eats and drinks a little too much does not feel the same effects from it as those who live in notorious instances of gluttony and intemperance. However, his course of indulgence, though it is not scandalous in the eyes of the world and does not seem to torment his conscience, constantly hinders his improvement in virtue; it gives him eyes that do not see and ears that do not hear (Jer. 5:21); it creates a sensuality in the soul, increases the power of bodily passions, and makes him incapable of entering into the true spirit of religion. This is also the case of those who waste their time in sleep: it does not disorder their lives or wound their consciences, as notorious acts of intemperance do, but, like any other more moderate course of indulgence, it silently, slowly wears away the spirit of religion, and sinks the soul into a state of dullness and sensuality.

If you think devotion is only a time for saying a few prayers, you will likely say your prayers but go on living in this daily indulgence. On the other hand, if you think devotion is a state of the heart that is deeply affected with a sense of its own misery and infirmities; if you consider it the fervor of a soul that desires the Spirit of God more than all things in the world; then you will find that the spirit of indulgence and the spirit of prayer cannot coexist. Self-denial is the very life and soul of piety; but one who cannot even deny himself enough to rise early to pray, has no reason to think that he has taken up his cross and is following Christ (Matt. 16:24).

Some people will not hesitate to tell you that they indulge themselves in sleep because they have nothing else to do; if they had either business or pleasure to rise to, they would not lose so much of their time in sleep. However, such people make a great mistake, for they have a great deal of business to do: they have a hardened heart to change, and they have the whole spirit of religion to get. Indeed, one who thinks devotion has less importance than business or pleasure, or that he has nothing to do because nothing but his prayers requires his time—he may be justly said to have the whole spirit of religion to seek.

Therefore, do not consider how small a crime it is to rise late; but consider how great a misery it is to lack the spirit of religion, to have a heart not rightly affected with prayer, and to live in such idleness that you are incapable of the most fundamental duties of a truly Christian and spiritual life. Do not consider the thing merely in itself, but consider its cause, what virtues it shows to be lacking, and what vices it naturally strengthens. Every habit of this kind reveals the state of the soul, and plainly shows the whole turn of your mind.

If Christ used to pray early before daylight (Mark 1:35); if He spent whole nights in prayer (Luke 6:12); if the devout Anna was day and night in the temple (Luke 2:36–37); if Paul and Silas at midnight sang praises unto God (Acts 16:25); if the first Christians, besides their hours of prayers in the daytime, met publicly in the churches at midnight to join in psalms and prayers; is it not certain that these practices showed the state of their hearts? Are they not evidence of their whole mind-set? Thus, if you waste a great part of every day in sleep, thinking that any time is soon enough to be at your prayers, is it not equally certain that you show the state of your heart and the disposition of your mind through such inaction?

If this indulgence is your way of life, you have as much reason to believe yourself destitute of the true spirit of devotion, as you have to believe the apostles and saints of the first church were truly devout. For as their way of life was a demonstration of their devotion, so a contrary way of life is as strong a proof of a lack of devotion.

When you read the Scriptures, you see a religion that is all life and spirit and joy in God; it supposes our souls risen from earthly desires and bodily indulgences, to prepare for another body, another world, and other enjoyments. You see Christians represented as temples of the Holy Spirit (1 Cor. 3:16), as "children of the day" (1 Thess. 5:5), as candidates for an eternal crown (James 1:12; 1 Pet. 5:4), as watchful virgins who have their lamps always burning, in expectation of the bridegroom (Matt. 25:1–13). How can one who does not have enough zeal to rise to his prayers, be thought to have this joy in God, this care of eternity, this watchful spirit?

When you look into the writings and lives of the first Christians, you see the same spirit that you see in the Scriptures. All is reality, life, and action. Watchfulness and prayer, self-denial and self-sacrifice, were the common business of their lives. Since that time, anyone who has been like them, as an eminent example of piety, has also been eminent in self-denial and prayer. This is the only royal way that leads to a kingdom. But, if you cannot even renounce the poor indulgence of sleep, so as to be able to rise to your prayers, how far you are from this way of life, and how contrary to it!

Self-denial and bodily suffering, watching and fasting, will be marks of glory at the Day of Judgment, but we who have slumbered away our time in sloth will have to hide our heads in shame. You might find some way to excuse yourself from the severity of fasting and self-denial, which the first Christians practiced: you may say that human nature is weaker than it used to be, or that the difference of climates makes it impossible for you to observe their methods of self-denial. However, all this is mere pretense; for the change is not in the outward state of things, but in the inward state of our minds. When we have the same spirit as the first Christians, when we feel the weight of religion as they did, when we have their faith and hope, we will take up our cross and deny ourselves (Matt. 16:24) and live in such methods of sacrifice as they did.

If Paul had lived in a cold country, if he had had a sickly stomach and frequent illnesses, he would have done as he advised Timothy; he would have mixed a little wine with his water (1 Tim. 5:23). Yet, he still would have lived in a state of self-denial and self-sacrifice. He would have given this same account of himself:

> *I therefore so run, not as uncertainly; so fight I, not as one that beateth the air: but I keep under my body, and bring it into subjection: lest that by any means, when I have preached to others, I myself should be a castaway.* (1 Cor. 9:26–27)

Is it not necessary for you to be as sober and vigilant, as fearful of yourself, as watchful over your passions, as apprehensive of danger, and as careful of your salvation as the apostles were? Or, do you somehow require less self-denial and sacrifice to subdue your body and purify your soul, than they required? Do you not need to have your loins girded (Eph. 6:14) and your lamps burning (Matt. 25:1–13), as they had? Or, will you make your life as constant a course of lethargy and indulgence, as theirs was of strictness and self-denial?

If, therefore, you think you have sufficient time for both prayer and other duties, even though you rise late, let me persuade you to rise early, as an instance of self-denial. It is such a small act of self-denial that, if you cannot comply with it, you have no reason to think yourself capable of any other. Wasting so much of your time in sleep is a great crime, but, more than that, this indulgence gives a sluggishness and idleness to your soul. It is contrary to the lively, zealous, watchful, and self-denying spirit that was not only the spirit of Christ and His apostles, all the saints, and all the martyrs, but must also be the spirit of everyone who would not sink into the common corruption of the world.

Therefore, we must set all that we have against this practice; we must blame it, not as having any particular evil, but as a general habit that extends itself through our whole spirit and supports a state of mind that is wholly wrong. It is contrary to piety in the way that a bad habit of the body is contrary to health. On the other hand, if you would rise early every morning as an instance of self-denial, as a method of renouncing indulgence, as a means of redeeming your time and preparing your spirit for prayer, you would find it greatly advantageous.

This method, though it seems such a small circumstance of life, would in all probability be a means of great piety. It would be a constant reminder to you that lethargy and idleness are to be avoided, and that self-denial is a significant part of Christianity. It would teach you to exercise power over yourself and to renounce other pleasures and dispositions that war against the soul. This one rule would teach you to think of others; it would dispose your mind to exactness, and would be very likely to bring the remaining part of the day under rules of prudence and devotion.

Yet, above all, one certain benefit from this method is that it will best prepare you for receiving the Holy Spirit. When you begin the day in the spirit of religion, renouncing sleep because you are to renounce sluggishness, you redeem your time. This disposition puts your heart into a good state and procures the assistance of the Holy Spirit: what is planted and watered in this manner will certainly have an increase from God. (See 1 Corinthians 3:6.) You will then speak from your heart; your soul will be awake; your prayers will refresh you like meat and drink; you will feel what you say; and you will begin to know what saints and holy men have meant by intensity of devotion.

One who is prepared in this way for prayer, who rises with these dispositions, is in a very different state from one who has no rules of this kind, who rises whenever he happens to be weary of his bed or is able to sleep no longer. If such a one prays only with his mouth; if his heart feels none of what he says; if he prays just to get his prayers over with; if they are a lifeless form of words that he only repeats because they are soon said; then we have nothing to wonder about, for such dispositions are the natural effect of such a state of life.

Hoping, therefore, that you are convinced of the necessity of rising early to your prayers, I will proceed to put before you a method of daily prayer. I do not take it upon myself to prescribe any particular forms of prayer; I only desire to show you the necessity of praying at certain times and in such a manner. You will find that I give you some ways to furnish yourself with forms of prayer that will be useful to you.

Although I think prepared forms of prayer are very necessary and suitable for public worship, if anyone can find a better way of raising his heart to God in private, then I have nothing to object against it. And if you are advanced in the spirit of devotion, so that your heart is always ready to pray in its own language, in this case I do not think it necessary to use borrowed forms.

Yet, without a doubt, I believe that most Christians should use set forms of prayer at all the regular times of prayer. It seems right for every believer to begin with a form of prayer; then, if he finds his heart ready, in the midst of his devotions, to break forth into new and higher strains of devotion, he should leave the prescribed words for a while and follow those fervors of his heart, until he again needs the assistance of his usual prayers. This seems to be the true liberty of private devotion: it should be under the direction of some form, but not so tied down to it that it cannot be free to take new expressions. Sometimes these new expressions are more affecting, and carry the soul more powerfully to God, than any that were ever used before.

Anyone who has ever reflected upon what takes place in his own heart, must know that the heart is extremely changeable in regard to devotion. Sometimes our hearts are so awakened, have such a strong sense of the divine presence, and are so full of deep remorse for our sins, that we cannot confess them in any language but that of tears. Sometimes the light of God's countenance (Ps. 89:15) shines so brightly upon us; we see so far into the invisible world; and we are so affected with the wonders of the love and goodness of God; that our hearts worship and adore in a language higher than that of words, and we feel the blessedness of devotion.

On the other hand, sometimes we are so sunk into our bodies, so dull and unaffected with that which concerns our souls, that our hearts are too low for our prayers; we cannot keep pace with our forms of confession or feel in our hearts even half of what we have in our mouths. We thank and praise God with forms of words, but our hearts have little or no share in them.

How can we prevent this inconstancy of our hearts? By having various forms of prayer at hand. Some will suit us when our hearts are in their best state, and others will be most likely to raise and stir them up when they have sunken into dullness. For, as words have the power to affect our hearts at all times, and as the same thing differently expressed has different effects upon our minds, so it is reasonable that we should use this advantage of language and provide ourselves with forms of expression that are most likely to move and enliven our souls.

One of the first things you can do to prevent inconstancy of devotion is to find a place to pray. If you were to accustom yourself (as far as you can) to pray always in the same place; if you were to be there only in times of devotion; if you were to reserve that place for devotion and not allow yourself to do anything common in it; if any particular place were used in this manner, being consecrated as a place holy unto God, it would very much assist your devotion. Such a sacred place as this in your home would in some measure resemble a chapel or house of God. This would dispose you to be always in the spirit of religion. Your own apartment would raise in your mind the kind of sentiments that you have when you stand near an altar; and you would be afraid of thinking or doing anything that was foolish near that place, which is the place of prayer and holy communion with God.

After you have set apart a place for devotion, the second thing you must do, once you are on your knees, is to shut your eyes, and with a short silence let your soul place itself in the presence of God; that is, separate yourself from all common thoughts, and make your heart as aware as you can of the divine presence. Think for a moment. If this contemplation of spirit is necessary—and who can say it is not?—then how poorly they must perform their devotions, who are always in a hurry, who begin them in haste and hardly allow themselves time to repeat their very form with any seriousness or attention! They are saying prayers, not praying.

Thirdly, when you begin your petitions, consider the greatness and power of the divine nature by using expressions of the attributes of God. Begin by saying,

> O Being of all beings, Fountain of all light and glory, gracious Father of men and angels,

> whose universal Spirit is everywhere present,
> giving life, and light, and joy, to all angels in
> heaven, and all creatures upon earth,

and so on. These representations of the divine attributes, which describe the majesty and greatness of God, are an excellent means of raising our hearts into lively acts of worship and adoration. Although prayer is not merely fine words or studied expressions, those words that speak of God in the highest manner, that most fully express the power and presence of God, and that raise in the soul thoughts most suitable to the greatness and providence of God, are the most useful and most edifying in our prayers.

When you pray to the Lord, let it be in expressions of this kind:

> O Savior of the world, You are the brightness
> of Your Father's glory and the express image
> of His person; You are the "Alpha and Omega,
> the beginning and the ending" (Rev. 1:8) of all
> things; You have destroyed the power of the
> Devil and have overcome death (John 16:33;
> Rev. 1:18); You have entered into the Holy of
> Holies (Heb. 9:12), to sit at the right hand of
> the Father and make intercession for all the
> world (Rom. 8:34), high above all thrones and
> principalities (Ps. 97:9); You are the Judge of
> the quick and dead (Acts 10:42); You will
> come in Your Father's glory to reward all men
> according to their works (Matt. 16:27). I ask
> You to be my Light and my Peace.

Such expressions, which describe our Savior's nature and power, are not only proper acts of adoration, but, if they are repeated with any attention, they will also fill our hearts with the highest sentiments of true devotion.

Again, if you would ask any particular grace of our Lord, let it be in some manner like this:

O Holy Jesus, Son of the Most High God, You who were scourged at a pillar, stretched and nailed upon a cross for the sins of the world, unite me to Your cross and fill my soul with Your holy, humble, and suffering spirit. O Fountain of mercy, You who saved the thief upon the cross (Luke 23:40–43), save me from the guilt of a sinful life; You who cast seven devils out of Mary Magdalene (Mark 16:9), cast out of my heart all evil thoughts and wicked desires.

O Giver of life, You who raised Lazarus from the dead (John 11:43–44), raise up my soul from the death and darkness of sin. You who gave to Your apostles "power over unclean spirits" (Mark 6:7), give me power over my own heart. You who appeared to Your disciples when the doors were shut (John 20:19), appear unto me in the secret place of my heart. You who cleansed the lepers, healed the sick, and gave sight to the blind (Matt. 11:5), cleanse my heart, heal the disorders of my soul, and fill me with heavenly light.

These appeals have a double advantage. First, they are proper acts of our faith, whereby we not only show our belief in the miracles of Christ, but also turn them at the same time into instances of worship and adoration. Secondly, they strengthen and increase the faith of our prayers by presenting to our minds so many instances of that power and goodness that we call upon for our own assistance. One who believes that Christ can cast out devils and raise the dead, has a good reason to pray earnestly and believe that his prayers will be answered.

It may be of use to you to observe a fourth rule in order to fill your prayers with a more excellent devotion. Whenever you happen to read a passage, either in Scripture or any book of piety, that more than ordinarily affects your mind and seems to incline your heart toward God, you should try to turn it into the form of a petition and give it a place in your prayers. By this, you will often improve your prayers and store up for yourself proper forms of making the desires of your heart known to God.

A fifth thing you will want to do in your devotions, at all the stated hours of prayer, will be to have something fixed and something at liberty. By this I mean that you should have some fixed subject that is constantly to be the chief matter of your prayer at that particular time; and yet, you should also have liberty to add other petitions that your condition may then require.

For instance, the morning is like the beginning of a new life, when God has given you a new enjoyment of yourself and a fresh entrance into the world. Therefore, it is highly proper that your first devotions should consist of praise and thanksgiving to God, as for a new creation, and that you should offer and devote body and soul, all that you are, and all that you have, to His service and glory.

Receive every day as a resurrection from death, as a new enjoyment of life; meet every rising sun with the kind of sentiments of God's goodness that you would possess if you had seen it newly created for you. Under the sense of so great a blessing, praise and thanksgiving and the offering of yourself to God, should always be the fixed and certain subject of your first prayers in the morning. After that, you may take the liberty of adding other devotions that are most needful and expedient for you.

One of the greatest benefits of private devotion comes from rightly adapting our prayers to two conditions: the difference of our state, and the difference of our hearts. By *the difference of our state,* I mean the differences in our external state or condition. Sickness, health, pains, losses, disappointments, troubles, particular mercies and judgments from God, all sorts of kindnesses, injuries, or reproaches from other people—these are great parts of our state of life because they are continually changing. Yet, when we turn all these changes of our state into prayers, our devotion will be made doubly beneficial to us. One who makes every change in his state a reason to pray in regard to that change, will soon find that he has taken an excellent means not only of praying with fervor, but of living as he prays.

The other condition to which we must always adapt some part of our prayers, is *the difference of our hearts.* By this I mean the different qualities of our hearts, not only of love, joy, peace, and tranquility, but also of dullness and dryness of spirit, anxiety, discontent, envy, ambition, dark and disconsolate thoughts, resentments, fretfulness, and irritability. Through the weakness of our nature, these things appear even in pious minds; therefore, we should constantly make some particular application to God concerning the present state of our hearts.

If we are in the delightful calm of sweet and easy passions, of love and joy in God, we should offer a grateful tribute of thanksgiving to God for the possession of so much happiness, thankfully acknowledging Him as the bountiful Giver of it all. If, on the other hand, we feel ourselves laden with heavy passions, with dullness of spirit, anxiety, and uneasiness, we must then look up to God in acts of humility, confessing our unworthiness, opening our troubles to Him, beseeching Him in His good time to lessen the weight of our infirmities and to deliver us from passions that oppose the purity and perfection of our souls. By this prudent and wise application of our prayers, we will get all the relief from them that is possible; and the very changeableness of our hearts will prove a means of exercising a greater variety of holy qualities.

Now, from all I have written here, you should easily perceive that people who have the greatest benefit from prayer, also share in the forming and composing of their own devotions. When their prayers are fixed on one certain subject, they often use the help of forms composed by other persons; but in that part of their prayers regarding the present state of their lives and the present state of their hearts, they let the sense of their own condition help them to the kinds of petition, thanksgiving, or resignation that their present states require.

Consider a man of leisure, who is often at a loss how to dispose of his time; who is forced into poor contrivances, idle visits, and ridiculous diversions, merely to get rid of hours that weigh heavily upon him. If he were to appoint certain times of the day to the study of devotion, searching after all the means and helps to attain a devout spirit; if he were to collect and transcribe the finest passages of Scripture-prayers to use for himself; if he were to collect the devotions, confessions, petitions, praises, resignations, and thanksgivings that are scattered throughout the Psalms, and classify them under different headings, as fuel for the flame of his own devotion; if he were to meditate upon them, memorize them, and make them as habitual as his own thoughts; how fervently he would pray, who came thus prepared to pray!

How much better it would be to use leisure time in this way, instead of wasting it in the poor impertinences of a playing, visiting, wandering life! How much better would it be, to be furnished with hymns and anthems of the saints, and to teach one's soul to ascend to God!

Now, businesspeople and workers must not think themselves excused from this, or from any better method of improving their devotion. Businesspeople, even more so than people of leisure, need a method such as this to prevent their work from overpowering their hearts, to keep them from sinking into worldly passions, and to preserve a sense and taste of heavenly things in their minds. Therefore, a little time, regularly and constantly employed in devotion, will do great things and produce great effects.

Few people consider devotion in this light, as something that is to be nursed and cherished with care; as something that is to be made part of our business, and improved with care and contrivance, by art and method, and through a diligent use of the best helps. For this reason, many people live and die strangers to the spirit of devotion, which, by a prudent use of proper means, they might have enjoyed in a high degree. For though the spirit of devotion is the gift of God and is not attainable by any mere power of our own, yet it is mostly given to, and never withheld from, those who prepare themselves for the reception of it by a wise and diligent use of proper means.

It is amazing to see how eagerly men employ their time in study, application, and exercise, when anything is intended and desired in worldly matters. Conversely, how dull, negligent, and unimproved they are, how little they use their discernment and abilities, when it comes to raising and increasing their devotion!

Mundanus[11] is a man of many talents and clear comprehension. He is well advanced in age and has gained much fame in business. Every part of trade and business that has reached his hands has benefited from him, and he aims at doing everything perfectly. The soundness and strength of his mind, and his just way of thinking, make him intent upon removing all imperfections. For example, he can tell you all the defects and errors in all the common methods of trade, building, land, or manufacturing. The clearness and strength of his understanding, which he is constantly improving by continual exercise in these matters and by often digesting his thoughts in writing and experiments, has rendered him a great master of most concerns in human life.

However, the one thing that he has not improved, the only thing that has not received any benefit from his judicious mind, is his devotion. It is in the same poor state as it was when he was only six years of age; and the old man now prays in the same words that his mother used to hear him repeat morning and night. This Mundanus, who considers how everything he sees might be made or used to better advantage, has gone all his life

---

[11]Mundanus: worldly-wise man.

praying in the same manner as when he was a child, without ever considering how much better or more often he might pray. He does not consider how many helps a wise and reasonable man may call to his assistance, and how necessary it is that our prayers should be varied and suited to the particular states and conditions of our lives.

How poor and contemptible is the conduct of this man of sense, who has so much judgment and understanding in everything but that which is the whole wisdom of man! And many people imitate this conduct! This seems to be the result of a strange and foolish state of negligence, which keeps people from considering what devotion is. For if they went so far as to think about it even once, or to ask themselves any questions about it, they would soon see that the spirit of devotion is like any other sense or understanding that is to be improved by study, care, and application.

If you were to ask Mundanus, or any man of business or learning, whether piety is not the highest perfection of man, or devotion the greatest attainment in the world, he would be forced to answer in the affirmative, or else give up the truth of the Gospel. For it is absurd for a Christian to set any accomplishment against devotion, or to think that anything in this world comes close to its excellency. Christianity supposes, intends, desires, and aims at nothing else but raising fallen men to a divine life, to habits of holiness and degrees of devotion that may ready him to enter among the holy inhabitants of the kingdom of heaven. One who does not believe this of Christianity may be considered an infidel; and one who believes it has faith enough to give him a right judgment of the value of things, to support him in a sound mind, and to enable him to conquer all the temptations that the world will set in his way.

Devotion is nothing but right understanding and right affections toward God. All practices, therefore, that heighten and improve our true understanding of God—all ways of life that tend to nourish, raise, and fix our affections upon Him—are to be considered helps and means to fill us with devotion. Prayer is the proper fuel of this holy flame, so we must use all our care and contrivance to give prayer its full power—by alms, self-denial, holy readings, and frequent times alone in our prayer closets; by composing forms for ourselves or using the best we can get; by observing hours of prayer; and by changing, improving, and suiting our devotions to the conditions of our lives and the state of our hearts.

Those who have much time for leisure seem more especially called to an eminent observance of these holy rules of a devout life. And those who, by the necessity of their state and not through their own choice, have only a little time to use in this way, must make the best use of the little time they have. This is the way in which devotion produces a devout life.

Chapter Fourteen

SING UNTO THE LORD

In the previous chapter, I pointed out to you some methods to help you raise and improve your devotion. I indicated how early you are to begin your prayers and what should be the subject of your first devotions in the morning. Yet, there is one thing still remaining that cannot be neglected without great injury to your devotions, and that is to begin all your prayers with a psalm.

I am not saying that you should simply read over a psalm. Rather, you should chant or sing one of those psalms that we commonly call the reading psalms, for a psalm that is only read is very much like a prayer that is only looked over. This is so beneficial to devotion and has so much effect upon our hearts, that it may be insisted upon as a common rule for every believer.

Now, everyone is able to chant a psalm, because chanting requires only a small and natural change of voice. Even so, this change is sufficient to raise and keep up the gladness of our hearts. You are, therefore, to consider chanting a psalm as a necessary beginning of your devotions, as something that awakens all that is good and holy within you—something that calls your spirit to its proper duty, sets you in your best posture toward heaven, and tunes all the powers of your soul to worship and adoration.

For nothing clears a way for your prayers, disperses dullness of heart, purifies the soul, opens heaven, or carries your heart so near it, as much as these songs of praise. They create a sense of and delight in God; they awaken holy desires; they teach you how to ask; and they prevail with God to give. They kindle a holy flame; they turn your heart into an altar and your prayers into incense; and they carry them as a sweet-smelling savor to the throne of grace.

The difference between singing and reading a psalm will easily be understood if you consider the difference between singing and reading a common song that you like. If you only read it, you may like it, but that is all. However, as soon as you sing it, then you enjoy it, you feel the delight of it; it has got hold of you, your passions keep pace with it, and you feel the same spirit within you that seems to be in the words.

If you were to tell a man with such a song, that he does not need to sing it and that it will be sufficient just to read it, he would wonder what you meant. It would be as if you were telling him that he should only look at his food, to see whether it is good, but that he does not need to eat it. Similarly, a song of praise not sung is very much like any other good thing not made use of.

Perhaps you will say, "Singing is a talent that belongs only to some people, and I have neither voice nor ear to make any music." If you had said that singing is a general talent, and that people differ in that as they do in all other things, you would have said something much truer.

Consider, in comparison, the different ways in which people think. Thinking is not only common to all men, but it seems to be the very essence of human nature. Yet, how vastly people differ in this talent! Some people readily use their reason about everything, and others will not think about anything at all. Some people discourse clearly on the most abstract matters, and others talk confusedly on the most ordinary subjects. Nevertheless, no one desires to be excused from thought or reason or discourse simply because he does not have these talents in the same measure that others have them.

If you think yourself excused from singing the praises of God because you do not have a fine ear or a musical voice, you may as well think yourself excused from thinking about God, from reasoning about your duty to Him, or from discoursing about the means of salvation, because you do not have these talents in any fine degree. Remember, it is speaking, not graceful speaking, that is a required part of prayer; it is bowing, not genteel bowing, that is a proper part of adoration; and it is singing, not artful, fine singing, that is a required way of praising God. A man may speak all his prayers in an odd tone, yet it will sufficiently answer all the ends of his own devotion. Likewise, a man may sing a psalm, though not in a very musical way, and yet it will sufficiently answer all the ends of rejoicing in and praising God.

Your objection to singing might be valid if you were singing to entertain other people; but it has no merit in the present case, where you are only required to sing the praises of God as a part of your private devotion. It is understandable for a person with a harsh voice and a bad way of speaking, to say that his voice is not proper to be the voice of the congregation. However, he would be very absurd if, for the same reason, he neglected his own private devotions.

This is exactly the case of singing psalms: you may not be able to entertain other people with your singing, and therefore it is reasonable to excuse yourself from it; but if for that reason you excuse yourself from this way of praising God, you are guilty of a great absurdity. We are no more required to sing for the purpose of making fine music than we are required to pray for the purpose of uttering fine words. Whether you make fine music or not, singing is the natural and proper expression of a heart rejoicing in God. And if you will live in such a way that your heart may truly rejoice in God, that it may feel itself affected with the praises of God, you will find that your heart will need neither voice nor ear to find a tune for a psalm.

Everyone, at some time or other, finds himself able to sing in some degree; the joy that they feel on holidays and other special occasions makes people ready to express their sense of it in some sort of harmony and to let their voices have a part in it. Therefore, a person who says he lacks a voice or an ear to sing a psalm, is quite mistaken: he actually lacks the spirit that really rejoices in God. The dullness is in his heart, not in his ear. When his heart feels a true joy in God, when it has a full relish of what is expressed in the Psalms, he will find it very pleasant to make the motions of his voice express the motions of his heart. If there are only a few singers of divine songs, if most people need to be urged to this part of devotion, it is because there are few whose hearts are raised to that height of piety at which they delight in the praises of God.

Singing, indeed, is not natural; it runs the voice through such a range of notes and such a variety of time changes, that it cannot be the result of any natural state of the mind. In this sense, it is not something that everyone can perform. Even so, the motion of the voice is suitable to the motions of the heart, and the changing of its tone goes according to the meaning of the words we utter. We know this to be as natural and common to all men as speaking loudly when one threatens in anger, or speaking low when one is dejected and asks for a pardon. All men, therefore, are singers in the same manner as all men think, speak, laugh, and lament.

Imagine that you were with Moses when he was led through the Red Sea. (See Exodus 14:21–29.) You would have seen the waters divide themselves and stand on a heap on both sides until you had passed through; then you would have seen them fall upon your enemies. Do you think you would have cared whether you had a voice or an ear for singing, when suddenly you sang with Moses, "The LORD is my strength and song, and he is become my salvation" (Exod. 15:2)? Surely, you will admit that everyone must have been a singer on such an occasion. Let this therefore teach you that it is the heart that tunes a voice to sing the praises of God; if you cannot sing the same words now with joy, it is because you are not as affected with the salvation of the world by Jesus Christ as the Jews were, or as you yourself would have been, with their deliverance at the Red Sea.

A few observations of human nature will easily prove that it is the state of the heart that disposes one to rejoice in singing. One who is strongly inclined to debauchery may, according to the language of the world, have neither voice nor ear if you sing a psalm to him; yet, if you sing something that celebrates his former debauches, he will show you, though he has no teeth in his head, that he has both a voice and an ear to join in such music. You awaken his heart, and he as naturally sings to such words as he laughs when he is pleased. This is the case with every song that touches the heart: if you celebrate the ruling passion of any man's heart, you put his voice in tune with yours.

Meanwhile, if you can find a man whose ruling temperament is devotion and whose heart is full of God, his voice will rejoice in those songs of praise that glorify God, though he has neither voice nor ear for other music. It is not necessary to learn a tune in order to delightfully perform this part of devotion, but it is necessary to prepare your heart; for, although holy joys, thanksgiving, and praise may proceed out of the heart, it is equally true that "out of the heart proceed evil thoughts, murders, adulteries, fornications, thefts, false witness, [and] blasphemies" (Matt. 15:19). If you can once say with David, "My heart is fixed, O God, my heart is fixed" (Ps. 57:7), it will be very easy and natural to add, as he did in the same verse, "I will sing and give praise."

Let us now consider another reason for this kind of devotion: as singing is a natural effect of joy in the heart, so does it also have a natural power of rendering the heart joyful. The soul and body are so united that they have power over one another in their actions. Certain thoughts and sentiments in the soul produce certain motions and actions in the body; and, on the other hand, certain motions and actions of the body have the same power of raising certain thoughts and sentiments in the soul. Thus, singing is the natural effect of joy in the mind, as truly as it is a natural cause of raising joy in the mind.

It is the same in all states of the mind: the inward state of the mind produces outward actions suitable to it, and those outward actions have the same power of raising an inward state of mind suitable to them. For example, anger produces angry words, and angry words increase anger. Likewise, singing or chanting the psalms is as proper and necessary to raise our hearts to a delight in God, as prayer is proper and necessary to excite us in the spirit of devotion.

Therefore, if you wish to know why singing psalms is so important, you must consider the importance of praising and rejoicing in God. The singing of psalms is as much the true exercise and natural language of the spirit of thanksgiving, as prayer is the true exercise and natural language of the spirit of devotion. If you think you can rejoice in God as you should without the practice of singing psalms, you may as well think that you can be as devout as you should without bothering to pray.

The union of soul and body is not a mixture of their substances, but it solely consists of the mutual power that they have of acting upon one another. If two persons were in such a state of dependence upon one another, that neither of them could act, move, think, feel, suffer, or desire anything without putting the other into the same condition, one might properly say that they were in a state of strict union, although their substances were not united together.

Of course, the union of the soul and body is such that the substance of the one cannot be mixed or united with the other; but they are held together in such a state of union, that all the actions and sufferings of the one are at the same time the actions and sufferings of the other. Every thought or passion of the soul concerns the body; every action or motion of the body in some degree affects the soul.

There is nothing in the nature of a human soul or body that is the cause of this union between the two. Rather, it is the will of God that they should be in such a state. Think of the eye. It is the organ of seeing, not because anything in the eye has the natural power of giving sight, but because God has made it so. And the ears are the instruments of hearing, not because the structure of the ear has any natural power over sounds, but merely because it is the will of God that hearing should be thus received. In like manner, it is the sole will of God, and not the nature of a human soul or body, that is the cause of this union between the soul and body. If you correctly understand the union of the soul and body, you will see a great deal into the reason and necessity of all the outward parts of religion.

This union of our souls and bodies is both the reason why we have so little and the reason why we have so much power over ourselves. We cannot prevent the effects of external objects on our bodies, and we cannot command outward causes; therefore, we cannot always command the inward state of our minds. Because outward objects act upon our bodies without our permission, our bodies act upon our minds by the laws of the union of the soul and the body; and because of this union, we have little power over ourselves.

On the other hand, it is because of this union that we have so much power over ourselves. Our souls depend on our bodies in great measure; and we can command our outward actions. We can oblige ourselves to habits of life that naturally produce habits in the soul, and we can subdue our bodies and remove ourselves from objects that inflame our passions. This gives us a great power over the inward state of our souls. We are masters of our outward actions because we can force ourselves to outward acts of reading, praying, singing, and the like. These bodily actions have an effect upon the soul, and they naturally tend to form certain dispositions in our hearts. Thus, by being masters of these outward, bodily actions, we have great power over the inward state of the heart.

Now, from this you ought to see the necessity and benefit of singing psalms, and of all the outward acts of religion; for if the body has so much power over the soul, it is certain that all such bodily actions that affect the soul are of great importance in religion. Of course, there is no true worship or piety in the actions themselves, but they raise and support that spirit that is the true worship of God. Therefore, we may use both outward helps and inward meditations in order to create and establish habits of piety in our hearts.

We must be careful that this doctrine is not carried too far, for by calling in too many outward means of worship, it may degenerate into superstition. On the other hand, some have been so overly careful of this, that they have renounced vocal prayer and other outward acts of worship, and they have resolved all religion into a quietism, or mystic intercourses with God in silence.

Now, these two extremes are equally harmful to true religion, injurious to both internal and external worship. I do not encourage the quietism of placing religion solely in the heart, and, even more so, I would not encourage the superstition of showing only the outward acts of worship. We are neither all soul nor all body, and none of our actions are exclusively of the soul or exclusively of the body. Therefore, it is certain that if we want to arrive at habits of devotion, we must not only meditate and exercise our souls, but we must also exercise our bodies in the outward actions that are conformable to these inward qualities.

If we desire to truly prostrate our souls before God, we must use our bodies in postures of lowliness; if we desire true devotion, we must make prayer the frequent labor of our lips. If we want to banish all pride and passion from our hearts, we must force ourselves to practice all outward actions of patience and meekness. If we want to feel inward motions of joy and delight in God, we must practice all the outward acts of it and make our voices call upon our hearts. From this you may plainly see the reason and necessity of the singing of psalms: outward actions are necessary to support inward dispositions; therefore, the outward act of joy is necessary to raise and support the inward joy of the mind.

If someone were to stop praying because he seldom finds his heart answering the words that he speaks, you would accuse him of absurdity. You would think it very reasonable that he should continue his prayers and be strict in observing all times of prayer, as the likeliest means of removing the dullness and lack of devotion from his heart.

This is also the case with the singing of psalms: people often sing without finding any inward joy suitable to the words that they are singing. Consequently, they are careless of it, or they wholly neglect it, not considering that they act as absurdly as one who neglects prayer because his heart was not affected enough by it. For it is certain that this singing is as much the natural means of raising emotions of joy in the mind, as prayer is the natural means of raising devotion.

I have spent so much time on this subject because of its great importance to true religion. There is no state of mind so holy, so excellent, and so truly perfect as that of thankfulness to God; and, consequently, nothing is of more importance in religion than that which exercises and improves this habit of mind. A dull, uneasy, complaining spirit, which is sometimes the spirit of those who seem careful of religion, is yet, of all spirits, the most contrary to religion because it disowns that God whom it pretends to adore. For whoever does not adore Him as a Being of infinite goodness, sufficiently disowns God.

If a man does not believe that all the world is as God's family, where nothing happens by chance, but all is guided and directed by the care and providence of a Being that is all love and goodness to all His creatures; if a man does not believe this from his heart, he cannot be said truly to believe in God. And yet, one who has this faith, has faith enough to overcome the world (1 John 5:4) and always be thankful to God. One who believes that everything happens to him for the best (Rom. 8:28), cannot possibly complain about the lack of something that is better.

If, therefore, you live in murmurings and complaints (see Philippians 2:14), blaming all the accidents of life for your hardships, it is not because you are a weak, infirm creature, but it is because you lack the first principle of religion—a right belief in God. For as thankfulness is an express acknowledgment of the goodness of God toward you, so complaints are plain accusations of God's supposed lack of goodness toward you.

On the other hand, do you want to know who is the greatest saint in the world? It is not the one who prays most or fasts most; it is not the one who gives the most alms or is most eminent in temperance, chastity, or justice; but it is the one who is always thankful to God, who wills everything that God wills, who receives everything as an instance of God's goodness, and who has a heart always ready to praise God for it.

All prayer and devotion, fasting and repentance, meditation and seclusion, all sacraments and ordinances, are simply means to render the soul divine and conformable to the will of God, to fill it with thankfulness and praise for everything that comes from God. This is the perfection of all virtues; and all virtues that do not lead to it or proceed from it, are like false ornaments of a soul not converted to God. Do not marvel, therefore, that I put so much stress upon singing a psalm during your devotions. This singing is intended to bring your spirit to such joy and thankfulness to God as are the highest perfections of a divine and holy life.

If anyone wishes to tell you the shortest, surest way to all happiness and all perfection, he must tell you to make it a rule to yourself to thank and praise God for everything that happens to you. For it is certain that whatever seeming calamity happens to you, if you thank and praise God for it, you turn it into a blessing. If you could work miracles, you could not do more for yourself than by this thankful spirit; for it heals with a word, and it turns all that it touches into happiness.

If, therefore, you would be so true to your eternal interest, as to make this thankfulness the end of all your religion; if you would simply settle it in your mind that this is the state that you are to aim for in all your devotions; you would then have something plain and visible to walk by in all your actions; you would then easily see the effect of your virtues, and safely judge whether you are improving in piety. Insofar as you renounce all selfish tempers and all motions of your own will; inasmuch as you seek no other happiness than in the thankful reception of everything that happens to you; then you may safely be considered to have advanced in piety.

Although this is the highest disposition that you can aim for, though it is the noblest sacrifice that the greatest saint can offer to God, it is not tied to any time or place or great occasion. Rather, it is always in your power, and it may be practiced every day. For the common events of every day are sufficient to discover and exercise this attitude, and they may plainly show you how far you are governed in all your actions by this thankful spirit. For this reason, I exhort you to this method in your devotion, that every day may be made a day of thanksgiving, and that the spirit of murmuring and discontentment may be unable to enter into the heart that is so often employed in singing the praises of God.

After all this, you may object that, although the great benefits and effects of this practice are very apparent, yet it does not seem proper if devotions are to be private. You say that one can hardly sing psalms without making his devotions public to other people—it is like sounding a trumpet at our prayers. I have a few replies to your complaint.

First, great numbers of people have it in their power to be as private as they please; such persons, therefore, are excluded from this excuse. In that case, let us take the benefit of this excellent devotion.

Secondly, many people, including prisoners and families in small houses, are forced to be continually in the presence or sight of other people. Now, are such persons to neglect their prayers because they cannot pray without being seen? No, they are obliged to be more exact in them, so that others may not be witnesses of their neglect and be corrupted by their example. This applies not only to the singing of psalms, but also to devotion as a whole. The rule is this: do not pray that you may be seen of men (Matt. 6:5-6); but if your confinement obliges you to be always in the sight of others, be more afraid of being seen neglecting your prayers than of being seen praying.

Thirdly, the short of the matter is this: either people can have privacy in this practice, or they cannot. If they can, then your objection has no relevancy; if they cannot, they should consider their confinement and the necessities of their state, as the confinement of a prison. In that case, they have an excellent pattern to follow—they may imitate Paul and Silas, who sang praises to God in prison, though we are expressly told that the prisoners heard them (Acts 16:25). They did not refrain from this kind of devotion for fear of being heard by others. Therefore, if anyone is in a similar situation, whether in prison or out of prison, what can he do better than to follow this example?

Observe how strongly we are called to this use of psalms, and what a mighty example Paul and Silas have given to us. In their great distress, in prison, in chains, under the soreness of stripes, in the horror of night, the divinest, holiest thing they could do was to sing praises to God. Furthermore, while these two holy men were thus employed in the most exalted part of devotion, doing on earth what angels do in heaven, "the foundations of the prison were shaken: and immediately all the doors were opened, and every one's bands were loosed" (Acts 16:26).

After this, will we need any exhortation to this holy practice? Will we let the day go by without the kind of thanksgiving that they would not neglect in the night? Will a prison, chains, and darkness furnish Paul and Silas with songs of praise, yet we do not sing in our prayer closets? And will we now ask for motivation to sing psalms, when, instead of arguments, we have such miracles to convince us of its mighty power with God? Could God by a voice from heaven more expressly call us to these songs of praise, than by showing us in this way how He hears, delivers, and rewards those who use them?

Yet, this is beside the point. I now return to the objection at hand, regarding the privacy of devotions; and my fourth response is that the privacy of our prayers is not destroyed by our having, but by our seeking, witnesses of them. If nobody hears you except those from whom you cannot separate yourself, then you are in secret, and your Father who "seeth in secret shall reward thee openly" (Matt. 6:6) for your secrecy, as if you were seen by Him only.

Fifthly, private prayer does not suppose that no one will witness it. Husbands and wives, brothers and sisters, parents and children, tutors and pupils are meant to be witnesses to one another of such private devotion. It is far from being a duty to conceal such devotion from near relations. Such relations may sometimes pray together in private and sometimes by themselves. In all these cases, therefore, the chanting of a psalm can have no valid argument against it.

Our Lord commands us, when we fast, to anoint our heads and wash our faces, "that thou appear not unto men to fast, but unto thy Father which is in secret" (Matt. 6:17–18). Simply put, this means that we must not make our fasting a public ostentation to the world. If no one were to fast in private, or could be said to fast in private, except those who had no witnesses of it, no one could keep a private fast but those who lived by themselves—for every family must know who fasts in it. Therefore, the privacy of fasting is not so private that it excludes everybody from knowing it, but it does not seek to be known abroad.

Cornelius, the devout centurion of whom the Scripture says, "gave much alms to the people, and prayed to God alway" (Acts 10:2), said to Peter, "Four days ago I was fasting until this hour" (Acts 10:30). We know that this fasting was sufficiently private and acceptable to God because of the vision of an angel, with which the holy man was blessed at that time (Acts 10:3–6). On the other hand, we also know that Cornelius's fasting was not entirely unknown to others, because we are told that he

> called two of his household servants, and a devout soldier of them that waited on him continually; and...[he] declared all these things unto them. *(Acts. 10:7–8)*

Cornelius's fasting was far from being unknown to his family, because the soldiers and the members of his household were made devout themselves by continually waiting upon him and seeing and partaking of his good works.

The whole of the matter is this: a great number of people can be as private as they please, and they may use this excellent devotion between God and themselves. Yet, as the privacy or excellency of fasting is not destroyed by being known to others, neither would the privacy or excellency of your devotions be hurt if some of your family heard you chanting a psalm.

If you are among those who have witnesses of several of their devotions, do not neglect the use of a psalm at such times. It is better that you be heard than be known to neglect your prayers, for surely there can be no harm in being known to sing a psalm when you are known to be at your prayers. If, at other times, you desire to have such secrecy in your devotions that no one will suspect it—and for that reason you do without your psalm—then I have nothing to say against it, provided that at the known hours of prayer, you never omit this practice.

My last response to the aforementioned objection is this: seeing that our imaginations have great power over our hearts and can mightily affect us with their representations, it would be of great use to you if, at the beginning of your devotions, you were to imagine things that might warm your heart to those prayers that you are then about to offer to God. In other words, before you begin your psalm of praise and rejoicing in God, make use of your imagination. Be still and imagine to yourself that you see the heavens open, and the glorious choirs of cherubim and seraphim about the throne of God. Imagine that you hear the music of those angelic voices, that cease not day and night to sing the glories of Him who is and was and is to come (Rev. 1:4).

It may help your imagination to use passages of Scripture such as this:

> *After this I beheld, and, lo, a great multitude, which no man could number, of all nations, and kindreds, and people, and tongues, stood before the throne, and before the Lamb, clothed with white robes, and palms in their hands; and cried with a loud voice, saying, Salvation to our God which sitteth upon the throne, and unto the Lamb. And all the angels stood round about the throne, and about the elders and the four beasts, and fell before the throne on their faces, and worshipped God, saying, Amen: Blessing, and glory, and wisdom, and thanksgiving, and honour, and power, and might, be unto our God for ever and ever. Amen.* (Rev. 7:9–12)

Think about this until your imagination has carried you above the clouds, until it has placed you among those heavenly beings and made you desire to have a part in their eternal music.

If you will accustom yourself to this method and let your imagination dwell on representations such as these, you will soon find it to be an excellent means of raising the spirit of devotion within you. Therefore, you should always begin your psalm, or song of praise, with these imaginations; and at every verse of it imagine that you are among those heavenly companions; that your voice is added to theirs; that angels join with you, and you with them; and that you, with a poor and low voice, are singing on earth what they are singing in heaven.

You may also imagine that you were one of those who joined with our blessed Savior when He sang a hymn. Try to imagine how majestic He looked; suppose that you stood close by Him, surrounded with His glory. Consider how your heart would have been inflamed and what ecstasies of joy you would have then felt, when singing with the Son of God. Imagine with what joy and devotion you would then have sung, had this really been your happy state; it would have been a punishment if you had had to remain silent. Let this representation teach you how to be affected with psalms and hymns of thanksgiving.

Again, imagine that you had seen David with his hands upon his harp (1 Sam. 16:23) and his eyes fixed upon heaven, passionately calling upon all creation—sun and moon, light and darkness, day and night, men and angels—to join with his rapturous soul in praising the Lord of heaven. Dwell upon this thought until you think you are singing with this divine musician; and let such a companion teach you to exalt your heart to God first thing in the morning.

You may use the words from Psalm 145:1: "I will extol thee, my God, O king; and I will bless thy name for ever and ever." Also, Psalms 34, 96, 103, 111, 146, and 147 set forth wonderfully the glory of God; and therefore you may keep to any one of them, at any particular hour, as you like. Or, you may take the finest parts of any of the psalms and add them together to make them more appropriate for your own devotion.

Chapter Fifteen

THE PRACTICE OF TRUE HUMILITY

Now we must come to another hour of prayer, which is nine o'clock in the morning. At this time, the devout Christian must look upon himself as called by God to renew his acts of prayer, and he must address himself again to the throne of grace.

There is indeed no express command in Scripture to repeat our devotions at this hour, which in Scripture is called the third hour of the day. However, neither is there any express command to begin and end the day with prayer, so this cannot be a reason for neglecting devotion at this hour. If the customs and practices of all the saints and of the first Christians and the pious Jews have any weight with us, we will need no persuasion to make this hour a constant season of devotion.

The Scriptures show us how this hour was consecrated to devotion by both Jews and Christians. As a result, if we desire to number ourselves among those whose hearts are devoted to God, we must not let this hour pass without presenting ourselves to Him in some solemnities of devotion. The reasonableness of it, alone, is sufficient to invite us to the observance of it.

If you were up at a good time in the morning, your first devotions will have been at a proper distance from this hour; you will have been long enough at other business to make it proper for you to return to this greatest of all business—the raising of your soul and affections unto God. However, if you have risen so late that you can hardly begin your first devotions at the hour that is proper for your second, you may then learn that indulging yourself in sleep in the morning is no small matter; it sets you far back in your devotions and robs you of those graces and blessings that are obtained by frequent prayers. For if prayer has power with God; if it looses the bands of sin (Isa. 58:6); if it purifies the soul, reforms our hearts, and draws down the aids of divine grace; how can something that robs us of an hour of prayer be considered a small matter?

Imagine that you could witness all the devotions that Christian people offer to God every day; imagine that you could see some of those Christians piously dividing the day and night, as the first Christians did—constant at all hours of devotion, singing psalms and calling upon God, at all those times that saints and martyrs received their gifts and graces from God. Now imagine that you could see others living without any rules regarding times and frequency of prayer, and that they are only at their devotions sooner or later, as sleep and laziness happen to permit them.

If you were to see this as God sees it, how do you suppose it would affect you? What judgment would you pass upon these different sorts of people? Could you think that those who were exact in their rules of devotion, got nothing by their exactness? Are their prayers received in the same manner as the prayers of those who prefer laziness and indulgence to times and rules of devotion? Do their prayers procure them no more blessings than that?

Could you take one group to be as true servants of God as the other? Could you imagine that those who were thus different in their lives, would find no difference in their states after death? Could you think it a matter of indifference to which of these people you were most similar? If not, let it be now your care to join yourself to that number of devout people, to that society of saints, among whom you desire to be found when you leave the world.

Although the bare number and repetition of our prayers is of little value, yet prayer, rightly and attentively performed, is the most natural means of amending and purifying our hearts. We may be sure that when we are frequent and importunate in our prayers, we are taking the best means of obtaining the highest benefits of a devout life, because importunity and frequency in prayer are as much stressed in the Scriptures as prayer itself. On the other hand, those who through negligence, laziness, or any other indulgence, render themselves either unable or disinclined to observe rules and hours of devotion, actually deprive themselves of those graces and blessings that an exact and fervent devotion procures from God.

This frequency of prayer is founded on the doctrines of Scripture, and is recommended to us by the practice of the true worshippers of God. Therefore, we should not think ourselves excused from it unless we are spending our time in some business equally acceptable, if not more acceptable, to God. Least of all must we imagine that dullness, negligence, indulgence, or diversions can be any pardonable excuses for not observing an exact and frequent method of devotion.

If you are of a devout spirit, you will rejoice at the fact that the hours of prayer come again and again to keep your soul in a holy enjoyment of God, and to fill your heart with stronger joys and consolations than you can possibly find in anything else. And, if you are not of a devout spirit, then you are even more obliged to this frequency of prayer, to train and exercise your heart into a true sense and feeling of devotion.

The spirit of holiness in the Christian religion, and the example of the saints of all ages, call upon you to divide the day into hours of prayer; so it will be highly beneficial to you to choose the subjects of your prayers and to keep every hour of prayer focused on some particular subject. Of course, you may alter or enlarge the subject, as the state you are in requires. Yet, by choosing your prayer topics, you will have an opportunity to be both general and particular in all the aspects of any virtue or grace that you have made the subject of your prayers. And, by asking for it in all its parts, and making it the substance of a whole prayer once every day, you will soon find a mighty change in your heart. A person cannot constantly pray for all the parts of any virtue every day of his life and yet live the rest of the day contrary to it.

If a worldly-minded man were to pray every day against all the instances of a worldly disposition; if he were to describe all his temptations of covetousness, and desire that God help him to reject them all and disappoint him in all his covetous designs; he would find his conscience so much awakened that he would be forced either to forsake such prayers or to forsake a worldly life. The same will hold true in any other instance.

If "ye ask, and receive not, [it is] because ye ask amiss" (James 4:3). We often ask in cold and general forms that name only the virtues without describing their particular parts, and therefore we make no change in our hearts. Whereas, when a man enumerates all the specifics of any virtue in his prayers, his conscience is thereby awakened, and he is frightened at seeing how far short he is of it. And this stirs him up to an ardor in devotion, when he sees how much he lacks of that virtue for which he is praying.

In the previous chapter, I recommended praise and thanksgiving as the subject of your first devotions in the morning. Now, I recommend humility to be made the constant subject of your devotions at this third hour of the day. A humble state of soul is the very state of religion; humility is the life and soul of piety, the foundation and support of every virtue and good work, and the best guard and security of all holy affections. No day is safe, nor is it likely to end well, in which you have not put yourself in this posture of humility early in the morning, and called upon God to carry you through the day in the exercise of a meek and lowly spirit.

Humility is so essential to the right state of our souls that one cannot live a reasonable or pious life without it. We may as well think we can see without eyes, or live without breath, if we think we can live in the spirit of religion without the virtue of humility. It is the soul and essence of all religious duties. Even so, humility is the least understood, the least regarded, the least intended, the least desired and sought after, of all other virtues among Christians.

No people have more occasion to be afraid of the approaches of pride, than those who have made some advances in a pious life: for pride can grow upon our virtues as well as our vices, and it steals up on us on all occasions. Every good thought that we have, every good action that we do, lays us open to pride and exposes us to the assaults of vanity and self-satisfaction. It is not only the beauty of our persons, the gifts of fortune, our natural talents, and the distinctions of life, but even our devotions, our alms, our fastings, and our humiliations that expose us to fresh and strong temptations of this evil spirit. For this reason, I earnestly advise every devout person to begin every day in this exercise of humility, that he may go on in safety under the protection of this good guide and not become a hindrance to his own progress in the virtues that are to save mankind from destruction.

Humility does not consist of having a worse opinion of ourselves than we deserve, or of putting ourselves lower than we really are; rather, as all virtue is founded in truth, humility is founded in a true and just sense of our weakness, misery, and sin. The weakness of our state comes from our inability to do anything of ourselves. In our natural state we are entirely without power. Yes, we are active beings, but we can only act by a power that is lent by God every moment. We have no more power of our own to move a hand or a foot, than to move the sun or stop the clouds. One who rightly feels and lives in this sense of his condition, lives in humility.

When we speak, we have no more power in ourselves to do so than we have power to raise the dead. Likewise, the apostles did not act within their own power or by their own strength, when a word from their mouth cast out devils and cured diseases; it was solely the power of God that enabled them to speak to such purposes. It is solely the power of God that enables us to speak at all. Indeed, we find that we can speak, as much as we find that we are alive; yet, the actual exercise of speaking is no more in our own power than the actual enjoyment of life.

This is the dependent, helpless poverty of our state—which is a profound reason for humility. We are not to be proud of anything that we are or of anything that we can do; we are not to ascribe glory to ourselves for these things, as if they were our own ornaments. Anything that we try to do or be in ourselves has the guilt both of stealing and lying. It has the guilt of stealing because it gives to ourselves those things that belong only to God, and it has the guilt of lying because it denies the truth of our state and pretends to be something we are not.

Another argument for humility is found in the misery of our condition. Now, the misery of our condition appears in that we use the borrowed powers of our nature to the torment and vexation of ourselves and our fellow creatures. God Almighty has entrusted us with the use of reason, and we use it to the disorder and corruption of our nature. We reason ourselves into all kinds of folly and misery, and make our lives the sport of foolish and extravagant passions—seeking after imaginary happiness in all shapes and sizes; creating a thousand desires for ourselves; amusing our hearts with false hopes and fears; using the world worse than irrational animals; and envying, vexing, and tormenting one another with restless passions and unreasonable contentions.

If any man were to look back upon his own life, he would see what use he has made of his reason, how little he has consulted it, and how much less he has followed it. What foolish passions, what vain thoughts, what needless labors, what extravagant projects have taken up the greatest part of his life! How foolish he has been in his words and conversation; how seldom he has judged well, and how often he has been kept from doing ill by accident; how seldom he has been able to please himself, and how often he has displeased others; how often he has changed his counsels, hated what he loved, and loved what he hated; how often he has been pleased and displeased with the very same trifles, constantly changing from one vanity to another!

Let a man simply take this view of his own life, and he will see reason enough to confess that pride was not made for man. If he would simply consider that, if the world knew of him what he knows of himself; if they saw what vanity and passions govern his inside, and what secret passions sully and corrupt his best actions; he would have no more pretense to be honored and admired for his goodness and wisdom, than a rotten and diseased body has to be loved and admired for its beauty and comeliness.

This is so true and so known to the hearts of almost everyone, that nothing would appear more dreadful to them than to have their hearts fully discovered to the eyes of all beholders. Perhaps there are very few people in the world who would not rather choose to die, than to have all their secret follies, the errors of their judgments, the vanity of their minds, the falseness of their pretenses, the frequency of their vain and disorderly passions, their uneasiness, hatred, envies, and vexations, made known to the world.

Should pride be entertained in a heart so conscious of its own miserable behavior? Should a creature who cannot support himself under the shame of being known to the world in his real state—should such a creature, because his shame is only known to God, to holy angels, and his own conscience—should he, in the sight of God and holy angels, dare to be vain and proud of himself?

We may find a still greater reason for humility if we add to this, thirdly, the shame and guilt of sin. Imagine a man who lives in complete innocence. Would he have any pretense for self-honor and esteem? No, because, as a creature, all that he is or has or does, is from God, and therefore the honor of all that belongs to him is rightly due to God. On the other hand, imagine that man as a sinner and under the displeasure of the great Governor of all the world. He deserves nothing from Him but pains and punishments for the shameful abuse of his powers. If such a creature pretends to self-glory for anything that he is or does, he can only be said to glory in his shame.

Now, the monstrous and shameful nature of sin is sufficiently apparent from the great atonement that was necessary to cleanse us from it. Nothing less than the sufferings and death of the Son of God has been required to take away the guilt of our sins. Had He not taken our nature upon Him (Heb. 2:16), we would have been forever separated from God, incapable of ever appearing before Him. Can there be any room for pride or self-glory while we are partakers of such a nature as this?

Our sins rendered us so abominable and odious to the One who made us, that He could not so much as receive our prayers or admit our repentance unless the Son of God made Himself man and became a suffering Advocate for our whole race. Can we, in this state, hold high thoughts of ourselves? Can we, who are not even worthy to ask pardon for our sins, presume to take delight in our own worth, without the mediation and intercession of the Son of God? In this way, the foundation of humility is laid deep in these deplorable circumstances of our condition. If man will boast of anything as his own, he must boast of his misery and sin; for there is nothing else but this that is his own property.

Turn your eyes toward heaven, and imagine that you see what is happening there, that you see cherubim and seraphim and all the glorious inhabitants of that place, all united in one work. They are not seeking glory from one another, not laboring for their own advancement, not contemplating their own perfections, not singing their own praises, not valuing themselves and despising others, but they are all employed in one and the same work, all happy in one and the same joy: casting their crowns before the throne of God (Rev. 4:10) and giving glory, honor, and power to Him alone (v. 11).

Then turn your eyes to the fallen world, and consider how unreasonable and odious it must be for such poor worms (Job 25:6), such miserable sinners, to take delight in their own fancied glories, while the highest and most glorious sons of heaven seek no other greatness and honor but that of ascribing all honor and greatness and glory to God alone. Pride is only the disorder of the fallen world; it has no place among other beings; it can only subsist where ignorance and sensuality, lies and falsehood, lusts and impurity reign.

Let a man, when he is most delighted with his own accomplishments, look upon a crucifix and contemplate our blessed Lord stretched out and nailed upon a cross. Then let him consider how absurd it must be for a heart full of pride and vanity to pray to God through the sufferings of such a meek and crucified Savior!

Meditate upon these reflections, that you may thereby be disposed to walk before God and man in a spirit of humility that becomes the weak, miserable, sinful state of fallen man. Then, when you have convinced your mind of the reasonableness of humility, you must not content yourself with this, as if you were humble by simply acknowledging its reasonableness. Instead, you must immediately enter into the practice of this virtue, like a young beginner who has everything to learn and can learn only a little at a time, with great difficulty. You must not only consider that you have this virtue to learn, but you must also be content to be a student of it all the time, endeavoring after greater degrees of it and practicing acts of humility every day, just as you practice acts of devotion every day.

You would not imagine yourself to be devout simply because you approved of prayers and often declared the favorableness of devotion. Yet, how many people imagine themselves humble for no other reason than because they often commend humility and make vehement declarations against pride!

Caecus[12] is a rich man of good upbringing. He is haughty and arrogant toward all his inferiors, is very full of everything that he says or does, and never imagines it possible for his judgment to be mistaken. He can bear no contradiction, and he discovers the weakness of your understanding as

---

[12]Caecus: blind.

198

soon as ever you oppose him. Caecus would have been very religious, if he had not always thought he was so. There is nothing so repulsive to Caecus as a proud man, and the misfortune is that he is so quick-sighted that he discovers some stroke of vanity in almost everybody. On the other hand, he is exceedingly fond of humble and modest persons. Humility, he says, is so amiable a quality that it increases our own worth wherever we meet with it.

Caecus no more suspects himself of pride than he suspects his lack of sense. This is because he always finds himself so in love with humility and so enraged at pride. Of course, he speaks sincerely when he says he loves humility and abhors pride. He is no hypocrite in that sense, for he speaks the true sentiments of his mind. However, Caecus only loves humility and hates pride in other people. He never once in his life thought of humility or pride in his own life.

The case of Caecus is a common case. Many people live in all the instances of pride, and indulge every vanity that can enter into their minds, and yet never suspect themselves to be governed by pride and vanity because they know how much they dislike proud people and how pleased they are with humility and modesty, wherever they find them. All their speeches in favor of humility, and all their railings against pride, are looked upon as proof of their own humble spirits.

Yet, in truth, these are far from being evidence of humility; rather, they are great evidence for the lack of it. For the fuller of pride anyone is himself, the more impatient he will be at the smallest instances of it in other people. Likewise, the less humility anyone has in his own mind, the more he will demand and be delighted with it in other people. Therefore, you must only consider yourself humble insofar as you impose every instance of humility upon yourself, and you must never call for it in other people unless you can spare it in yourself.

Now, in order to do this, you must realize that pride and humility mean nothing to you, and they do you neither good nor harm, except to the extent that they are the qualities of your own heart. Consequently, it is of no benefit or advantage to you to love humility unless you also love to see all your own thoughts, words, and actions governed by it. Similarly, it does you no good to hate pride unless you also hate to harbor any degree of it in your own heart.

In order to begin and set out well in the practice of humility, you must take it for granted that you are proud, that you have all your life been more or less infected with this unreasonable temperament. You should also believe that it is your greatest weakness, that your heart is most subject to it, and that it is so constantly stealing upon you that you have reason to watch and suspect its approaches in all your actions.

This is what most people, especially new beginners in a pious life, may with great truth think of themselves. For there is no one vice that is more deeply rooted in our nature, or that receives such constant nourishment from almost everything that we think or do. There is hardly anything in the world that we want or use, or any action or duty of life, that pride does not take hold of. As a result, we can hardly be surer of anything than that we have a great deal of pride to repent of, regardless of when we begin to offer ourselves to God.

If you find that you cannot put yourself among those who need to be cured of pride, you may be sure that you have not only much, but all, of your humility to seek. For you can have no greater sign of pride than when you think that you are humble enough. One who thinks he loves God enough, shows himself to be a complete stranger to that holy passion. Likewise, one who thinks he has enough humility, shows that he has not even begun the practice of true humility.

Chapter Sixteen

A LIFE CONTRARY TO THE WORLD

Every person, when he first applies himself to the exercise of this virtue of humility, must, as I said before, consider himself a learner; that is, he must learn something that is contrary to former states and habits of mind, something that can only be obtained by daily and constant practice.

He also has a great deal to unlearn: he is to forget and lay aside his own spirit, which has been a long while fixing and forming itself; he must forget and depart from passions and opinions that the spirit of the world has made natural to him. He must lay them aside because they are, in many respects, contrary to humility; and before he can be governed by the spirit of humility, he must unlearn what the spirit of the world has taught him. He must lay aside his own spirit, because we are born in sin and therefore in pride, which is as natural to us as self-love, and continually springs from it. This is one reason why Christianity is so often represented as a new birth (John 3:7) and a new spirit (2 Cor. 5:17).

The Devil is called in Scripture the prince of this world (John 12:31) because he has great power in it and because many of its rules and principles were invented by this evil spirit, the father of all lies and falsehoods (John 8:44), to separate us from God (Matt. 25:41) and to prevent our return to happiness.

Now, according to the spirit of this world, whose corrupt air we have all breathed, there are many things that seem great and honorable and desirable. Yet these things are so far from being so, that the true greatness and honor of our nature consists in not desiring them. To abound in wealth, to have fine houses and rich clothes, to be beautiful in our persons, to have titles of dignity, to be above our fellow creatures, to command the deference and obeisance of other people, to be looked upon with admiration, to overcome our enemies with power, to subdue all who oppose us, to set out ourselves in as much splendor as we can, to live highly and magnificently, to eat and drink and delight ourselves in the most costly manner—these are the great, the honorable, the desirable things to which the spirit of the world turns the eyes of all people. And many a man is afraid of standing still and not engaging in the pursuit of these things, lest the world should take him for a fool.

The history of the Gospel is chiefly the history of Christ's conquest over the spirit of the world (John 16:33). "If any man have not the Spirit of Christ, he is none of his" (Rom. 8:9). "Whatsoever is born of God overcometh the world" (1 John 5:4). "Set your affection on things above, not on things on the earth. For ye are dead, and your life is hid with Christ in God" (Col. 3:2–3). This is the language of the whole New Testament, and the mark of Christianity: you are to be dead, that is, dead to the spirit and temper of the world, and to live a new life in the Spirit of Jesus Christ (Rom. 6:8–11). The number of true Christians is only the number of those who, following the Spirit of Christ, have lived contrary to this spirit of the world.

Yet, as clear and plain as these doctrines that renounce the world may seem, a great number of Christians live and die slaves to the customs and attitudes of the world. How many people swell with pride and vanity for things that they would not know how to value at all if these things were not admired in the world? A man works in business for ten additional years to add two more horses to his coach, because he knows that the world admires such. How fearful are many people of having their houses poorly furnished, or themselves poorly clothed, lest the world should look down upon them or place them among low and poor people! How often would a man have yielded to the haughtiness and ill nature of others, and shown a submissive temper, but that he dares not pass for such a weak man in the opinion of the world! Many a man would often drop a resentment and forgive an affront, but that he is afraid the world would not forgive him if he did so.

Many more people would practice Christian temperance and sobriety, in its utmost perfection, if it were not for the censure that the world passes upon such a life. Many have frequent intentions of living up to the rules of Christian perfection, but they are frightened by what the world would say of them. In this way, the impressions that we have received from living in the world enslave our minds, so that we dare not attempt to be eminent in the sight of God and holy angels, for fear of being little in the eyes of the world.

From this arises the greatest difficulty of humility, because it cannot exist in a mind that is not dead to the world or that has not parted with all desires of enjoying its greatness and honors. So, in order to be truly humble, you must unlearn all those notions that you have been learning all your life from this corrupt spirit of the world. You can make no stand against the assaults of pride, and the meek affections of humility can have no place in your soul, until you stop the power of the world over you and set yourself firmly against a blind obedience to its laws.

When you have advanced far enough to be able to stand still against the torrent of worldly fashions and opinions, and examine the worth and value of things that are most admired and valued in the world, you have gone a great way in the gaining of your freedom, and have laid a good foundation for the amendment of your heart. For as great as the power of the world is, it is all built upon a blind obedience; we need only open our eyes to get rid of its power over us.

Ask whom you will, learned or unlearned; everyone seems to know and confess that the general attitude and spirit of the world is nothing else but humor, folly, and extravagance. Who will not admit that the wisdom of theology and the piety of religion have always been confined to a small number of people? Is this not due simply to the fact that the common spirit and attitude of the world is neither according to the wisdom of theology nor the piety of religion? The world, therefore, seems condemned enough even by itself, to make it very easy for a thinking man to be of the same judgment.

I hope you will not think it a hard saying that, in order to be humble, you must withdraw your obedience from that vulgar spirit that gives laws to the fools of this world, and form your judgments according to the wisdom of theology and the piety of religion. Who would be afraid of making such a change as this?

To lessen your regard to the opinion of the world, think how soon the world will disregard you and have no more thought or concern about you than about the poorest animal that died in a ditch. Your friends, if they can, may bury you with some distinction and set up a monument to let posterity see that your dust lies under such a stone; and when that is done, all is done. Your place is filled up by another; the world is just in the same state it was; you are blotted out of its sight; and you are as much forgotten by the world as if you had never belonged to it.

Think about the rich, the great, and the learned persons who have become very famous and been high in the esteem of the world; many of them died in your lifetime, yet they are buried and gone and as much disregarded by the world as if they had been bubbles in water. Think again how many poor souls see heaven lost, and lie now expecting a miserable eternity for their service and homage to a world that thinks itself just as well-off without them, and is just as merry as it was when they were in it.

Is it therefore worth your while to lose the smallest degree of virtue for the sake of pleasing so bad a master, and so false a friend, as the world is? Is it worth your while to bow the knee to such an idol as this, that so soon will have neither eyes, nor ears, nor a heart to regard you, instead of serving that great and holy and mighty God, who will make all His servants partakers of His own eternity? Will you let the fear of a false world, which has no love for you, keep you from the fear of that God who has only created you that He may love and bless you to all eternity?

After you have thought about this, you must consider what behavior the profession of Christianity requires of you with regard to the world. This is plainly set forth in these words: "Who gave himself for our sins, that he might deliver us from this present evil world" (Gal. 1:4). Christianity implies a deliverance from this world, and whoever claims to be a Christian, claims also to live contrary to every thing and every passion that is peculiar to this evil world.

John declared this opposition to the world in this manner: "They are of the world: therefore speak they of the world, and the world heareth them. We are of God" (1 John 4:5–6). No one who in his heart belongs to this world, is to be considered a Christian in reality. "We know," said the same apostle, "that we are of God, and the whole world lieth in wickedness" (1 John 5:19).

Christians, therefore, cannot know that they are of God, unless they know that they are not of the world; that is, that they do not live according to the ways and the spirit of the world. For all the ways, maxims, politics, and passions of the world, lie in wickedness. And he is only of God, or born of God in Christ Jesus, who has overcome this world (1 John 5:4); that is, who has chosen to live by faith and govern his actions by the principles of a wisdom revealed from God by Christ Jesus.

Paul said in all certainty that Christians are no longer to be considered as living in this world. He said it as an undeniable principle, so well known to Christians; and he applied it to the abolishment of the rites of the Jewish law:

Wherefore if ye be dead with Christ from the rudiments of the world, why, as though living in the world, are ye subject to ordinances?   *(Col. 2:20)*

The apostle took it as an irrefutable truth, that Christians knew that their profession of faith required them to be done with all the tempers and passions of the world, to live as citizens of the New Jerusalem (Rev. 3:12; 21:2), and to have their conversation in heaven (Phil. 3:20).

Our blessed Lord Himself has fully settled this point in these words: "They are not of the world, even as I am not of the world" (John 17:16). This is the state of Christianity with regard to this world: if you are not living contrary to the world, you lack the distinguishing mark of Christianity; you cannot belong to Christ except by being out of the world as He was out of it.

We may deceive ourselves, if we please, with vain and euphemistic comments upon these words; but they are, and will be, understood in their simplicity and plainness by everyone who reads them in the same spirit that our blessed Lord spoke them. To give them any lower, less significant meaning, is to let carnal wisdom explain away that doctrine by which it was to be destroyed.

The Christian's great conquest over the world is all contained in the mystery of Christ upon the cross. It was there that He taught all Christians how they are to come out of and conquer the world, and what they are to do in order to be His disciples. All the doctrines, sacraments, and institutions of the Gospel are only amplifications of the meaning, and applications of the benefit, of this great mystery. Indeed, the state of Christianity implies nothing else but an entire, absolute conformity to the attitude that Christ showed in the mysterious sacrifice of Himself upon the cross.

Every man, therefore, is only a Christian insofar as he partakes of this attitude of Christ. It was this that made Paul so passionately express himself: "God forbid that I should glory, save in the cross of our Lord Jesus Christ" (Gal. 6:14). But, why does he glory? Is it because Christ had suffered in his stead, and had excused him from suffering? No, by no means. Rather, it was because his profession of faith had called him to the honor of suffering with Christ, and of dying to the world under reproach and contempt, as He had done upon the cross. For Paul immediately added, "By whom the world is crucified unto me, and I unto the world" (Gal. 6:14). This, you see, was the reason of his glory in the cross of Christ; it had called him to a similar state of death and crucifixion to the world.

In this manner, the cross of Christ was, in Paul's day, the glory of Christians, not because it meant they were not ashamed to have a Master who was crucified, but because it signified their glorying in a religion that was nothing else but a doctrine of the Cross, which called them to the same suffering spirit, the same sacrifice of themselves, the same renunciation of the world, the same humility and meekness, the same patient bearing of injuries, reproaches, and contempts, and the same dying to all the greatness, honors, and happiness of this world, which Christ showed upon the cross.

To have a true idea of Christianity and to make our joining with Him acceptable to God, we must not only consider our blessed Lord as suffering in our stead, but we must also consider Him as our Representative, acting in our name. He suffered and was made a sacrifice in order to make our sufferings and the sacrificing of ourselves fit to be received by God. We are to suffer, be crucified, die, and rise with Christ; or else His crucifixion, death, and resurrection will profit us nothing.

The necessity of this conformity to all that Christ did and suffered on our account is very plain from the whole tone of Scripture. First, in regard to His sufferings, the only condition of our being saved by them is this: "If we suffer [with Him], we shall also reign with him" (2 Tim. 2:12). Secondly, as to His crucifixion, we know "that our old man is crucified with him" (Rom. 6:6). Here we see that Christ is not crucified in our stead; rather, we are crucified with Him. Unless our old man is really crucified with Him, the Cross of Christ will profit us nothing.

Thirdly, as to the death of Christ, the condition is this: "If we be dead with [Christ], we shall also live with him" (2 Tim. 2:11). If, therefore, Christ has died alone, and if we are not dead with Him, we know from this Scripture that we will not live with Him. And, lastly, regarding the resurrection of Christ, the Scripture shows us how we are to partake of the benefit of it:

> *If ye then be risen with Christ, seek those things which are above, where Christ sitteth on the right hand of God.* (Col. 3:1)

From this you see how plainly the Scriptures set forth our blessed Lord as our Representative, acting and suffering in our name, binding and obliging us to conform to all that He did and suffered for us.

It was for this reason that Jesus said of His disciples, and therefore of all true believers, "They are not of the world, even as I am not of the world" (John 17:14). All true believers, conforming to the sufferings, crucifixion, death, and resurrection of Christ, live no longer after the spirit and temper of this world, but their lives are "hid with Christ in God" (Col. 3:3).

All orders of Christians are called to this state of separation from the world. They must so far renounce all worldly temperaments, be so far governed by the things of another life, that their lives show that they are really and truly crucified, dead, and risen with Christ. It is as necessary for all Christians to conform to this great change of spirit, to be new creatures in Christ (2 Cor. 5:17), as it was necessary that Christ should suffer, die, and rise again for our salvation.

Paul, in these words, described how high the Christian life is placed above the ways of this world:

> *Wherefore henceforth know we no man after the flesh: yea, though we have known Christ after the flesh, yet now henceforth know we him no more. Therefore if any man be in Christ, he is a new creature: old things are passed away; behold, all things are become new.* (2 Cor. 5:16–17)

If you will only feel the force and spirit of these words, you will hardly be able to bear any human interpretation of them.

"Henceforth," said Paul; that is, since the death and resurrection of Christ, "the state of Christianity has become so glorious a state, that we do not even consider Christ Himself as in the flesh upon earth, but as a God of glory in heaven. In other words, we know and consider ourselves not as men in the flesh, but as members of a new society; we will all place our hearts, our spirits, and our conversation in heaven." In this way, Christianity has placed us out of and above the world; and we fall from our calling as soon as we fall into the ways of the world.

Now, as it was the spirit of the world that nailed our blessed Lord to the cross, so every man who has the Spirit of Christ, who opposes the world as He did, will certainly be crucified by the world in some way. For Christianity still lives in the same world that Christ did; and these two will be utter enemies until the kingdom of darkness is entirely at an end.

If you had lived with our Savior as His true disciple, you would have been hated as He was; and if you live now in His Spirit, the world will be the same enemy to you that it was to Him.

If ye were of the world, the world would love his own: but because ye are not of the world, but I have chosen you out of the world, therefore the world hateth you.   (John 15:19)

We are apt to lose the true meaning of these words of Christ by considering them only as a historical description of the state of our Savior and His disciples at that time. Indeed, this is reading the Scripture as a dead letter; for these words describe exactly the state of true Christians at this and all other times, to the end of the world.

True Christianity is nothing else but the Spirit of Christ, so whether that Spirit appears in the person of Christ Himself or His apostles or followers in any age, it is the same thing; whoever has His Spirit will be hated, despised, and condemned by the world, as He was. For the world will always love its own, and none but its own: this is as certain and unchangeable as the difference between light and darkness.

When Jesus said to His disciples, "If the world hate you" (John 15:18), He did not add by way of consolation that it may cease its hatred, or that it will not always hate them. Instead, the only reason He gave why they should bear it was, "ye know that it hated me before it hated you" (John 15:18). What he meant was that He, that is, His Spirit, by reason of being contrary to the world, was then, and always would be, hated by it.

You will perhaps say that the world has now become Christian, at least that part of it where we live, and that therefore the world is not now to be considered in that state of opposition to Christianity as when it was heathen. True, the world now professes to be Christian, but will anyone say that this Christian world is of the Spirit of Christ? Are its general qualities the qualities of Christ? Are the passions of sensuality, self-centeredness, pride, covetousness, ambition, and vainglory, less contrary to the spirit of the Gospel now, among Christians, than when they were among heathens? Or will you say that the tempers and passions of the heathen world are lost and gone?

Consider what is meant by the words, *the world*. John described it for us in 1 John 2:16:

> *All that is in the world, the lust of the flesh,*
> *and the lust of the eyes, and the pride of life,*
> *is not of the Father, but is of the world.*

This is an exact and full description of the world. After reading these words, will you say that this world has become Christian? The world we live in now is the same world that John condemned as being not of the Father. If all this still exists, then the same world is now in existence, and it is the same enemy to Christianity that it was in John's time.

Therefore, whether it openly professes or persecutes Christianity, it is still just as contrary to the true spirit and holiness of the Gospel. Indeed, by professing Christianity, the world is so far from being a less dangerous enemy than it was before, that it has destroyed more Christians than it ever did by the most violent persecution. We must, therefore, be far from considering the world as in a state of less enmity and opposition to Christianity than it was in the first times of the Gospel; we must, instead, guard against it as a greater and more dangerous enemy now than it was in those times.

It is a greater enemy because it has greater power over Christians by its favors, riches, honors, rewards, and protection, than it had by the fire and fury of its persecutions. It is a more dangerous enemy by having lost its appearance of enmity. Its outward profession of Christianity makes it no longer considered as an enemy, and therefore most people are easily persuaded to resign themselves to be governed and directed by it.

How many consciences are not awakened because they sin under the authority of the Christian world! How many directions of the Gospel lie disregarded, and how indifferently some people read them, because the rest of the Christian world seems to disregard them! How many conformities people make to the Christian world, without any hesitation or remorse—conformities that would have been refused as contrary to the holiness of Christianity, if they had been required of them only by heathens!

Many people are content with seeing how contrary their lives are to the Gospel, because they see that they live as the Christian world does. How could anyone who reads the Gospel need to be persuaded of the great necessity of self-denial, humility, and poverty of spirit, unless the authority of the world had banished the doctrine of the Cross? There is nothing, therefore, that a good Christian ought to be more suspicious of, or to more constantly guard against, than the authority of the Christian world. All the passages of Scripture that represent the world as contrary to Christianity, that require our separation from it as from a mammon of unrighteousness (Luke 16:9), a monster of iniquity, are all to be taken in the same strict sense in relation to the present world. For the change that the world has undergone has only altered its methods, not lessened its power, of destroying religion.

Christians had nothing to fear from the heathen world but the loss of their lives; however, the world became a friend, and made it difficult for them to save their religion. When pride, sensuality, covetousness, and ambition had only the authority of the heathen world, Christians were made more intent upon the contrary virtues. Yet, when pride, sensuality, covetousness, and ambition have the authority of the Christian world, then private Christians are in the utmost danger, not only of being ashamed out of the practice of, but of losing the very notion of, the piety of the Gospel.

There is, therefore, hardly any possibility of saving yourself from the present world, unless you consider it the same wicked enemy to all true holiness as it was in the Scriptures; unless you are convinced it is as dangerous to conform to the attitudes and passions of the world now that it is Christian as when it was heathen.

Ask yourself, "Is the piety, the humility, the sobriety of the Christian world, the same piety, humility, and sobriety of the Christian spirit?" And if it is not, how can you be more ruined by any world, than by conforming to that which is considered Christian? In every order and position of life, whether in learning or business, church or state, you cannot live up to the spirit of religion without renouncing the most general qualities and behavior of those who are of the same order and business as you are.

Does a man need to do more to make his soul unfit for the mercy of God, than be greedy and ambitious? Yet, how can a man renounce this disposition without renouncing the spirit and disposition of the world in which he lives? Along the same lines, how can a man be made more incapable of the Spirit of Christ, than by a wrong regard for money? And yet, he could not be more wrong in his value of it if he followed the authority of the Christian world.

Human prudence seems to talk wisely about the necessity of avoiding minute details, yet the one who dares not be so particular because he thinks it is a weakness, will often be obliged to avoid the most substantial duties of Christian piety.

The reflections in this chapter will, I hope, help you to break through those difficulties and resist those temptations that the authority and fashion of the world have raised against the practice of Christian humility.

Chapter Seventeen

A WAY OF LIFE FOR EVERYONE

Perhaps some people will think that the hours of prayer come too frequently, that they can only be observed by people of great leisure, and should not be pressed upon the majority of men, who have the cares of families and employments, nor upon the upper classes, whose state and position in the world cannot allow this frequency of devotion; and that it is only fit for monasteries and nunneries, or for people who have no more to do in the world than monks and nuns.

My response to this argument is that this method of devotion is not pressed upon any sort of people as absolutely necessary; but it is recommended to all people as the best, the happiest, and the most perfect way of life. If a great and exemplary devotion is as much the greatest happiness and perfection of a merchant, a soldier, or a man of quality, as it is the greatest happiness and perfection of the most retired, contemplative life, then it is as proper to recommend it without any modifications to every order of men, because happiness and perfection are of the same worth and value to all people.

The gentleman and the tradesman may, indeed, spend much of their time differently from the pious monk in the monastery or the contemplative hermit in the desert. Even so, the monk and the hermit will lose the meaning of such retirement unless they make it all serviceable to devotion. Thus, the gentleman and businessman fail to live up to the greatest ends of a more social life, and they live to their loss in the world, unless devotion is their chief and governing temper.

It is certainly very creditable for people to engage in trades and employments; it is reasonable for people to manage well their estates and families, and to find proper refreshment for themselves. However, every gentleman and tradesman, if he does not live more to piety and devotion than to anything else in the world, loses the greatest happiness of his creation, and he is robbed of something that is greater than all employments, distinctions, and pleasures of the world.

Therefore, no excuses can be made here for men of business and reputation in the world. First, because we cannot excuse them from the greatest meaning of living, we cannot give them reasons for making themselves less beneficial and less serviceable to God and the world.

Secondly, most businesspeople engage too far in worldly matters, much farther than the reasons of human life or the necessities of the world require. Merchants and tradesmen, for instance, are generally ten times farther engaged in business than they need to be; this is so far from being a reasonable excuse for their lack of time for devotion, that it is a crime, and must be censured as a blamable instance of covetousness and ambition.

The gentry and people of status either give themselves up to state employments, or to the gratifications of their passions, in a life of gaiety and debauchery. If these things can be considered as allowable diversions from devotion, then devotion must be considered a poor circumstance of life. Unless gentlemen can show that they have another God than the Father of our Lord Jesus Christ; another nature than that which is derived from Adam; another religion than Christianity; it is in vain to plead their state and dignity and pleasures as reasons for not preparing their souls for God by a strict and regular devotion.

For since piety and devotion are the common, unchangeable means of saving all the souls in the world that will be saved, there is nothing left for the gentleman, the soldier, and the tradesman, but to take care, by prayer and watchfulness, by meditation and heedfulness, that their various positions are made into positions of exact and solid piety. Devotion is not only the best and most desirable practice in a monastery, but it is also the best and most desirable practice of men in every state of life. Those who desire to be excused from it because they are men in business or in the upper classes, are no wiser than those who desire to be excused from health and happiness for the same reasons.

I cannot see why every gentleman, merchant, or soldier should not put these questions seriously to himself:

* What is the best thing for me to intend and drive at in all my actions?
* What will I do to make the most of human life?
* What ways will I wish that I had taken, when I am leaving the world?

Now, to be this wise and to make use of our reason in this way, seems to be but a small and necessary piece of wisdom. For how can we pretend to have any sense and judgment, if we dare not seriously consider and answer and govern our lives by that which such questions require of us? Yet, if people will live in so much ignorance as never to ask themselves these questions, but they continue in quest of they know not what, nor why, without ever considering the worth, value, or tendency of their actions, without considering what God, reason, eternity, and their own happiness require of them—then it is for the honor of devotion that none but those who are thus thoughtless, who dare not inquire after that which is the best and most worthy of their choice, can neglect it.

Will a nobleman think his birth too high a dignity to condescend to such questions as these? Or will a tradesman think his business too great, to take any care about himself? If devotion is not a greater advantage to a man than anything else that he can do in its stead; if devotion does not procure an infinitely greater good than can be got by neglecting it; then there is no use in it.

You would think it very absurd for a man not to value his own health because he was not a physician. Yet, it is more absurd to neglect the improvement of your soul in piety because you are not an apostle or a bishop. Consider this text of Scripture:

If ye live after the flesh, ye shall die: but if ye through the Spirit do mortify the deeds of the body, ye shall live. For as many as are led by the Spirit of God, they are the sons of God. (Rom. 8:13–14)

Do you think that this Scripture does not equally relate to all mankind? Can you find any exception here for men of fame and fortune? Is not a spiritual and devout life here made the common condition on which all men are to become sons of God? Will you leave hours of prayer and rules of devotion to particular states of life, when nothing but the same spirit of devotion can save you, or any man, from eternal death?

Consider this text:

> For we must all appear before the judgment seat of Christ; that every one may receive the things done in his body, according to that he hath done, whether it be good or bad.
>
> (2 Cor. 5:10)

Now, if something about your life could excuse you from appearing before this judgment seat, if your fame could protect you from receiving according to your works, there would be some pretense for your leaving devotion to other people. However, if you, who are now distinguished, must then appear naked among common souls, without any other distinction from others but such as your virtues or sins give you, does it not concern you, as much as any prophet or apostle, to make the best provision for the best rewards at that great Day?

Again, consider this doctrine of the apostle: "For none of us," that is, none of us Christians,

> liveth to himself, and no man dieth to himself. For whether we live, we live unto the Lord; and whether we die, we die unto the Lord....For to this end Christ both died, and rose, and revived, that he might be Lord both of the dead and living. (Rom. 14:7–9)

Is anyone an exception to the doctrine of this text? Will you, because of your condition, leave it to any particular sort of people to live and die unto

Christ? If so, you must also leave it to them to be redeemed by the death and resurrection of Christ. For the doctrine of the text is that Christ died and rose again so that none of us should live to himself. It is not that priests or apostles or monks or hermits should live no longer to themselves, but that none of us, that is, no Christian of any state whatsoever, should live unto himself.

If, therefore, there are any instances of piety, any rules of devotion, that you can neglect and yet live as truly unto Christ as if you observed them, this text calls you to no such devotion. If you neglect such devotion for any worldly consideration, that you may live more to your own mind and taste, more to the fashions and ways of the world, then you forsake the terms on which all Christians are to receive the benefit of Christ's death and resurrection.

Furthermore, observe how the same doctrine was taught by Peter: "As he which hath called you is holy, so be ye holy in all manner of conversation" (1 Pet. 1:15). If, therefore, you are one of those who are here called, you see what it is that you are called to. You are not called to have a religion suitable to your opinions, your business, or your pleasures; you are not called to a particular sort of piety that may be sufficient for gentlemen of fame or much property. Instead, you are called, first, to be holy, as "he which hath called you is holy"; secondly, you are called to be "holy in all manner of conversation," that is, to carry this spirit and degree of holiness into every part of your life.

The reason that the apostle immediately gives as to why this spirit of holiness must be the common spirit of Christians, is very affecting; it equally calls upon all sorts of Christians. In 1 Peter 1:18–19, we read,

> *Forasmuch as ye know that ye were not redeemed with corruptible things, as silver and gold, from your vain conversation...but with the precious blood of Christ.*

It is as if he said, "You know you were made capable of this state of holiness, brought into a society with Christ, and made heirs of His glory, not by any human means, but by a mysterious instance of love that infinitely exceeds everything that can be thought of in this world. Since God has redeemed you to Himself, how base and shameful it must be if you do not henceforth devote yourselves wholly to the glory of God, and become holy, as He who has called you is holy!"

If, therefore, you consider your fame and fortune; or if, in the words of the text, you consider your gold and silver and the corruptible things of this life, as any reason why you may live to your own humor and fancy, why you may neglect a life of strict piety and great devotion; if you think anything in the world can be an excuse for your not imitating the holiness of Christ in the whole course and form of your life; then you make yourself as guilty as if you neglected the holiness of Christianity for the sake of gathering straw.

For the greatness of this new state of life, to which we are called in Christ Jesus (1 Pet. 5:10) in order to be forever "as the angels of God in heaven" (Matt. 22:30), and the greatness of the price by which we are made capable of this state of glory, has turned everything that is worldly, temporal, and corruptible into an equal littleness.

Thus, it is great baseness and folly, and a contempt of the blood of Christ, to neglect any degrees of holiness because you are a man of some estate and quality.

In 1 Corinthians 6, Paul asked,

> *Know ye not that your body is the temple of the Holy Ghost which is in you...and ye are not your own? For ye are bought with a price: therefore glorify God in your body, and in your spirit, which are God's.*
>
> *(1 Cor. 6:19–20)*

How poorly you have read the Scriptures, how little you know of Christianity, if you can yet talk of your estate and condition as a pretense for a freer kind of life. Are you any more your own than one who has no state or dignity in the world? Must lowly people preserve their bodies as temples of the Holy Spirit by watching, fasting, and prayer, while you indulge yours in idleness, lusts, and sensuality because you have much property or some title of distinction? How poor and ignorant are such thoughts as these!

And yet, if you cannot think in this way, you must acknowledge that the holiness of saints, prophets, and apostles, is the holiness that you are to seek with all the diligence and care that you can. For if you leave it to others to live in piety and devotion—in the kind of self-denial, humility, and temperance that renders them able to glorify God in their bodies and in their spirits—then you must also leave it to them to have the benefit of the blood of Christ.

Perhaps you have often heard the following words of Paul to the Thessalonians, without ever thinking how much they require of you:

> *Ye know how we exhorted and comforted*
> *and charged every one of you...that ye would*
> *walk worthy of God, who hath called you*
> *unto his kingdom and glory.*
>
> *(1 Thess. 2:11–12)*

And yet, you cannot consider them without perceiving to what a high state of holiness they call you.

For how can the holiness of the Christian life be set before you in higher terms than walking worthy of God? Can you think of any abatements of virtue, any neglects of devotion, that are consistent with a life that is worthy of God? Can you suppose that any man can walk in this manner unless he watches all his steps and considers how everything he does may be done in the spirit of holiness? To whatever height these expressions may carry this holiness, it is here plainly made the necessary holiness of all Christians; for the apostle does not here exhort his fellow apostles and saints to this holiness, but he commands all Christians to endeavor after it. "We...charged every one of you," he said, "that ye would walk worthy of God, who hath called you unto his kingdom and glory."

Also note what Peter said:

> *If any man speak, let him speak as the ora-*
> *cles of God; if any man minister, let him do*
> *it as of the ability which God giveth: that*
> *God in all things may be glorified through*
> *Jesus Christ.*   *(1 Pet. 4:11)*

From this, do you not plainly perceive your high calling? Is not the one who speaks to have such regard to his words, that he appears to speak by the direction of God? Is not the one who gives to give in such a way that whatever he disposes of may appear to be a gift received from God? And is not all this to be done that God may be glorified in all things?

Must not every man of nobility, dignity of state, or reputation in the world, use his nobility and fame as the gifts of God, for the greater setting forth of His glory? Is there anything contrived or far-fetched in this conclusion? Do the words plainly intend that everything in life is to be made a matter of holiness unto God? If so, then your estate and dignity are so far from excusing you from great piety and holiness of life, that they lay you under a greater necessity of living more to the glory of God, because you have more of His gifts that may be made serviceable to it.

Therefore, if people of fame and fortune leave great piety and eminent devotion to any particular orders of men or to those they think have little else to do, they also leave the kingdom of God to them. For it is the purpose of Christianity to redeem all orders of men into one holy society, that rich and poor, high and low, may in one and the same spirit of piety become

a chosen generation, a royal priesthood, an holy nation, a peculiar people; that [are to] show forth the praises of him who hath called [them] out of darkness into his marvellous light. (1 Pet. 2:9)

Great devotion and holiness are not to be left to any particular sort of people, but they are to be the common spirit of all who desire to live up to the terms of common Christianity.

Chapter Eighteen

LOVE DEMONSTRATED TO ALL

I now proceed to consider the nature and necessity of universal love, which is here recommended to be the subject of your devotion at twelve o'clock, or at what the Scriptures call the sixth hour of the day. You are also called at this time to intercession, the most proper exercise to raise and preserve that love.

By *intercession* I mean praying to God and interceding with Him for our fellow creatures. Our blessed Lord has given His love to us as the pattern and example of our love to one another. Therefore, as He is continually making intercession for us all (Rom. 8:27), so ought we to intercede and pray for one another. He says,

> *A new commandment I give unto you, That ye love one another; as I have loved you, that ye also love one another. By this shall all men know that ye are my disciples, if ye have love one to another.* (John 13:34–35)

The newness of this precept was not that men were commanded to love one another; for this was an old precept, both of the law of Moses and of nature. But it was new in this respect, that it was to imitate a new and, until then, unheard-of example of love; it was to love one another as Christ has loved us. If men are to know that we are disciples of Christ by our love for one another, according to His new example, then if we are void of this love, we make it plainly known unto men that we are not His disciples.

There is no principle of the heart that is more acceptable to God than a universal, fervent love to all mankind, wishing and praying for their happiness. This is because there is no principle of the heart that makes us more like God, who is love (1 John 4:8) and goodness itself (Mark 10:18), and created all beings for their enjoyment of happiness. The highest notion, therefore, that we can form of man is when we imagine him to be like God in this respect, as far he can be—using all his infinite faculties, whether of wisdom, power, or prayers, for the common good of all his fellow creatures; heartily desiring that they may have all the happiness they are capable of, and as many benefits and assistances from him as his position in the world will permit him to give them.

On the other hand, what baseness and iniquity there is in all instances of hatred, envy, spite, and ill will, if we consider that every instance of them is in opposition to God, intending mischief and harm to those creatures that God favors and protects and preserves for their happiness! An ill-natured man among God's creatures is the most perverse creature in the world, acting contrary to that love by which he himself subsists, which alone gives subsistence to the variety of beings that enjoy life in any part of the creation. "Whatsoever ye would that men should do to you, do ye even so to them" (Matt. 7:12).

For love is the measure of our actions toward ourselves, and we can never act in the same manner toward other people until we look upon them with that love with which we look upon ourselves. We cannot be disposed toward others as we are toward ourselves, until we universally renounce all instances of spite, envy, and ill will, even in the smallest degrees.

If we had in our eyes any imperfection that made us see any one thing wrong, for the same reason they would show us a hundred things wrong. In the same way, if we have any disposition of our hearts that makes us envious or spiteful or ill-natured toward anyone, the same disposition will make us envious, spiteful, and ill-natured toward a great many more. If, therefore, we desire this divine virtue of love, we must exercise our hearts in the practice of love for all, because it is not Christian love until it is the love of everyone.

A love that is not universal may indeed have tenderness and affection, but it has nothing of righteousness or piety in it: it is but self-pleasing passion, or interest, or the kind of love that heathens practice. For it is as much a law of Christ to treat everybody as your neighbor, and to love your neighbor as yourself, as it is a law of Christ to abstain from theft.

If a man could keep this whole law of love, and yet offend in one point, he would be guilty of all (James 2:10). As one allowed instance of injustice destroys the justice of all our other actions, so one allowed instance of envy, spite, and ill will renders all our other acts of benevolence and affection worth nothing.

Now, the noblest motive for this universal tenderness and affection is founded in this doctrine: "God is love; and he that dwelleth in love dwelleth in God" (1 John 4:16). Who, therefore, whose heart has any tendency toward God, would not aspire after this divine temper that so changes and exalts our nature into a union with Him? We ought to rejoice in the exercise and practice of this love that is so pure and universal that it imitates the love that God bears to all His creatures.

God wills the happiness of all beings, though it is no happiness to Himself. Therefore, we must desire the happiness of all beings, though no happiness comes to us from it. God delights equally in the perfections of all His creatures; therefore, we should rejoice in those perfections, wherever we see them, and be as delighted to have other people as perfect as ourselves.

As God forgives all and gives grace to all, so we should forgive all those injuries and affronts that we receive from others, and do all the good that we can to them. God Almighty, besides His own great example of love, which ought to draw all His creatures after it, has so provided for us and made our happiness so common to everyone, that we have no occasion to envy or hate one another. As we cannot be happy but in the enjoyment of God, so we cannot rival or rob one another of this happiness. And, in regard to the enjoyments and prosperities of this life, they are so little in themselves, so foreign to our happiness, and, generally speaking, so contrary to that which they appear to be, that they are no foundation for envy, spite, or hatred.

How silly it would be to envy a man who was drinking poison out of a golden cup! And yet, who can say that he is any wiser than one who envies any instance of worldly greatness? How many saints has adversity sent to heaven! And how many poor sinners has prosperity plunged into everlasting misery! A man may seem to be in the most glorious state when he has conquered, disgraced, and humbled his enemy; however, it may be that same conquest that has saved his adversary and ruined himself.

A woman who is envied for her beauty may perhaps owe all her misery to it; and another may be forever happy, for having had no admirers at all. One man succeeds in everything, and then loses all; another meets with nothing but losses and disappointments, and thereby gains more than all the world is worth. (See Matthew 16:26 and 19:30.)

How envied was Alexander, when, conquering the world, he built towns, set up his statues, and left marks of his glory in so many kingdoms! And how despised was the poor preacher Paul, when he was beaten with rods (2 Cor. 11:25)! And yet, how strangely was the world mistaken in their judgment! How much Paul was to be envied; how much Alexander was to be pitied! Thus, we see that the different conditions of this life have nothing in them to excite our uneasy passions, nothing that can reasonably interrupt our love and affection to one another. This being said, let us turn our attention to another motive for this universal love.

Our power of doing external acts of love and goodness is often very narrow and restrained. There are, it may be, few people to whom we can contribute any worldly relief. However, while our outward means of doing good are often limited in this way, yet, if our hearts are full of love and goodness, we get, as it were, an infinite power, because God will attribute to us those good works, those acts of love, and those tender charities that we sincerely desired, and would gladly have performed, had it been in our power.

You cannot heal all the sick or relieve all the poor; you cannot comfort all in distress or be a father to all the fatherless; you cannot, it may be, deliver many from their misfortunes or teach them to find comfort in God. Nevertheless, if there is a love and tenderness in your heart, that delights in these good works and excites you to do all that you can; if your love has no bounds, but continually wishes and prays for the relief and happiness of all who are in distress; you will be received by God as a benefactor to those who have had nothing from you but your good will and tender affections.

You cannot build hospitals for the incurable; you cannot erect monasteries for the education of persons in holy solitude, continual prayer, and self-denial. However, if you join in your heart with those who do, and thank God for their pious designs; if you are a friend to these great friends to mankind, and rejoice in their eminent virtues; you will be received by God as a sharer of those good works that, though they had none of your hands, yet had all your heart. This consideration is sufficient to make us watch over our hearts with all diligence, to study the improvement of our inward dispositions, and to aspire after every height and perfection of a loving, charitable, and benevolent mind.

On the other hand, there is a great evil and mischief in all wrong turns of mind—in envy, spite, hatred, and ill will. For if the goodness of our hearts could entitle us to the reward of good actions that we never performed, then the badness of our hearts, our envy, ill nature, and hatred, will certainly bring us under the guilt of actions that we have never committed. As he that lusts after a woman will be considered an adulterer, though he has only committed the crime in his heart (Matt. 5:28), so the malicious, spiteful, ill-natured man, who only secretly rejoices at evil, will be considered a murderer, though he has shed no blood.

Therefore, since our hearts are always naked and open to the eyes of God, and because they give such an exceeding extent and increase either to our vices or virtues, it is our best and greatest business to govern the motions of our hearts, to watch, correct, and improve the inward state and quality of our souls. And there is nothing that exalts our souls so much as this heavenly love: it cleanses and purifies like a holy fire, and all ill tempers fall away before it. It makes room for all virtues and carries them to their greatest height. Everything that is good and holy grows out of it, and it becomes a continual source of all holy desires and pious practices.

By *love* I do not mean any natural tenderness, which is more or less in people according to their constitutions; but I mean a larger principle of the soul, founded in reason and piety, which makes us tender, kind, and benevolent to all our fellow creatures, as creatures of God, and for His sake. It is this love—which loves all things in God as the images of His power, as the creatures of His goodness, as parts of His family, and as members of His society—that becomes a holy principle of all great and good actions.

The love of our neighbor is only a branch of our love to God. When we love God with all our hearts, and with all our souls, and with all our strength (Mark 12:30), our love for those beings that are so nearly related to God, that have everything from Him and are created by Him to be objects of His own eternal love, will follow. If I hate or despise any one man in the world, I hate something that God cannot hate, and I despise what He loves. Can I think that I love God with all my heart, while I hate what belongs only to God, has no other master but Him, bears His image, is part of His family, and exists only by the continuance of His love toward it? It was the impossibility of this that made John say, "If a man say, I love God, and hateth his brother, he is a liar" (1 John 4:20).

In this way, we may see that no love is holy or religious until it becomes universal. For if religion requires me to love all persons as God's creatures that belong to Him, that bear His image, enjoy His protection, and make up parts of His family and household; if these are the great and necessary reasons why I should live in love and friendship with every man in the world; then I offend all these reasons whenever I lack love toward any one man. The sin of hating or despising any one man is like the sin of hating all God's creation; and the necessity of loving any one man is the same necessity of loving every man in the world.

Many people may appear to us ever so sinful, repulsive, or strange in their conduct, yet we must never look upon that as the least motive for any contempt or disregard of them. Rather, we must look upon them with compassion, as if they are in the most pitiable condition that can be. The sins of the world made the Son of God become a compassionate, suffering Advocate for all mankind. Therefore, no one is of the Spirit of Christ except he that has the utmost compassion for sinners. There is no greater sign of your own perfection than when you find yourself entirely full of love and compassion toward those who are very weak and defective.

On the other hand, you never have more reason to be displeased with yourself than when you find yourself angry and offended at the behavior of others. All sin is certainly to be hated and abhorred, wherever it is; but we must set ourselves against sin, as we do against sickness and diseases, by showing ourselves tender and compassionate to the sick and diseased. All other hatred of sin that does not fill the heart with the softest, tenderest affections toward persons miserable in it, is the servant of sin at the same time that it seems to be hating it.

A man naturally imagines that it is his own love of virtue that makes him not able to bear with those who lack it. When he abhors one man, despises another, and cannot bear the name of a third, he supposes it all to be a proof of his own high sense of virtue and his just hatred of sin. He needs no other cure for this way of thinking than this one reflection: if this had been the spirit of the Son of God, if He had hated sin in this manner, there would have been no redemption of the world; if, day and night, God had hated sinners in this manner, the world itself would have ceased long ago.

Therefore, we may take for certain, that the more we partake of the divine nature, the more improved we are ourselves; and the higher our sense of virtue is, the more we will pity those who lack it. The sight of such people will then, instead of raising in us a haughty contempt or peevish indignation toward them, fill us with the kind of compassion we have when we see the miseries of a hospital. Therefore, so that the follies, crimes, and ill behavior of our fellow creatures may not lessen that love and tenderness that we are to have for all mankind, we should often consider the reasons on which the duty of love is founded.

We are not told to love our neighbors, that is, all mankind, because they are wise, holy, virtuous, or well behaved; all mankind neither ever was, nor ever will be so. Indeed, the reason of our being obliged to love them is not founded in their virtue; if it were, we would have no rule to proceed by; for, generally speaking, we are very poor judges of the virtue and merit of other people. We can be sure that the virtue or merit of persons is not the reason of our being obliged to love them, because we are commanded to pay the highest instances of love to our worst enemies: we are to love and bless and pray for those who most injuriously treat us (Matt. 5:44).

Furthermore, let us consider what that love is that we owe to our neighbor. It is to love him as ourselves, that is, to have all those sentiments toward him that we have toward ourselves; to wish him everything that we may lawfully wish to ourselves; to be glad of every good, and sorry for every evil, that happens to him; and to be ready to do him such acts of kindness as we are always ready to do to ourselves. This love, you see, is nothing but a love of benevolence; it requires nothing of us except the good wishes, tender affections, and acts of kindness that we show to ourselves. This is the love that we owe to the best of men, and to the worst or most unreasonable man in the world.

Now, what are the reasons why we are to love every man in this manner? Our obligation to love all men is founded upon many reasons.

First, by reason of equity, every man is of the same nature and in the same condition as ourselves. Therefore, if it is just to love ourselves in this manner, it must be unjust to deny any degree of this love to others.

Another reason for this love is founded in the authority of God, who has commanded us to love every man as ourselves (Matt. 19:19).

Thirdly, we are obliged to this love in imitation of God's goodness, that we "may be children of [our] Father which is in heaven," who wills the happiness of all His creatures and "maketh his sun to rise on the evil and on the good" (Matt. 5:45).

Fourthly, our redemption by Jesus Christ, who came from heaven and laid down His life out of love to the whole sinful world, calls us to the exercise of this love.

Fifthly, we must love in this manner by the command of our Lord and Savior, who has required us to love one another as He has loved us (John 13:34).

These are the great, perpetual reasons on which our obligation to love all mankind as ourselves is founded. These reasons never vary or change, and so at all times we are obliged to demonstrate this love to all persons. God loves us, not because we are wise and good and holy, but in pity of us because we lack this happiness. Our love, therefore, must take this course, not looking for or requiring the merit of our fellow Christians, but pitying their disorders and wishing them all the good that they need and are capable of receiving.

It appears, from what has been said, that the love that we owe to our fellow believers is only a love of benevolence. This duty of benevolence is founded upon reasons that never vary or change, that have no dependence upon the qualities of persons. It follows that it is the same great sin to lack this love toward a bad man as to lack it toward a good man. Therefore, when you let loose any ill-natured passion, either of hatred or contempt, toward one you suppose to be a bad man, consider what you would think of another that was doing the same toward a good man, and be assured that you are committing the same sin.

You will perhaps say, "How is it possible to love a good and a bad man in the same degree?" Do you find it difficult to show justice and faithfulness to a bad man? Do you doubt whether you need to be as just and faithful to him as you need be to a good man? Why is it that you are in no doubt about it? It is because you know that justice and faithfulness are founded upon reasons that never vary or change, that have no dependence upon the merits of men, but are founded in the nature of things, in the laws of God, and are to be observed with an equal exactness toward good and bad men. If you will think about this in regard to your neighbor, you will find it possible to perform the same exact charity, the same exact justice, to all men, whether good or bad.

You will, perhaps, further ask, "Am I not to have a particular esteem, veneration, and reverence for good men?" Yes, but this high esteem and veneration is very different from that love of benevolence that we owe to our neighbors. The high esteem and veneration that you have for a man of eminent piety, is no act of charity to him—it is not out of pity and compassion that you so reverence him; rather, it is an act of charity to yourself, that such esteem and veneration may excite you to follow his example. We do not love virtue with the love of benevolence, as anything that needs our good wishes, but as something that is our proper good.

The whole of the matter is this: the actions that you are to love, esteem, and admire are the actions of good and pious men; but the persons to whom you are to do all the good you can, in all sorts of kindness and compassion, are all persons, whether good or bad. This distinction between the love of benevolence, and esteem or veneration, is very plain and obvious: no man is to have a high regard or honor for his own accomplishments or behavior; yet every man is to love himself, that is, to wish well to himself.

If you think it hardly possible to dislike the actions of unreasonable men and still have a true love for them, consider this in relation to yourself. It is very possible, I hope, for you not only to dislike, but also to detest and abhor a great many of your own past actions, and to accuse yourself of great folly for them. However, do you then lose any of those tender sentiments toward yourself that you used to have? Do you then cease to wish well to yourself? Is not the love of yourself as strong as at any other time?

At the same time, what is possible in this way with ourselves, is in the same manner possible with others. We may have the highest good wishes toward them, desiring for them every good that we desire for ourselves, and yet, at the same time, dislike their way of life. Remember, all the love that we may justly have for ourselves, we are, in strict justice, obliged to exercise toward all other men. We offend the great law of our nature, and the greatest laws of God, when our attitudes toward others are different from those we have toward ourselves. If, therefore, you do not feel these kind dispositions toward all other people, you may be assured that you are not in that state of love that is the very life and soul of Christian piety.

You know how it hurts you to be made the jest and ridicule of other people, how it grieves you to be robbed of your reputation and deprived of the favorable opinion of your neighbors. If, therefore, you expose others to scorn and contempt in any degree, if it pleases you to see or hear of their frailties and infirmities, or if you are hardly reluctant to conceal their faults, then you are far from loving such people as yourself. For such attitudes are as truly the proper fruits of hatred as the contrary attitudes are the proper fruits of love. Just as it is a certain sign that you love yourself because you are sensitive about everything that concerns you, so it is as certain a sign that you hate your neighbor when you are pleased with anything that hurts him.

But, now, if the need for a true and exact love is so great that, as Paul said, it renders our greatest virtues as "sounding brass, or a tinkling cymbal" (1 Cor. 13:1), how highly it concerns us to study every art and to practice every method of raising our souls to this state of love! It is for this reason that you must not let this noon hour of prayer pass without a full and solemn supplication to God for a universal love and benevolence to all mankind. Such daily, constant devotion is the only likely means of preserving you in a state of love necessary to prove you to be a true follower of Jesus Christ.

Chapter Nineteen

THE NECESSITY OF INTERCESSION

It is very evident from Scripture that intercession is a great and necessary part of Christian devotion. The first followers of Christ seemed to support all their love and maintain all their conversation and correspondence by mutual prayers for one another. The apostle Paul, whether he wrote to churches or particular persons, showed his intercession to be perpetual for them; they were the constant subject of his prayers. He wrote to the Philippians,

> I thank my God upon every remembrance of you, always in every prayer of mine for you all making request with joy.   (Phil. 1:3–4)

Here, we see a continual intercession performed with so much gladness, that it was an exercise of love in which he highly rejoiced.

His devotion also had the same care for particular persons, which is shown by the following passage:

> I thank God, whom I serve from my forefathers with pure conscience, that without ceasing I have remembrance of thee in my prayers night and day.   (2 Tim. 1:3)

How holy an acquaintance and friendship this was; how worthy of persons who were raised above the world and related to one another as new members of a kingdom of heaven!

Apostles and great saints did not only benefit and bless particular churches and private persons, but they themselves also received graces from God by the prayers of others. This is what Paul said to the Corinthians:

> *Ye also helping together by prayer for us, that for the gift bestowed upon us by the means of many persons thanks may be given by many on our behalf.*   *(2 Cor. 1:11)*

This was the ancient friendship of Christians, uniting and cementing their hearts together, not by worldly considerations or human passions, but by the mutual communication of spiritual blessings, by prayers and thanksgivings to God for one another.

It was this holy intercession that raised Christians to a state of mutual love that far exceeded all that had been praised and admired in human friendship. When the same spirit of intercession is again in the world, when Christianity has the same power over the hearts of people that it then had, this holy friendship will again be in fashion, and Christians will again be the wonder of the world for that exceeding love that they bear to one another.

A frequent intercession with God, earnestly beseeching Him to forgive the sins of all mankind, to bless them with His providence, enlighten them with His Spirit, and bring them to everlasting happiness, is the divinest exercise that the heart of man can be engaged in. Therefore, be daily on your knees in a solemn, deliberate performance of this devotion, praying for others in such forms, and with such length, importunity, and earnestness, as you use for yourself. You will find all little, ill-natured passions die away, and your heart will grow great and generous, delighting in the common happiness of others, as you once delighted only in your own.

One who prays daily to God that all men may be happy in heaven, will also delight in their happiness on earth. It is hardly possible for you to ask God to make anyone happy and yet be troubled to see him enjoy the much smaller gifts of God in this short and low state of human life. How strange and unnatural would it be, for instance, to ask God to grant health and a longer life to a sick man, and at the same time to envy him the simple pleasure of agreeable medicines!

We receive the greatest benefits of a general intercession when it descends to the particular instances that our state and condition in life more particularly require of us. We are to treat all mankind as neighbors, no matter the occasion; yet we can only live in the actual society of a few, and are, by our state and condition, more particularly related to some than others. Consequently, when our intercession is made an exercise of love and care for those among whom our lot is fallen, or who belong to us in a nearer relation, it then becomes the greatest benefit to ourselves and produces its best effects in our own hearts. Therefore, when you have accustomed your heart to a serious performance of this holy intercession, you will have done a great deal to render it incapable of spite and envy and to make it naturally delight in the happiness of all mankind.

It would do your heart much good for you to always change and alter your intercessions according to the needs and necessities of your neighbors or acquaintances. When you ask God to deliver them from particular evils, or to grant them particular gifts or blessings, you exercise toward such persons every virtue that so often has a place in your own prayers. This would make it easier for you to be courteous, civil, and kind to everyone around you; you would be made unable to say or do a rude or hard thing to those for whom you had been so kind and compassionate in your prayers.

There is nothing that makes us love a man so much as praying for him. (See Matthew 5:44.) If ever you can do this sincerely for any man, you have fitted your soul for the performance of everything that is kind and civil toward him. This will fill your heart with a generosity and tenderness that will give you a better and sweeter behavior than anything that is called fine upbringing and good manners. Consider yourself an advocate with God for your neighbors and acquaintances, and you will never find it hard to be at peace with them. It becomes easier for you to bear with and forgive those for whom you have particularly implored the divine mercy and forgiveness.

Such prayers as these among neighbors and acquaintances would unite them to one another in the strongest bonds of love and tenderness. It would exalt and ennoble their souls, and teach them to consider one another in a higher state, as members of a spiritual society that are created for the enjoyment of the common blessings of God, and as fellow heirs of the same future glory. By desiring that everyone should have his full share of the favors of God, we would not only be content, but glad to see one another happy in the little enjoyments of this temporary life.

Celestius[13] is a priest in a poor country village, and he is full of the spirit of the Gospel. Every soul in the village is as dear to him as himself, and he prays for them all as often as he prays for himself. His whole life is one continual exercise of great zeal and labor; he is hardly ever satisfied with any degrees of care and watchfulness, because he has learned the great value of souls by so often appearing before God as an intercessor for them.

He never thinks he can love or do enough for the members of his flock, because he never considers them as anything but people who, by receiving the gifts and graces of God, are to become his hope, his joy, and his crown of rejoicing (1 Thess. 2:19). He goes about his parish and visits everybody in it, but he visits in the same spirit of piety that he preaches to them: he visits them to encourage their virtues, to assist them with his advice and counsel, to discover their manner of life, and to know the state of their souls, that he may intercede with God for them according to their particular needs.

When Celestius first entered into holy orders, he had a haughtiness in his temperament and a great contempt and disregard for all foolish and unreasonable people. When he first came to his little village, it was as disagreeable to him as a prison, and every day seemed too tedious to be endured in so retired a place. He thought his parish was too full of poor and lowly people, and that none of them were fit for the conversation of a gentleman. However, he has prayed away this attitude, and now has the greatest tenderness for the

---

[13]Celestius: heavenly.

most obstinate sinners. Now his days are far from being tedious, and the solitude of his little parish has become a matter of great comfort to him, because he hopes that God has placed him and his flock there to make it their way to heaven.

His prayers for others have altered and amended the state of his own heart. He now thinks the poorest creature in his parish great enough to deserve the humblest attendances, the kindest friendships, and the tenderest services he can possibly show them. He is now daily watching over the weak and infirm, humbling himself to perverse, rude, and ignorant people, wherever he can find them; and he desires to be used as the servant of all. In the spirit of his Lord and Master, he girds himself and is glad to kneel down and wash any of their feet (John 13:5–7). All these noble thoughts and divine sentiments are the effects of his great devotion; he presents every person so often before God in his prayers that he never thinks he can esteem, reverence, or serve enough, those for whom he implores so many mercies from God.

Celestius is greatly affected with this passage of Holy Scripture: "The effectual fervent prayer of a righteous man availeth much" (James 5:16). He reads how God Himself said unto Abimelech, concerning Abraham: "He is a prophet, and he shall pray for thee, and thou shalt live" (Gen. 20:7). Again, He said of Job, "And my servant Job shall pray for you: for him will I accept" (Job 42:8). From these passages Celestius justly concludes that the prayers of men who strive for piety and perfection in the Christian life, have an extraordinary power with God. This makes him practice every manner of holy living and aspire after every instance of piety and righteousness, so that his prayers for his flock may have their full force and avail much with God.

These are the favorable effects that a devout intercession has produced in the life of Celestius. If people were to imitate this example in ways that suited their particular states of life, they would certainly find the same effects from it. For instance, if parents would make themselves advocates and intercessors with God for their children, constantly applying to heaven on behalf of them, nothing would be more likely not only to bless their children, but also to form and incline their own minds to the performance of everything that is excellent and praiseworthy.

I am not implying a general remembrance of one's children, but a regular method of recommending all their particular needs and necessities to God. The state of parents is a holy state, in some degree like that of the priesthood; they are called to bless their children with their prayers and sacrifices to God. Job watched over and blessed his children; he sanctified them; he "rose up early in the morning, and offered burnt offerings according to the number of them all" (Job 1:5). If parents would daily call upon God in a solemn, deliberate manner, changing their intercessions as the state of their children required, such devotion would have a mighty influence on the rest of their own lives. It would make them very careful of how they govern themselves: prudent and heedful of everything they said or did, lest their example should hinder what they so constantly desired in their prayers.

If a father thus considered himself an intercessor with God for his children, and he prayed daily that God would inspire his children with true piety, great humility, and strict temperance, what could be more likely to make the father himself become exemplary in these virtues? How naturally he would grow ashamed of lacking the virtues that he thought necessary for his children! Such thoughts would make him avoid everything that is sinful and displeasing to God, lest when he prayed for his children, God should reject his prayers. The father's prayers for their piety would be a certain means of exalting his own to its greatest height.

How tenderly, how religiously, would such a father converse with his children, whom he considered his little spiritual flock, whose virtues he was to form by his example, encourage by his authority, nourish by his counsel, and prosper by his prayers to God for them. How fearful he would be of all greedy and unjust ways of raising their fortune, of bringing them up in pride and indulgence, or of making them too fond of the world, lest he should thereby render them incapable of those graces that he was so often asking God to grant them.

If everyone, when feeling the first approaches of resentment, envy, or contempt toward others, or in all little disagreements and misunderstandings, instead of indulging their minds with little, low reflections, if they would resort to a more particular and extraordinary intercession with God for those who raised their envy, resentment, or discontentment, this would certainly prevent the growth of all uncharitable dispositions. It would also be an excellent means of raising their hearts to the greatest state of perfection.

For instance, when you find in your heart envy toward any person, whether on account of his riches, power, reputation, learning, or advancement, if you immediately take yourself at that time to your prayers, and pray to God to bless and prosper him in that very thing that raised your envy; if you express and repeat your petitions in the strongest terms, asking God to grant him all the happiness from the enjoyment of it that can possibly be received; you will soon find it to be the best antidote in the world to expel the venom of that poisonous passion. This would be such a triumph over yourself, would so humble and reduce your heart into obedience and order, that the Devil would even be afraid of tempting you again in the same manner, when he saw the temptation turned into so great a means of amending and reforming the state of your heart.

In another case, if, in any differences or misunderstandings that you happen to have at any time with a relation, a neighbor, or anyone else, you would pray for them in a more extraordinary manner than you ever did before—asking God to give them every grace and blessing and happiness you can think of—you will have taken the speediest method possible of reconciling all differences and clearing up all misunderstandings. You will then think nothing too great to be forgiven. This would be the mighty power of such Christian devotion: it would remove all peevish passions, soften your heart into the most tender condescensions, and be the best arbitrator of all differences that happen between you and anyone else.

The greatest resentments among friends and neighbors most often arise from poor manners and little mistakes in conduct. This is a certain sign that their friendship is merely human, not founded upon religious considerations or supported by a course of mutual prayer for one another such as the first Christians used. For such devotion must necessarily either destroy such tendencies or be itself destroyed by them; you cannot possibly have any ill temper or show any unkind behavior to a man for whose welfare you are so much concerned as to be his advocate with God in private.

From this we may also learn the repulsive nature and exceeding guilt of all spite, hatred, contempt, and angry passions. They are not to be considered as defects in good nature and sweetness of spirit, nor as failings in civility of manners or good upbringing, but as such base tempers that they are entirely inconsistent with the charity of intercession.

You may think it a small matter to ridicule one man and despise another, but you should consider whether it is a small matter to lack the charity toward these people that Christians are not allowed to lack toward even their most inveterate enemies. For if you are charitable to these men, if you bless and pray for them as you are obliged to bless and pray for your enemies, then you will find that you have enough charity to make it impossible for you to treat them with any degree of scorn or contempt. For you cannot possibly despise and ridicule that man whom your private prayers recommend to the love and favor of God.

When you despise and ridicule a man, it is for no other reason but to make him ridiculous and contemptible in the eyes of other men, and in order to prevent their esteem of him. How, therefore, can it be possible for you to ask God sincerely to bless a man with the honor of His love and favor, when you desire men to treat him as worthy of their contempt? Could a nobleman, out of love to his poor neighbor, desire his king to honor the poor man with every mark of his esteem and favor, and yet, at the same time, expose the man to the scorn and derision of his own servants? Yet, this is entirely too common.

From these considerations we may plainly discover the reasonableness and justice of this doctrine of the Gospel:

> *Whosoever shall say to his brother, Raca, shall be in danger of the council: but whosoever shall say, Thou fool, shall be in danger of hell fire.* (Matt. 5:22)

We are not to believe that every hasty word or unreasonable expression that slips from us by chance or surprise, and is contrary to our intention, is the great sin mentioned in this verse. However, what is meant by "whosoever shall say...Raca" [14] and "whosoever shall say, Thou fool," is one who allows himself deliberate, designed acts of scorn and contempt toward his brother, and speaks to him and of him in reproachful language.

Now, since it appears that at the root of these dispositions is the worst uncharitableness; since no one can be guilty of them unless he does not have enough charity even to pray to God for his brother; it cannot be thought hard or rigorous justice that such dispositions endanger the salvation of Christians. For who would think it unfair that a Christian cannot obtain the favor of God for himself, unless he reverences and esteems his Christian brother as one who bears the image of God, as one for whom Christ died, as a member of Christ's

---

[14] Raca: ignorant, or empty.

body, and as a member of that holy society on earth, which is in union with that triumphant church in heaven? All these considerations are forgotten when a man treats one who has such glorious privileges as an object of scorn and contempt.

To scorn or despise a brother, or, as our blessed Lord says, to call him Raca or fool, must be looked upon as one of the most repulsive, unjust, and guilty states of mind that can be supported in the heart of a Christian, justly excluding him from all his hopes in the salvation of Jesus Christ. For to despise one for whom Christ died is to be as contrary to Christ as one who despises anything that Christ has said or done.

Imagine if a Christian who had lived with the Virgin Mary, had begun, after the death of our Lord, to treat her with contempt. You would certainly say that he had lost his piety toward our blessed Lord, for a true reverence for Christ would have forced him to treat her with respect who was so nearly related to Him. Does this not tell you that this relation of the Virgin Mary to our blessed Lord must have obliged all those who lived and conversed with her to treat her with great respect and esteem? Might not a man have justly dreaded the vengeance of God upon him for any scorn or contempt that he had shown to her?

Now, if this is plain and obvious reasoning, if a contempt of the Virgin Mary must be interpreted as a contempt of Christ because of her near relation to Him, then let the same reasoning show you the great impiety of despising any brother or sister in Christ. You cannot despise a brother without despising him as one who stands in a high relation to God, to His Son Jesus Christ, and to the Holy Trinity.

You would certainly think it a great wrong to treat with great contempt a book that had been written by the finger of God. Can it be any less of an impiety to scorn and vilify a brother or sister who is not only the workmanship (Eph. 2:10) but also in the image of God (Gen. 1:27)? You would justly think it great irreverence to scorn and trample upon an altar because it was appropriated to holy uses and had had the body of Christ so often placed upon it. Can you suppose it to be any less profane to scorn and trample upon a brother, who belongs to God in such a way that his very body is to be considered as the temple of the Holy Spirit (1 Cor. 6:19)?

If you had despised and mistreated the Virgin Mary, you would have been guilty of the impiety of despising her of whom Christ was born. And if you scorn and despise a brother, you are guilty of the impiety of despising him for whom Christ laid down His life. Now, if this scornful temper is founded upon a disregard of all these relations that every Christian bears to God and Christ and the Holy Trinity, can you think it unfair that a Christian who allows himself to despise a brother should be in danger of hell fire?

Although the great sin condemned in the words, "Whosoever shall say, Thou fool" (Matt. 5:22), and so on, is the intentional despising of a brother, we must consider that all hasty expressions and words of contempt, though spoken by surprise or accident, are by this text condemned as great sins and notorious breaches of Christian charity. They proceed from great lack of Christian love and meekness, and they call for great repentance. They are only little sins when compared to habits and settled dispositions of treating a brother spitefully, but they fall as directly under the condemnation of this text as the grossest habits of uncharitableness.

We are always to recognize our guilt and call ourselves to a strict repentance for these hasty expressions of anger and contempt, because they seldom are what they seem to be; that is, mere reactions of temper that were occasioned purely by surprise or accident, are actually much more our own acts than we imagine. One man says a number of bitter things, and he immediately forgives himself because he supposes it was only the suddenness of the occasion or something accidental that carried him so far beyond himself. However, he should consider that perhaps the accident, or surprise, was not the occasion of his angry expressions; perhaps it was only his angry temper showing itself.

Generally speaking, this is the case, because all haughty, angry language generally proceeds from some secret habits of pride in the heart. (See Matthew 12:34.) Therefore, people who are subject to it, though only now and then as accidents happen, have great reason to repent of more than their present behavior, to charge themselves with greater guilt than accidental passion, and to bring themselves to the kind of repentance and self-denial that will destroy habits of a haughty spirit.

This may be the reason why the text looks no farther than the outward language, why it only says, "Whosoever shall say, Thou fool." Few can go so far as to accidentally use haughty, disdainful language, except those whose hearts are more or less possessed with habits and settled dispositions of pride and haughtiness.

Now, returning to my point, intercession is not only the best arbitrator of all differences, the best promoter of true friendship, the best cure and preservative against all unkind tempers, all angry and haughty passions, but through it we may also discover the true state of our own hearts. There are many attitudes that we think lawful and innocent, that we never suspect of any harm; however, if they were to be tried by this devotion, they would soon show us how we have deceived ourselves.

Susurrus[15] is a pious, temperate man, constantly at the service of the church. His charity is so great that he almost starves himself to be able to give greater alms to the poor. Even so, Susurrus has had an unusual failing: he once had a strong inclination to find out all the defects and weaknesses of everyone around him. You were welcome to tell him anything about anybody, provided that you did not do it in the style of an enemy. He never disliked a man for speaking evil, unless his language was rough and passionate. If you were to whisper anything gently, though it were ever so bad in itself, Susurrus was ready to receive it.

When he visited, you generally heard him relating how sorry he was for the defects and failings of a neighbor. Of course, he was always letting you know how sensitive he was about the reputation of his neighbor, how reluctant he was to say what he was forced to say, and how gladly he would conceal it if it could be concealed. Susurrus had such a tender, compassionate manner of relating the most prejudicial things, that he seemed to be exercising a Christian charity at the same time that he was indulging a whispering, evil-speaking temperament.

---

[15]Susurrus: whisper.

He once whispered to a particular friend in great secrecy, something too terrible to be spoken of publicly. He ended by saying how glad he was that it had not yet taken wind, and that he had some hopes it might not be true, though the suspicions were very strong. His friend made him this reply:

> You say, Susurrus, that you are glad it has not yet taken wind, and that you may have some hopes it may not prove true. Go home, therefore, to your closet, and pray to God for this man in such a manner, and with such earnestness, as you would pray for yourself on the like occasion.
>
> Beseech God to interpose in his favor, to save him from false accusers, and to bring all those to shame who, by uncharitable whispers and secret stories, wound him, like those that stab in the dark. And when you have made this prayer, then you may, if you please, go tell the same secret to some other friend, that you have told to me.

Susurrus was exceedingly affected by this rebuke, and he felt the force of it upon his conscience in as lively a manner as if he had seen the books opened at the Day of Judgment (Rev. 20:12). All other arguments might have been resisted; but it was impossible for Susurrus either to reject or to follow this advice without being equally self-condemned in the highest degree.

Since that time, he has constantly practiced this method of intercession, and his heart is so entirely changed by it that he can no longer whisper anything to the prejudice of another. Whisperings and evil speaking now hurt his ears like curses, and he has appointed one day in the week to be a day of penance as long as he lives, to humble himself before God in the sorrowful confession of his former guilt.

You may wonder how a man of so much piety could be so deceived in himself as to live in such a state of scandal and evil speaking, without suspecting himself to be guilty of it. However, it was the tenderness and seeming compassion with which Susurrus heard and related everything that deceived both himself and others. This was a falseness of heart, which was only to be fully discovered by the true charity of intercession. If people of virtue, who think as little harm of themselves as Susurrus did, were to try their spirits by such an intercession, they would often find themselves to be what they suspected least of all.

I have laid before you the many great advantages of intercession. You have seen what a divine friendship would be formed among Christians by it; how dear it would render all relations and neighbors to one another; how it tends to make clergymen and parents exemplary and perfect in all the duties of their positions; how certainly it destroys all envy, spite, and ill-natured passions; how speedily it reconciles all differences; and with what a piercing light it discovers to a man the true state of his heart.

These considerations will, I hope, persuade you to make intercession the constant and chief matter of your devotions at twelve o'clock, the sixth hour of prayer.

Chapter Twenty

CONFORMING TO HIS WILL

I have recommended certain subjects to be made the fixed matter of your devotions at all the hours of prayer that have been already considered. Your first prayers in the morning are to focus on thanksgiving and the offering of yourself to God. At nine o'clock, the great virtue of Christian humility is to be the chief part of your petitions. At twelve, you are called upon to pray for all the graces of universal love, and to raise it in your heart by such general and particular intercessions as your own state and your relation to other people seem to require of you.

Now, at the ninth hour of the day, or three o'clock in the afternoon, the principal matter of your prayers ought to be resignation and conformity to the will of God. There is nothing wise, holy, or just, but the great will of God. This is as strictly true in the most rigid sense, as to say that nothing is infinite and eternal except God. Therefore, no beings, whether in heaven or on earth, can be wise, holy, or just, but insofar as they conform to the will of God. It is conformity to this will that gives virtue and perfection to the highest services of the angels in heaven; and it is conformity to the same will that makes the ordinary actions of men on earth become an acceptable service unto God.

The whole nature of virtue consists in conforming to, and the whole nature of vice in declining from, the will of God. All God's creatures are created to fulfill His will; the sun and moon obey His will by the necessity of their nature; angels conform to His will by the perfection of their nature. If, therefore, you would show yourself not to be a rebel and apostate from the order of the creation, you must act like beings both above and below you; it must be the great desire of your soul that God's will may be done by you on earth as it is done in heaven (Matt. 6:10). It must be the settled purpose and intention of your heart to will nothing, plan nothing, do nothing, but insofar as you have reason to believe that it is the will of God that you should so desire, plan, and do. (See Psalm 127:1.)

You are therefore to consider yourself as a being that has no other business in the world, but to be what God requires you to be; to have no rules of your own, to seek none of your own designs or ends, but to fill some place and act some part in strict conformity and thankful resignation to the divine pleasure. (See John 5:30.) To think that you are your own, or are at your own disposal, is as absurd as to think that you created and can preserve yourself. It is as necessary to believe you are thus God's, that you belong to Him and are to act and suffer all in a thankful resignation to His pleasure, as to believe that in Him you "live, and move, and have [your] being" (Acts 17:28).

Resignation to the divine will signifies a cheerful approval and a thankful acceptance of everything that comes from God. It is not enough to submit patiently, but we must thankfully receive and fully approve of everything that happens to us by the order of God's providence. For there is no reason why we should be patient, but what is as good and strong a reason why we should be thankful. If we were under the hands of a wise physician who could do nothing to us that was not for our benefit, it would not be enough to be patient and abstain from murmurings against such a physician. No, it would be as great a breach of duty and gratitude to him not to be pleased and thankful for what he did, as it would be to murmur against him.

Now, this is our true state with relation to God: we cannot be said so much as to believe in Him unless we believe Him to be of infinite wisdom. Every argument, therefore, for patience under His actions toward us, is as strong an argument for acceptance of and thankfulness for everything that He does to us. We need nothing more to dispose us to this gratitude toward God than a full belief in Him, that He is this Being of infinite wisdom, love, and goodness.

If you will assent to this truth in the same manner as you assent to things of which you have no doubt, then you will cheerfully approve of everything that God has already approved for you. You cannot possibly be pleased with the behavior of any person toward you, unless it is for your good, is wise in itself, and is an effect of his love and goodness toward you. Likewise, when you are satisfied that God does not only do what is wise, good, and kind, but also what is the effect of an infinite wisdom and love in the care of you, it will be as necessary as wishing your own happiness, while you have this faith, to be thankful and pleased with everything that God chooses for you.

Therefore, whenever you find yourself disposed to uneasiness or murmuring at anything that is the effect of God's providence over us, you must look upon yourself as denying either the wisdom or goodness of God, for every complaint necessarily supposes this. You would never complain about your neighbor unless you meant to show his unwise, unjust, or unkind behavior toward you. In the same way, every murmuring, impatient reflection under the providence of God is the same accusation of God. A complaint always supposes ill usage.

You may also see the great necessity and piety of this thankful state of heart in that the lack of it implies an accusation of God's lack, either of wisdom or goodness, in His actions toward us. Thankfulness is not, therefore, any high degree of perfection, founded in any uncommon nicety of thinking or refined notions, but a plain principle, founded in this plain belief, that God is a Being of infinite wisdom and goodness.

Now, this resignation to the divine will may be considered in two respects: first, as it signifies a thankful approval of God's general providence over the world; secondly, as it signifies a thankful acceptance of His particular providence over us.

First, every man is, by the law of his creation, obliged to consent to and acknowledge the wisdom and goodness of God in His general providence over the whole world. He is to believe that it is the effect of God's great wisdom and goodness that the world itself was formed at such a time and in such a manner; that the general order of nature, the whole frame of things, is contrived and formed in the best manner. He is to believe that God's providence over states and kingdoms, times and seasons, is all for the best; that the revolutions of state and changes of empire, the rise and fall of monarchies, persecutions, wars, famines, and plagues, are all permitted and conducted by God's providence to the general good of man in this state of trial.

A good man is to believe all this with the same fullness of assent as he believes that God is in every place, though he neither sees nor can comprehend the manner of His presence. This is a noble magnificence of thought, a true religious greatness of mind, to be affected with God's general providence in this manner—admiring and magnifying His wisdom in all things, never murmuring at the course of the world or the state of things, but looking all around at heaven and earth as a pleased spectator, and adoring that invisible hand that gives laws to all motions and rules over all events to ends suitable to the highest wisdom and goodness.

Every person thinks he may justly say what a wretched, abominable climate he lives in. It is very common for people to allow themselves great liberty in finding fault with things that have only God for their cause. They frequently tell you what a dismal, cursed day it is and what intolerable seasons we have. Others think they have very little to thank God for, that it is hardly worth their while to live in a world so full of changes and revolutions. Even so, these are attitudes of great impiety, and they show that religion does not yet have its place in such hearts.

Indeed, it sounds much better to murmur at the course of the world or the state of things, than to murmur at Providence; to complain about the seasons and weather than to complain about God. However, if these things have no other cause but God and His providence, it is a poor distinction to say that you are only angry at the things, but not at the Cause and Director of them.

Our Lord taught us, in the case of oaths, how the whole frame of the world is sacred, and how all things are to be considered as God's and are to be associated with Him:

> But I say unto you, Swear not at all; neither by heaven; for it is God's throne: nor by the earth; for it is his footstool: neither by Jerusalem; for it is the city of the great King. Neither shalt thou swear by thy head, because thou canst not make one hair white or black. (Matt. 5:34–36)

Here you see that all things in the whole order of nature, from the highest heavens to the smallest hair, are always to be considered, not separately as they are in themselves, but as in some relation to God. If it is good reasoning not to swear by the earth, a city, or your hair, because these things are God's, and in a certain manner they belong to Him, is it not exactly the same reasoning to say you cannot complain about the seasons of the earth, the states of cities, and the changing of times, because all these things are in the hands of God, have Him for their Author, and are directed and governed by Him as He sees fit?

If you think you can murmur against the state of things without murmuring at Providence or complain of seasons without complaining of God, hear what our blessed Lord says further about oaths:

> Whoso therefore shall swear by the altar, sweareth by it, and by all things thereon. And whoso shall swear by the temple, sweareth by it, and by him that dwelleth therein. And he that shall swear by heaven,

Now, does this Scripture not clearly oblige us to reason after this manner? Whoever complains about the course of the world also complains about the God who governs the course of the world. Whoever complains about the seasons and the weather, whoever speaks impatiently of times and events, complains and speaks impatiently about God, who is the sole Lord and Governor of times, seasons, and events.

Therefore, just as we are to have no sentiments but of praise and thanksgiving when we think of God Himself, we are to receive with the same sentiments of praise and gratitude those things that are under the direction of God and are governed by His providence. Of course, we are not to think that everything permitted by the providence of God is right, just, or lawful, because then nothing that exists by His permission could be unjust. Yet, we must adore God even in the greatest public calamities and the most grievous persecutions, such as plagues and famines, because such things are suffered for purposes suitable to His wisdom and glory in the government of the world.

There is nothing more suitable to the piety of a reasonable creature, or to the spirit of a Christian, than to approve, admire, and glorify God in all the acts of His general providence, considering the whole world as His, and all events as directed by His wisdom. Everyone seems to consent to this as an undeniable truth, that all things must be as God pleases. Is this not enough to make every man pleased with them himself?

How can a man complain about anything that is the effect of Providence, without showing that his own self-will and self-wisdom are of more weight with him than the will and wisdom of God? And what can religion be said to have done for a man whose heart is in this state?

If a man cannot thank and praise God in calamities and sufferings as much as he does in prosperity and happiness, he is far from the piety of a Christian. For to thank God only for such things as you like, is no more a proper act of piety than to believe that only what you see is an act of faith. Resignation and thanksgiving to God are only acts of piety when they are acts of faith, trust, and confidence in the divine goodness.

The faith of Abraham was an instance of true piety because it stopped at no difficulties; it was not altered or lessened by any human appearances. It first of all carried him, against all show of happiness, from his own kindred and country, into a strange land, "not knowing whither he went" (Heb. 11:8). It afterwards made him, against all appearances of nature, when he was about a hundred years old and his body was near death, depend on the promise of God, being fully persuaded that what God had promised, He was able to perform. (See Genesis 18:1–12; 21:1–3; Romans 4:16–22.) It was this same faith that, against so many pleas of nature, so many appearances of reason, prevailed upon him to offer up Isaac, "accounting that God was able to raise him up, even from the dead" (Heb. 11:19).

This faith is the true pattern of Christian resignation to the divine pleasure; you are to thank and praise God, not only for things agreeable to you, that have the appearance of happiness and comfort, but also when you are, like Abraham, called from all appearances of comfort to be a pilgrim in a strange land (Heb. 11:13), to part with an only son, being as fully persuaded of the divine goodness in all things that happen to you, as Abraham was of the divine promise when there was the least appearance of its being performed.

True Christian resignation to God requires no more to support it than the kind of plain assurance of the goodness of God that Abraham had of His truthfulness. If you ask yourself what greater reason Abraham had to depend on the divine truth than you have to depend on the divine goodness, you will find that none can be given. You cannot, therefore, look upon this as an unnecessary height of perfection, since the lack of it implies the need, not for any high notions, but for a plain and ordinary faith in the most certain doctrines both of natural and revealed religion.

I have said this much concerning resignation to the divine will: that it signifies a thankful approval of God's general providence. We will now consider it as it signifies a thankful acceptance of God's particular providence over us.

Every man is to consider himself a particular object of God's providence, under the same care and protection of God as if the world had been made for him alone. It is not by chance that any man is born at such a time, of such parents, and in such a place and condition. Rather, it is certain that every soul comes into the body at such a time and in such circumstances according to some purpose in the will of God and for some particular ends; this is as certain as that some beings are angels and others are men by the specific purpose of

God. It is as much by the counsel and eternal purpose of God that you were born in your particular state and that Isaac was the son of Abraham, as that Gabriel is an angel and Isaac was a man.

The Scriptures assure us that it was by divine appointment that our blessed Savior was born at Bethlehem, and at such a time (Matt. 2:3–6; John 7:42). Although it was because of the dignity of His person and the great importance of His birth, that much of the divine counsel was declared to the world concerning the time and manner of it, we are as sure from the same Scriptures that the time and manner of every man's birth is according to some eternal purposes and the direction of divine providence. The time, place, and circumstances are directed and governed by God for particular ends of His wisdom and goodness. (See Jeremiah 1:5; Ephesians 1:4.)

We are as certain of this from plain revelation as we can be of anything. For if we are told that not one sparrow falls to the ground without our heavenly Father's knowledge (Matt. 10:29), can anything more strongly teach us that much greater beings, such as human souls, do not come into the world without His care and direction? If it is said, "The very hairs of your head are all numbered" (Matt. 10:30), is it not to teach us that nothing, not even the smallest thing imaginable, happens to us by chance? But, if the smallest things we can conceive are declared to be under the divine direction, do we need to be, or can we be, more plainly taught that the greatest things of life, such as the manner of our coming into the world, our parents, the time, and other circumstances of our birth and condition, are all according to the eternal purposes, direction, and appointment of divine providence?

The disciples asked our Lord concerning the blind man, "Master, who did sin, this man, or his parents, that he was born blind?" (John 9:2). And He that was the eternal Wisdom of God made this answer: "Neither hath this man sinned, nor his parents: but that the works of God should be made manifest in him" (John 9:3). We gather from this verse that the particular circumstances of every man's birth, the body that he receives, and the condition and state of life into which he is born, are appointed by a secret providence, which directs all things to their particular times and seasons and manner of existence, that the wisdom and works of God may be made manifest in them all.

We are certain of our birth, time, and condition of entering into the world, and these particulars of our state are the effect of God's particular providence over us, intended for some particular ends both of His glory and our own happiness. Therefore, by the greatest obligations of gratitude, we are called upon to conform and resign our wills to the will of God in all these respects, thankfully approving and accepting everything that is particular to our lives; praising and glorifying His name for our birth of such parents, and in such circumstances of state and condition; being fully assured that it was for some reasons of infinite wisdom and goodness that we were born into our particular states of life.

If the man mentioned above was born blind so that the works of God might be manifested in him, did he not have great reason to praise God for appointing him, in such a particular manner, to be the instrument of His glory? Likewise, if one person is born here, and another there; if one falls among riches, and another into poverty; if one receives his flesh and blood from these parents, and another from those; does not every person have the greatest reason to bless God and to be thankful for his particular state and condition, because all that is particular in it is directly intended for the glory of God and his own good—just as the man was born blind so that the works of God might be manifested in him?

How noble an idea this gives us of the divine omniscience, presiding over the whole world, governing such a long chain and combination of seeming accidents and chances, to the common and particular advantage of all beings! Every person, in such a wonderful variety of causes, accidents, and events, falls into a foreseen and foreordained state—to his best advantage and to the wise and glorious ends of God's government of the whole world.

If you had been anything else than what you are, you would have, all things considered, been less wisely provided for than you are now. You would have lacked some circumstances and conditions that are best suited to make you happy and serviceable to the glory of God. If you could see all that God sees, the whole chain of causes and motives that are to move and invite you to a right course of life, you would see something intended exclusively for you, to put you into a state similar to your own. However, because you cannot see this, it is here that your Christian faith and trust in God are to exercise themselves and render you as grateful and thankful for the happiness of your state as if you could see everything that contributes to it with your own eyes.

Now, if this is the case of every man in the world, blessed in such a way with some particular state that is most convenient for him, how reasonable it is for every man to will what God has already willed for him! How reasonable to adore and magnify, by a pious faith and trust in the divine goodness, the wise Providence that has made the best choice for him of those things that he could not choose for himself!

Every uneasiness at our own state is founded upon comparing it with that of other people; we are like a sick man who is angry at those who prescribe things to him different from those that are prescribed to people in health. For all the different states of life are like the different states of diseases; what is a remedy to one man in his state may be poison to another. Therefore, to complain because you are not as some others are, is as if a man in one disease should complain that he is not treated like one who is in another. Whereas, if he were to have his will, he would be killed by that which will prove to be the cure of another.

It is the same in the various conditions of life; if you give yourself up to uneasiness or complain about anything in your state, you may, for all you know, be so ungrateful to God that you actually complain about the very thing that is to be the cause of your salvation. If you had it in your power to get what you think is so grievous to lack, it might perhaps be that very thing that, of all others, would most expose you to eternal damnation. Therefore, whether we consider the infinite goodness of God, which cannot choose amiss for us, or our own great ignorance of what is most advantageous to us, there can be nothing so reasonable and pious as to have no will but that of God's, and to desire nothing for ourselves, in our persons, our state, or our condition, except what the good providence of God appoints to us.

Furthermore, as the providence of God introduces us into the world, into such states and conditions of life that are most convenient for us, so the same unerring Wisdom orders all events and turns in the whole course of our lives, in such a manner as to render them the best means to exercise and improve our virtue. Nothing hurts us, nothing destroys us, except the ill use of that liberty with which God has entrusted us. Nothing happens to us by chance, just as the world itself was not made by chance; all things happen and work together for our good (Rom. 8:28), just as God is goodness itself. A man has as much reason to will everything that happens to him because God wills it, as to think that the wisest things are directed by infinite wisdom.

This is not cheating or soothing ourselves into any false contentment or imaginary happiness; but it is a satisfaction grounded upon as great a certainty as the existence and attributes of God. For if we are right in believing God to act over us with infinite wisdom and goodness, we cannot carry too high our notions of conformity and resignation to the divine will; nor can we ever be wrong in thinking that God has brought upon us only what He knows to be best for us.

The providence of God is not more concerned about the government of night and day, and the variety of seasons, than about the common course of events that seem most to depend upon the mere wills of men. Therefore, it is as strictly right to look upon all worldly accidents and changes, all the various turns and alternations in your own life, to be as truly the effects of divine providence as the rising and setting of the sun, or the alternations of the seasons of the year. Because you are always to adore the wisdom of God in the direction of these things, so it is the same reasonable duty always to magnify God as an equal Director of everything that happens to you in the course of your own life.

This holy resignation and conformity of your will to the will of God being so much the true state of piety, I hope you will think it proper to make this hour of prayer a constant season of applying to God for so great a gift. I hope that, by constantly praying for it in this way, your heart may be habitually disposed toward it, and always in a state of readiness to look at everything as God's and to consider Him in everything; so that everything that befalls you, may be received in the spirit of piety and made a means of exercising some virtue.

There is nothing that so powerfully governs the heart, that so strongly excites us to wise and reasonable actions, as a true sense of God's presence. But, just as we cannot entirely comprehend the essence of God, so nothing will so constantly keep us under a lively sense of the presence of God as this holy resignation, which attributes everything to Him and receives everything as from Him.

If we could see a miracle from God, how our thoughts would be affected with a holy awe and veneration of His presence! However, if we consider everything as God's doing, either by order or permission, we will then be affected with common things as if we had seen a miracle. When you consider God as acting in all things and all events, then all things will become venerable to you, like miracles, and fill you with the same sentiments of awe toward the divine presence.

Now, you must not reserve the exercise of this pious temper to any particular times or occasions, or imagine how resigned you will be to God if particular trials were to happen. For this is amusing yourself with the notion or idea of resignation, instead of acting out the virtue itself. Therefore, do not please yourself with thinking how piously you would act and submit to God in a plague or famine or persecution, but be intent upon the perfection of the present day; and be assured that the best way of showing a true zeal is to make little things the occasions of great piety.

Begin in the smallest matters and the most ordinary occasions, and accustom your mind to the daily exercise of this pious disposition in the lowest occurrences of life. And, when a contempt, an affront, a little injury, loss, or disappointment, or the smallest events of every day continually raise your mind to God in proper acts of resignation, then you may justly hope that you will be numbered among those who are resigned and thankful to God in the greatest trials and afflictions.

Chapter Twenty-One

A LOOK WITHIN OURSELVES

We now come to six o'clock in the evening, which, according to the Scripture account, is called the twelfth, or last, hour of the day. This is a time so proper for devotion that I suppose nothing needs to be said to recommend it as a season of prayer to everyone who professes any regard to piety.

The labor and action of every state of life is generally over at this hour, so this is the proper time for every person to call himself to account and review all his behavior from the first action of the day. The necessity of this examination is founded upon the necessity of repentance. For if it is necessary to repent of all our sins, if the guilt of unrepented sins remains with us, then it is necessary that not only all our sins, but also all the particular circumstances and magnifications of them, be known, recollected, and brought to repentance.

The Scriptures say, "If we confess our sins, he is faithful and just to forgive us our sins, and to cleanse us from all unrighteousness" (1 John 1:9). In other words, our sins are forgiven, and we are cleansed from the guilt and unrighteousness of them, when they are repented of and confessed in this fashion. Therefore, it seems to be the greatest necessity that *all* our daily actions be constantly observed and brought to account, lest by negligence we load ourselves with the guilt of unrepented sins.

This examination of ourselves every evening is not only to be considered as a commendable rule that is suitable for a wise man to observe, but as something that is as necessary as a daily confession and repentance of our sins. This daily repentance has very little significance and loses all its chief benefits, unless it is a particular confession and repentance of the sins of that day. This examination is necessary to repentance, in the same manner as time is necessary; you cannot repent or express your sorrow unless you allow some time for it; nor can you repent unless you know what it is that you are repenting of. So, when I say that it is necessary to examine and call your actions to account, I am only saying that it is necessary to know what and how many things you are to repent of.

Perhaps, until now, you have only confessed yourself a sinner in general, and you have always asked for an overall forgiveness, without any particular remembrance or contrition for the particular sins of that day. By this practice you are brought to believe that the same short and general form of confession of sin is a sufficient repentance for every day.

Suppose another person held the opinion that a confession of our sins in general once at the end of every week was sufficient, and that it was as well to confess the sins of seven days altogether, as to have a particular repentance at the end of every day. You may sufficiently see the unreasonableness and impiety of this opinion, and you may think it is easy enough to show the danger and folly of it. Yet, there is no express text of Scripture against it. For this reason, you must take all your arguments from the nature of repentance and the necessity of a particular repentance for particular sins. Nothing can be said against leaving the sins of the whole week to be repented for in general, that cannot also be said against a daily repentance that considers the sins of that day only in general. Therefore, every argument must fully prove the necessity of being very particular in our repentance of the sins of every day.

Would you tell such a man that a daily confession is necessary to keep up an abhorrence of sin, that the mind would grow hardened and senseless of the guilt of sin without it? And is this not a good reason for requiring that your daily repentance be very specific and particular for your daily sins? For if confession is to raise an abhorrence of sin, surely a confession that considers and lays open your particular sins, that brings them to light with all their circumstances, that requires a particular sorrowful acknowledgment of every sin, must fill the mind with an abhorrence of sin in a much greater degree than that which only, in the same form of words, confesses you to be a sinner in general. This is nothing but what the greatest saint may justly say of himself; therefore, the daily repeating of such a general confession has nothing in it to make you truly ashamed of your own way of life.

Furthermore, must you not tell such a man that, by leaving himself to such a weekly general confession, he is in great danger of forgetting a great many of his sins? Yet, is there any sense or force in this argument unless you suppose that our sins are all to be remembered and brought to a particular repentance? Is it not necessary that our particular sins not be forgotten, but particularly remembered in our daily repentances, as we would remember them in a repentance at any other time?

As you can see, every argument for a daily confession and general repentance is the same argument for the confession and repentance of the particular sins of every day. Daily confession has no other reason or necessity but our daily sins; and therefore it is nothing of what it should be, unless it is a repentance and sorrowful acknowledgment of the particular sins of the day.

I suppose you would think yourself guilty of great impiety if you were to go to bed without confessing yourself to be a sinner and asking pardon of God; you would not think it sufficient that you did so yesterday. And yet, if, without any regard to the present day, you only repeat the same form of words that you used yesterday, the sins of the present day may justly be looked upon to have had no repentance. The sins of the present day require a new confession, because it is the state and condition of every day that is to determine the state and manner of your repentance in the evening; otherwise, the same general form of words is an empty formality that has the appearance of a duty, rather than a true performance of repentance that is necessary to make it truly useful to you.

Let us suppose that, on a certain day, you were guilty of the following sins: you lied, ascribing something falsely to yourself through pride; you made disparaging, belittling remarks; and you indulged yourself in some degree of intemperance. Let us also suppose that, on the next day, you lived in a contrary manner: you neglected no duty of devotion, and you spent the whole day innocently employed in your proper business.

Now, imagine that on the evening of both these days, you used the same general confession, having considered it a duty that is to be performed every night, rather than a repentance that is to be suited to the particular state of the day. Is it at all reasonable to say that each day has had its proper repentance? Is there no difference in the guilt of these days, that you can say they need no different repentance at the ends of them? How can each of them have its proper repentance except by having a repentance as large, as extensive, and as particular as the guilt of each day?

Again, let us suppose that, on that day when you had been guilty of the three notorious sins mentioned above, you had only called one of them to mind in your evening repentance. Is it not obvious that the other sins are unrepented of, and that, therefore, their guilt still abides upon you? You are then as a man who commits himself to the night without repenting for the day that had betrayed him into such great sin.

Now, these are not needless particulars or scrupulous niceties that a man does not need to trouble himself about. Rather, they are such plain truths that they essentially concern the very life of piety. For if repentance is necessary, then it is necessary that it be rightly performed, and in due manner. I have entered into all these particulars only to show you, in the plainest manner, that examination and a careful review of all the actions of the day, is not only to be looked upon as a good rule, but as something as necessary as repentance itself.

If a man is to account for his expenses at night, can it be thought a needless exactness in him to take notice of every particular expense in the day?

And if a man is to repent of his sins at night, can he be considered too conscientious if he knows and calls to mind what sins he is to repent of?

Some may think that a confession in general should be a sufficient repentance for the end of days that have only the unavoidable frailties of our nature to lament. However, even this folly proves the absolute necessity of this self-examination; for without this examination, who can know that he has gone through any day in this manner? An evening repentance, which brings all the actions of the day to account, is not only necessary to wipe off the guilt of sin, but it is also the most certain way to amend and perfect our lives. It is only such a repentance as this that touches the heart, awakens the conscience, and leaves a horror and detestation of sin upon the mind.

For instance, if, on a particular evening, all that you could charge yourself with was a hasty, negligent performance of your devotions, or too much time spent in an impertinent conversation; if the unreasonableness of these things were fully reflected upon and acknowledged; if you were then to condemn yourself before God for them and implore His pardon and assisting grace; what could be so likely a means to prevent your falling into the same faults the next day? Or, if you do fall into them again the next day, if they were again brought to the same examination and condemnation in the presence of God, their happening again would be such a proof to you of your own folly and weakness that your shame and confusion at yourself would, in all probability, make you exceedingly desirous of greater perfection.

In the case of repeated sins, the mind would be made humble and full of sorrow and deep conviction, and, by degrees, forced into amendment by this examination and confession. A formal, general confession, on the other hand, that is only considered as an evening duty, that overlooks the particular mistakes of the day, and is the same whether the day is spent ill or well, has little or no effect upon the mind. A man may use such a daily confession and yet go on sinning and confessing all his life, without any remorse of mind or any true desire of amendment.

For if your own particular sins are left out of your confession, your confessing of sin in general has no more effect upon your mind than if you had only confessed that all men in general are sinners. There is nothing in any confession to show that it is yours, but insofar as it is a self-accusation, not of sin in general or sin that is common to all others, but of particular sins that are your own proper shame and reproach. A confession that does not discover and accuse your own particular guilt cannot be an act of true sorrow or real concern at your own condition. A confession that is without this sorrow and contrition of heart, has nothing in it either to atone for past sins or to produce in us any true reformation and amendment of life.

In addition, in order to make this examination still more beneficial, every man should oblige himself to a certain method in it. Every man has something particular in his nature: stronger inclinations to some vices than others, and some infirmities that stick closer to him and are harder to be conquered than others; it is as easy for every man to know this of himself, as to know whom he likes or dislikes. Therefore, it is highly necessary that these particularities of our natures and temperaments should never escape a severe trial at our evening repentance. I say, "a severe trial," because nothing but a rigorous severity against these natural dispositions is sufficient to conquer them.

They are the right eyes that are not to be spared, but are to be plucked out and cast from us. (See Matthew 5:29.) They are the infirmities of nature; they have the strength of nature; and they must be treated with great opposition, or they will soon be too strong for us. Therefore, if you know yourself to be subject to anger and passion, you must be very exact and constant in your examination of this disposition every evening. You must find out every slip that you have made of that kind, whether in thought, word, or action; you must shame, reproach, and accuse yourself before God for everything that you have said or done in obedience to your anger. You must no more allow yourself to forget the examination of this disposition than to forget any of your prayers.

Again, if you find that vanity is your prevailing quality—that is, if you are preoccupied with the adornment of your person and pursuing everything that compliments or flatters your abilities—never spare nor forget this quality in your evening examination. Instead, confess to God every vanity of thought, word, or action that you have been guilty of, and put yourself to all the shame for it that you can.

Every person should act in this manner with regard to the chief frailty to which his nature most inclines him. Of course, this will not immediately do all that he would wish; yet, by a constant practice, it will certainly produce its desired effect in a short time.

Further, all states and employments of life have their particular dangers and temptations, exposing people more to some sins than to others. Consequently, every man who wishes his own improvement should make it a necessary part of his evening examination, to consider how he has avoided or fallen into sins that are most common to his state of life. Our businesses and conditions of life have great power over us, so nothing but watchfulness such as this can secure us from those temptations to which we are exposed daily.

The poor man, for example, is always in danger of complaining and uneasiness; the rich man is most exposed to sensuality and indulgence; the tradesman to lying and unreasonable gains; the scholar to pride and vanity: so that in every state of life, a man should always, in his examination of himself, be very watchful of and exact about those faults to which his state of life most of all exposes him.

Again, it is reasonable to suppose that every good man has entered into, or has at least proposed to himself, some method of holy living, and has set himself some rules to observe that are known only to himself. It should be a constant part of his evening devotions to examine how, and in what degree, he has observed them, and to reproach himself before God for every neglect of them.

By *rules*, I mean rules that relate to the well-ordering of our time and the business of our everyday lives, rules that prescribe a certain order to all that we are to do: our businesses, devotions, sacrifices, readings, seclusions, conversations, meals, refreshments, sleep, and the like. Good rules relating to all these things are certain means of great improvement, and all serious Christians must propose these rules to themselves. However, they will hardly ever be observed to any purpose unless they are made the constant subject of our evening examinations.

Lastly, you are not to content yourself with a hasty, general review of the day, but you must enter upon it with deliberation. Begin with the first action of the day, and proceed, step-by-step, through every particular matter that you have been concerned in; and let no time, place, or action be overlooked. In a little time, such an examination will make you as different from yourself as a wise man is different from an idiot. It will give you a newness of mind and a spirit of wisdom and desire for perfection that you were an entire stranger to before.

Now, would it not be a great help to you in your evening examination, if you also were to possess a great horror of sin, such as would lead you to confess your sins in deep sorrow? I proceed now to set before you the sort of considerations that may fill your mind with a just dread and horror of all sin, and help you to confess your own in the most passionate contrition and sorrow of heart.

Consider, first, how hateful all sin is to God, what a mighty baseness it is, and how abominable it renders sinners in the sight of God. It is sin alone that makes the great difference between an angel and the Devil; and every sinner is, so far as he sins, a friend of the Devil (1 John 3:8), carrying on his work against God. Sin is a greater blemish and defilement of the soul than any filth or disease is a defilement of the body. And to be content to live in sin is a much greater baseness than to desire to wallow in the mire (see 2 Peter 2:22) or to love any bodily impurity.

Consider how you abhor a creature that delights in nothing but filth and nastiness, that hates everything that is decent and clean. Let this teach you to understand how repulsive that soul that delights in nothing but the impurity of sin, must appear unto God. For all sins, whether of sensuality, pride, or falseness, or of any other irregular passion, are nothing but the filth and impure diseases of fallen man. And all righteousness is nothing but the purity, the decency, the beauty, and the perfection of that spirit that is made in the image of God (Gen. 1:27).

Again, learn, from the greatness of the Atonement that has been made for it, what horror you ought to have for the guilt of sin. In the first chapter of Genesis, we learn that God made the world by the breath of His mouth, by the mere spoken word; how easily God can create beings! However, the redemption of the world has been a work of longer labor. From the costly Atonement, the bloody sacrifices, the pains and repentances, the sicknesses and deaths, which all had to be undergone before the guilty sinner was fit to appear in the presence of God, we learn how difficult it is for infinite mercy to forgive sins.

Ponder these great truths. First, the Son of God was forced to become man; to be a partaker of all our infirmities; to undergo a poor, painful, miserable, and contemptible life; to be persecuted, hated, and at last nailed to a cross; that, by such sufferings, He might cause God to have more sympathy with and favor toward that nature in which Christ suffered.

Secondly, all the bloody sacrifices and atonements of the Jewish law were to represent the necessity of this great sacrifice and the great displeasure God bore to sinners.

Thirdly, the world is still under the curse of sin, and certain marks, such as famines, plagues, tempests, sicknesses, diseases, and death, show God's displeasure at it.

Fourthly, all the sons of Adam are to go through a painful, sickly life, denying their natural appetites, and crucifying the lusts of the flesh, in order to have a share in the atonement of our Savior's death.

Fifthly, all their penances and self-denials, all their tears and repentances, are only made available by that great intercession that is still being made for them at the right hand of God (Rom. 8:34).

Sixthly, this mysterious redemption and all these sacrifices and sufferings, both of God and man, are only to remove the guilt of sin.

After this general consideration of the guilt of sin, do you not see with what tears and contrition you ought to purge yourself from it? Sin has done so much mischief to our nature, exposed it to so great a punishment, and made it so repulsive to God, that nothing less than the great Atonement of the Son of God, and a great repentance of our own, can restore us to the divine favor.

Consider, next, your own particular share in the guilt of sin. And if you wish to know with what zeal you ought to repent, consider how you would exhort another sinner to repentance. What repentance and amendment would you expect from him whom you judged to be the greatest sinner in the world?

Now, perhaps you may fairly look upon yourself to be the greatest sinner that you know in the world. For though you may know an abundance of people to be guilty of some gross sins, with which you cannot charge yourself, yet you may justly condemn yourself as the greatest sinner that you know. This may be true for the following reasons.

First, because you know more of the folly of your own heart than you do of other people's, you can charge yourself with various sins that you know of yourself but of which you cannot be sure that other sinners are guilty. You know more of the folly, baseness, pride, deceitfulness, and negligence of your own heart, than you do of anyone else's; therefore, you have good reason to consider yourself as the greatest sinner that you know.

Secondly, the greatness of our guilt arises chiefly from the greatness of God's goodness toward us, from the particular graces and blessings, the favors, insights, and instructions that we have received from Him. These graces and blessings, and the multitude of God's favors toward us, are the great magnifiers of our sins against God, so they are known only to ourselves. And, therefore, every sinner knows more of the aggravations of his own guilt than he does of other people's; consequently, he may justly look upon himself to be the greatest sinner that he knows.

How good God has been to other sinners, what light and instruction He has vouchsafed to them, what blessings and graces they have received from Him, how often He has touched their hearts with holy inspirations, you cannot tell. However, you know all this of yourself; therefore, you know greater aggravations of your own guilt and are able to charge yourself with greater ingratitude than you can charge other people with. The greatest saints have in all ages condemned themselves as the greatest sinners, because they knew the aggravations of their own sins, which they could not know of other people's.

The right way, therefore, to fill your heart with true contrition and a deep sense of your own sins, is this: do not consider or compare the outward course of your life with that of other people's, and then think yourself to be less sinful than they because the outward forms of your life are less sinful than theirs. In order to know your own guilt, you must consider your own particular circumstances: your health or sickness; your youth or age; your particular calling; your education; the degrees of light and instruction that you have received; the good men that you have conversed with; the admonitions that you have had; the books that you have read; the numberless multitude of divine blessings, graces, and favors that you have received; the good motions of grace that you have resisted; the resolutions of amendment that you have often broken; and the checks of conscience that you have disregarded.

It is from these circumstances that everyone is to determine the measure of his own guilt. You are the only one who knows the circumstances of your own sins, so you must necessarily know how to charge yourself with higher degrees of guilt than you can charge other people with. It may be that God Almighty knows greater sinners than you, because He sees and knows the circumstances of all men's sins. However, your own heart, if it is faithful to you, can discover no guilt so great as your own; it can only see in you those circumstances on which a great part of the guilt of sin is founded.

You may see sins in other people that you cannot charge yourself with; but then you know a number of circumstances of your own guilt that you cannot lay to their charge. And perhaps that person, who appears at such a distance from your virtue and so hateful in your eyes, would have been much better than you are had he been in your circumstances and received all the same favors and graces from God that you have had.

This is a very humbling reflection for those people who measure their virtue by comparing the outward course of their lives with that of other people's. Look at whom you will, however different from you in his way of life, yet you can never know how much divine grace he has been given, or that he would not have been much truer to his duty than you are if he had your circumstances.

Now, this is why I desired you to consider how you would exhort that man to confess and bewail his sins whom you looked upon to be one of the greatest sinners. If you will deal justly, you must fix the charge at home and look no farther than yourself. For God has given no one any power of knowing the true weight of any sins besides his own; therefore, the greatest sinner that every man knows is himself.

A serious and frequent reflection upon these things will tend to humble us in our own eyes, make us very aware of the greatness of our own guilt, and make us very cautious about censuring and condemning other people. For who would dare to be severe against other people when, for all he can tell, the severity of God may be more due to himself than to them? Who would exclaim against the guilt of others when he considers that he knows more of the greatness of his own guilt than he does of theirs?

How often you have resisted God's Holy Spirit, how many motives to goodness you have disregarded, how many particular blessings you have sinned against, how many good resolutions you have broken, how many checks and admonitions of conscience you have stifled, you very well know; but how often this has been the case of other sinners, you do not know. Therefore, the greatest sinner that you know must be yourself. Whenever you are angry at sin or sinners, whenever you read or think of God's indignation and wrath at wicked men, let this teach you to be the most severe in your censure, and the most humble and contrite in the acknowledgment and confession, of your own sins, because you know of no sinner equal to yourself.

In conclusion, once you have examined and confessed your sins at this hour of the evening, you must afterwards look upon yourself as still obliged to pray again, just before you go to bed. The subject that is most proper for your prayers at that time is death. Imagine that your bed is your grave; that all things are ready for your burial; that you are to have no more to do with this world; and that it will be only by God's great mercy if you ever see the light of the sun again or have another day to add to your works of piety. Then commit yourself to sleep, as into the hands of God, as if you will have no more opportunities of doing good, but will awake among spirits that are separate from the body and waiting for the judgment of the Last Day.

Such a solemn resignation of yourself into the hands of God every evening, and parting with all the world as if you were never to see it anymore, is a practice that will soon have excellent effects upon your spirit. For this time of the night is exceedingly proper for such prayers and meditations; and the likeness that sleep and darkness have to death, will make your thoughts about it the more deep and affecting.

Let your last prayers of the day, therefore, be wholly upon death, considering all the dangers, uncertainties, and terrors of death; let them contain everything that can make you more aware of it. Let your petitions be all for right sentiments of the approach and importance of death; and beg of God that your mind may be possessed with such a sense of its nearness, that you may have it always in your thoughts, do everything as in sight of it, and make every day a day of preparation for it.

Chapter Twenty-Two

A DEVOUT SPIRIT

I have now finished what I intended in this treatise. I have explained the nature of devotion, both as it signifies a life devoted to God, and as it signifies a regular method of daily prayer. I have now only to add a word or two in recommendation of a life governed by this spirit of devotion.

It is reasonable to suppose that all Christians desire to arrive at Christian perfection, yet experience shows us that nothing needs more to be pressed, repeated, and forced upon our minds than the plainest rules of Christianity. I have recommended voluntary poverty, virginity, and devout seclusion as things not necessary, yet highly beneficial, to those who would make the way to perfection the easiest and the most certain. However, Christian perfection itself is tied to no particular form of life; it is to be attained, though not with the same ease, in every state of life.

In another book, entitled *On Christian Perfection,* I have asserted that Christian perfection does not necessarily call anyone to a monastery, but it does call everyone to the full performance of those duties that are necessary for all Christians and common to all states of life. The whole of the matter is plainly this: virginity, voluntary poverty, and other such restraints of lawful things, are not necessary to Christian perfection; but they are much to be commended in those who choose them as the means of a safer and speedier arrival at it. It is only in this manner and in this sense that I would recommend any particularity of life, not as if perfection consisted in the thing itself, but because of its great tendency to produce and support the true spirit of Christian perfection.

Nevertheless, the life I am advocating to every man is a life of a great and strict devotion, which, I think, has been sufficiently shown to be equally the duty and happiness of all orders of men. There is nothing in any particular state of life that can be argued as a reason for any abatements of a devout spirit. Yet, in this polite age of ours, we have lived apart from the spirit of devotion to such an extent that many seem afraid even to be suspected of it, imagining great devotion to be great bigotry. Many believe that devotion is founded in ignorance and poorness of spirit, and that little, weak, and dejected minds are generally the greatest experts in it.

Great devotion, in truth, is the noblest temper of the greatest and noblest souls; and whoever thinks devotion is only for the ignorant or poor in spirit, is himself entirely ignorant of the nature of devotion, the nature of God, and the nature of man. People who are well learned or possess great knowledge in worldly matters may perhaps think it unfair to have their lack of devotion charged to their ignorance. However, if they will let themselves be tried by reason and Scripture, it will soon appear that a lack of devotion, either among the learned or unlearned, is founded in gross ignorance and the greatest blindness and insensibility that can happen to a rational creature. Devotion is so far from being the effect of a little and dejected mind, that it must and will be always highest in the most perfect natures.

Who considers it a sign of a poor, little mind, for a man to be full of reverence and duty to his parents, to have the truest love and honor for his friend, or to excel in the highest instances of gratitude to his benefactor? Are not these qualities, in the highest degree, in the most exalted and perfect minds? And yet, what is high devotion if it is not the highest exercise of duty, reverence, love, honor, and gratitude to the amiable and glorious Parent, Friend, and Benefactor of all mankind?

The higher these dispositions are, the more they are esteemed among men and are allowed to be the greater proofs of a true greatness of mind. Likewise, the higher and greater these same dispositions are toward God, so much more do they prove the nobility, excellence, and greatness of the mind. So long as duty to parents, love to friends, and gratitude to benefactors, are thought great and honorable qualities, then devotion, which is nothing but duty, love, and gratitude to God, must have the highest place among our highest virtues.

Furthermore, that part of devotion that expresses itself in sorrowful confessions and penitential tears of a broken and a contrite heart, is very far from being any sign of a little and ignorant mind. For who does not acknowledge it as an instance of an honorable, generous, and brave mind, to Are acknowledge a fault and ask pardon for any offense? not the finest and most improved minds the ones that are most remarkable for this excellent quality? Is not the excellence of a man's spirit shown when his sorrow and indignation at himself rises in proportion to the folly of his crime, and the goodness and greatness of the person he has offended?

Now, if things are like this, then the greater any man's mind is and the more he knows of God and himself, the more he will be disposed to prostrate himself before God in all the humblest acts and expressions of repentance. Also, the greater the generosity and judgment of his mind, the more he will exercise and indulge a passionate, tender sense of God's just displeasure. And the more he knows of the greatness, goodness, and perfection of the divine nature, the fuller of shame and confusion he will be at his own sins and ingratitude. On the other hand, the more ignorant and dull any soul is, the more base and ungenerous it naturally is, and the more senseless it is of the goodness and purity of God, the more averse it will be to all acts of humble confession and repentance.

Devotion, therefore, is so far from being best suited to little, ignorant minds, that a true elevation of soul, a lively sense of honor, and great knowledge of God and ourselves, are the greatest natural helps that our devotion has. On the other hand, the lack of devotion is founded on the most excessive ignorance—a point I will make clear by a number of examples.

First, our blessed Lord and His apostles were eminent instances of great and frequent devotion. Now, if we will grant (as all Christians must) that their devotion was founded in a true knowledge of the nature of devotion, the nature of God, and the nature of man, then everyone who is insensible of the duty of devotion is in an excessive state of ignorance: they neither know God, nor themselves, nor devotion. For if a right knowledge in these three respects produces great devotion, as in the case of our Savior and His apostles, then a neglect of devotion must be due to ignorance.

Again, why do we find that most people have recourse to devotion when they are in sickness, distress, or fear of dying? Is it not because their state shows them more of their need for God and more of their own weakness than they perceive at other times? Is it not because their weakness, their approaching end, convinces them of something that they did not half perceive before? Now, if devotion at these seasons is the effect of a better knowledge of God and ourselves, then the neglect of devotion at other times is always the result of a great ignorance of God and ourselves.

The lack of devotion is ignorance, and the most shameful ignorance at that, to be charged with the greatest folly. This will be obvious to anyone who considers by what rules we are to judge the excellency of any knowledge, or the shamefulness of any ignorance. Of course, there would be no excellence in knowledge itself, nor any reproach to us in ignorance, if we were not rational creatures. Therefore, the knowledge most suitable to our rational nature is our highest, finest knowledge; and the ignorance that relates to things most essential to us as rational creatures is the most gross and shameful ignorance.

If a judge has fine skill in painting, architecture, and music, but at the same time has confused ideas of equity and a poor, dull comprehension of the value of justice, who would hesitate to consider him an ignorant judge? If a bishop is a man of great skill in raising and enriching his family in the world, but has no taste nor sense of the maxims and principles of the saints and Fathers of the church; if he does not comprehend the holy nature and great obligations of his calling, and judge it better to be crucified to the world than to live idly in pomp and splendor; who would delay in charging such a bishop with a lack of understanding?

If a gentleman were to imagine that the moon is no bigger than it appears to the eye, that it shines with its own light, that all the stars are only spots of light; and if, after reading books of astronomy, he continues in the same opinion; most people would think he lacked understanding. However, if the same person were to think it better to provide for a short life here than to prepare for a glorious eternity hereafter; that it was better to be rich than to be eminent in piety; his ignorance and dullness would be too great to be compared to anything else.

There is no knowledge that so much deserves the name knowledge as that which we call *judgment*. The clearest and most improved understanding is able to judge best the value and worth of things. All the rest is but the capacity of an animal; it is merely seeing and hearing. And there is no excellence of any knowledge in us, until we exercise our judgment and judge well the value and worth of things.

If a man had eyes that could see beyond the stars or pierce into the heart of the earth, but could not see the things that were before him or discern anything that was serviceable to him, we would think that he had very bad eyesight. If another had ears that received sounds from the moon, but could hear nothing that was said or done upon earth, we would look upon him as deaf. In like manner, if a man has a memory that can retain a great many things; if he has a wit that is sharp and acute in arts and sciences, or an imagination that can wander agreeably in fictions; but has a poor understanding of his duty and relation to God, of the value of piety, or the worth of moral virtue; he may very justly be considered to have a bad understanding. He is like the man that can only see and hear such things that are of no benefit to him.

Piety, virtue, and eternal happiness are certainly of the most concern to man, and the immortality of our nature and relation to God are certainly our most glorious circumstances. It is certain that he who dwells most in contemplation of them, whose heart is most affected with them, who sees farthest into them, who best comprehends the value and excellency of them, who judges all worldly attainments to be mere air and shadows in comparison to them, proves himself to have the finest understanding and the strongest judgment among men.

If we do not reason after this manner or allow this method of reasoning, we have no arguments to prove that there is any such thing as a wise man or a fool. For a man is proved to be an idiot, not because he lacks any of his senses or is incapable of everything, but because he has no judgment and is entirely ignorant of the worth and value of things. He would choose a fine coat rather than a large estate. As the essence of stupidity consists in the entire lack of judgment, in an ignorance of the value of things, so, on the other hand, the essence of wisdom and knowledge must consist in the excellency of our judgment, or in the knowledge of the worth and value of things.

This is an undeniable proof that he who knows most about the value of the best things, who judges most rightly of the things that are of most concern to him, who would rather have his soul in a state of Christian perfection than the greatest share of worldly happiness, has the highest wisdom and is at the farthest distance from fools that any knowledge can place him. On the other hand, one who can speak several languages and repeat a great deal of history, but prefers the indulgence of his body to the purity and perfection of his soul; who is more concerned to get a name or an estate here than to live in eternal glory hereafter; is in the nearest state to that idiot who chooses a fancy coat rather than a large estate. He is not called a fool by men, but he must appear to God and heavenly beings to be in a more excessive state of stupidity, and he will sooner or later certainly appear so to himself.

Now, if it is undeniably clear that we cannot prove a man to be a fool, unless we show that he has no knowledge of things that are good and evil for himself, then it is equally as clear that we cannot prove a man to be wise unless we show that he has the fullest knowledge of things that are his greatest good and his greatest evil. If, therefore, God is our greatest good; if there can be no good but in His favor, nor any evil but in departing from Him; then it is obvious that he who judges that the best thing he can do is to please God to the utmost of his power, who worships and adores Him with all his heart and soul, who would rather have a pious mind than all the dignities and honors in the world, shows himself to be in the highest state of human wisdom.

We know how our blessed Lord acted in a human body; it was His meat and drink to do the will of the Father (John 4:34). And if any number of heavenly spirits were to leave their habitations in the light of God, to be for a while united to human bodies, they would certainly tend toward God in all their actions and be as heavenly as they could in a state of flesh and blood. They would act in this manner because they would know that God is the only good of all spirits, and that whether they are in the body or out of the body, in heaven or on earth, they must have every degree of their greatness and happiness from God alone.

Therefore, as for human spirits, the more exalted they are, the more they know their divine source, and the nearer they come to heavenly spirits, that is how much more they will live to God in all their actions and make their whole lives a state of devotion. Devotion, therefore, is the greatest sign of a great and noble mind; it is practiced by a soul in its highest state of knowledge; and none but little and blinded minds, sunk into ignorance and vanity, are destitute of it.

If a man were to imagine some mighty prince to be greater than God, we would take him for a poor, ignorant creature; everyone would acknowledge such an imagination to be the height of stupidity. And, if this same man thought it better to be devoted to some mighty prince than to be devoted to God, would this not be still greater proof of a poor, ignorant, and blinded nature? Yet, everyone who thinks that anything is better, greater, or wiser than a devout life, does exactly the same as this man. However we may consider this matter, it plainly appears that devotion is an instance of great judgment, of an elevated nature; and the lack of devotion is a certain proof of a lack of understanding.

The greatest minds of the heathen world, such as Pythagoras, Socrates, Plato, Epictetus, and Marcus Antonius, owed all their greatness to the spirit of devotion. They were full of God; their wisdom and deep contemplations tended only to deliver men from the vanity of the world and the slavery of bodily passions, that they might act as spirits that came from God and were soon to return to Him.

To see the dignity and greatness of a devout spirit, we need only compare it with other qualities that are chosen in lieu of it. John told us that everything in the world (that is, all the ways of a worldly life) is the lust of the flesh, the lust of the eyes, and the pride of life (1 John 2:16). Let us, therefore, consider what wisdom or excellency of mind is required to qualify a man for these delights.

Think of a man who is given up to the pleasures of the body. Surely this can be no sign of a fine mind or an excellent spirit; for if he had only the mind of an animal, he would be great enough for these enjoyments.

Now suppose him to be devoted to honors and splendors, to be fond of glitter and fame. Yet, this second state of mind requires no great mind or fine understanding to make a man capable of it; otherwise, it would prove the world to abound with great wits.

Thirdly, let us suppose him to be in love with riches, and to be so eager in the pursuit of them that he never believes he has enough. Now, this passion is so far from any excellent sense or great understanding, that blindness and folly are the best supports that it has.

Imagine this man, lastly, to be not exclusively devoted to any of these passions, but, as it usually happens, to be governed by all of them in their turns. Does this show a more exalted nature than to spend his days in the service of just one of them? No, because to have a taste for these things and to be devoted to them is far from any tolerable understanding. A love for riches, or any similar passion, is suitable only to the dullest, weakest minds, and it requires only a great deal of pride and folly to be greatly admired.

Now, let libertines bring any such charge as this, if they can, against devotion. They may as well endeavor to accuse light of having everything that belongs to darkness. If they will simply admit that there is a God and providence, then they will have admitted enough to justify the wisdom, and support the honor, of devotion. For if there is an infinitely wise and good Creator, in whom we live, move, and have our being (Acts 17:28), whose providence governs all things in all places, surely it must be the highest act of our understanding to conceive rightly of Him.

It must be the noblest instance of judgment, the most exalted disposition of our nature, to worship and adore this universal providence, to conform to its laws, to study its wisdom, and to live and act everywhere as in the presence of this infinitely good and wise Creator. One who lives in this manner, lives in the spirit of devotion. For if God is wisdom, surely the wisest man in the world is one who most conforms to the wisdom of God, who best obeys His providence, who enters farthest into His designs, and who does all he can that God's will may be done on earth as it is done in heaven (Matt. 6:10).

A devout man makes a true use of his reason: he sees through the vanity of the world, and he discovers the corruption of his nature and the blindness of his passion. He lives by a law that is not visible to vulgar eyes; he enters into the world of spirits; he compares the greatest things, sets eternity against time; and he chooses to be forever great in the presence of God, when he dies, rather than to have the greatest share of worldly pleasure while he lives. (See Matthew 6:19–20.)

He that is devout is full of these great thoughts; he lives upon these noble reflections and conducts himself by rules and principles that can only be understood, admired, and loved by reason. There is nothing, therefore, that shows so great a genius, nothing that so raises us above vulgar spirits, nothing that so plainly declares a heroic greatness of mind, as great devotion. Keep in mind that when you suppose a man to be a saint because his life is filled entirely with devotion, you have raised him as much above all other conditions of life as a philosopher is above an animal.

Lastly, courage and bravery are words that sound wonderful; they seem to signify a heroic spirit. Yet, humility, which seems to be the lowest part of devotion, is a more certain argument of a noble and courageous mind. Humility contends with greater enemies, is more constantly engaged and more violently assaulted, bears more, suffers more, and requires greater courage to support itself than any instances of worldly bravery. (See 1 Corinthians 13:7.)

A man who dares to be poor and contemptible in the eyes of the world, in order to approve himself to God; who resists and rejects all human glory; who opposes the clamor of his passions; who meekly puts up with all injuries and wrongs; and who dares to wait for his reward until the invisible hand of God gives to every man his proper place (see Revelation 22:12)—this man endures a much greater trial and exerts a nobler fortitude than one who is bold and daring in the fire of battle. For the boldness of a soldier, if he is a stranger to the spirit of devotion, is weakness rather than fortitude; it is at best a mad passion and heated tempers, and it has no more true valor in it than the fury of a tiger.

We cannot lift a finger or move a foot except by a power lent to us from God (Acts 17:28); as a result, bold actions that are not directed by the laws of God are no more true bravery than sedate malice is Christian patience. It is as base and cowardly to be bold and daring against the principle of reason and justice, as to be bold and daring in lying and perjury.

Reason is our universal law, which obliges us in all places and at all times; and no actions have any honor, but insofar as they are instances of our obedience to reason. If we, therefore, wish to exercise a true fortitude, we must do everything in the spirit of devotion, be valiant against the corruptions of the world, the lusts of the flesh, and the temptations of the Devil; for to be daring and courageous against these enemies is the noblest bravery that a human mind is capable of.

I have made this digression for the sake of those who think great devotion to be bigotry and poorness of spirit, that by these considerations they may see how poor and low all other dispositions are if compared to it; that they may see that all worldly attainments, whether of greatness, wisdom, or bravery, are but empty sounds. May they see that there is nothing wise or great or noble in a human spirit, but rightly to know and heartily to worship and adore the great God who is the support and life of all spirits, whether in heaven or on earth.